© 1994, Benjamin W. Powell, Sr.

LABRADOR BY CHOICE
First Printing, 1979
Second Printing, 1984
Third Printing, 1988
Fourth Printing, 1994

Printed by:
Robinson-Blackmore Printing and Publishing Limited
St. John's, Newfoundland, Canada

Published by:
Benjamin W. Powell, Sr.
Charlottetown, Labrador, Newfoundland, Canada
A0K 5Y0

in cooperation with ℞ Books
P.O. Box 8660
St. John's, Newfoundland, Canada
A1B 3T7

ISBN 0-920884-36-9

Contents

I dedicate this book in memory of

Alex Campbell, Sr. –

friend and fellow trapper on the Labrador.

Introduction

In late August 1971 I was aboard the two hundred-foot Canadian National steamer *Cabot Strait* as she glided into the channel just outside the harbour at Square Islands, Labrador. Before she dropped anchor I could hear the dull putt-putt of the motorboats in the harbour, making their way out to the steamer. These twenty-eight-foot crafts seemed to be filled with fishermen and their families, the children eagerly leaning over the bows and a few of the women shyly sitting with hands folded in their laps. I was amazed at the bustle of activity in this tiny isolated community on the coast.

Deck hands lowered the *Cabot*'s gangway to the water's edge; I dared not think how many fathoms deep that channel might be! Regardless of the deck sign stating "No Visitors Allowed," the Square Islanders lashed their motorboats to the gangway and climbed aboard. The crew didn't prevent them, for this was local custom at all ports-of-call. The steamer was a link with the outside world – it brought tourists with their cameras and curious questions; fishermen could sell a few salmon or cod to the ship's cook; messages from other parts of the coast could be delivered by captain or crew; interesting freight could be unloaded over the side, hopefully fresh fruit and vegetables, maybe a bicycle from a mail order catalogue, perhaps a crated snowmobile in preparation for the winter.

Amidst this flurry of activity, my friend and I descended the gangway and stepped into the nearest boat. Square Islands, the summer community, and Charlottetown, the winter community, would be our home for the year. We were teachers who had requested positions on the Labrador coast.

I hardly remember sailing back into the harbour or climbing the dock. But I do recall Mrs. Ben Powell – Aunt Effie, as we learned to call her – scurrying down the steps of her bright yellow house that sat on a solid rock shoreline. Years later I could still recognize her at a distance by her characteristic, quick step. She was wearing a red print, sleeveless dress and her arms were filled with freshly-washed clothes. She was a woman in her late forties with a welcoming smile and expressive, joyful eyes. She greeted us hurriedly on her way to the clothesline, saying she had to hang out the wash while the weather was fine but that we must stop there for a cup of tea "'t once."

We sat down on the extensive rocky slope that graduated to the dock and watched the white smoke billow from the stack of the *Cabot Strait* as she signalled her departure for ports north. Aunt Effie bustled back shortly. She motioned us into her home where we sat down to "tea" – cold meat, mustard potato salad, homemade bread, and fruit – a meal very characteristic of the hospitable Labrador folk. There we met some of the family — Lisa, Irving, Benny who were the younger ones; Blanche who was in grade 5; Ramsay, in his early teens, who shyly took his lunch into the pantry and ate it while standing at the counter; and Marie, in her late teens, who had just returned from a short holiday. The older boys – Tony, Sandy and Lewis – were fishing on their father's long liner at the time. Pilot Lester was flying tourists in and out of his father's fishing camp on White Bear Arm.

And of course we met Ben, Sr., the one who makes this book possible. He appeared to be a quiet, almost shy man, with few words to add to the general conversation at the table. But over the next seven years I came to know the depth of experience and knowledge that this man had to share. His ambitions had not been limited by the natural restrictions of living on the Labrador coast. And he still believed in the old ethic – that the days of free labour were not over if they could help a man or a community achieve something beneficial.

Ben's love for the Labrador is genuine; although born a Newfoundlander, he has no intention of ever moving back across the Strait of Belle Isle. He had adopted that beautiful coast of Labrador for a lifetime, and I'm sure that the nameless little cemetery at the head of the bay, which you will read about, will one day claim the remains of Ben Powell, a man who lived his life for the people and place he loved.

Uncle Ben, as he is fondly called by young and old alike, exemplifies a generation that soon will fade along the coast. Although he cannot be classified among the old-timers, for he is only now in his late fifties, he does represent many in Labrador who know what hard times were and who had little or no formal education. He demonstrates the fact that a determined goal with the consistent force of hard work behind it can bring lasting results, even in a small seemingly isolated village on the Labrador coast.

In *Labrador by Choice* Ben shares some of the fondest memories of his life. You will walk with him so closely by means of his words that you will visualize the wilderness life he talks about.

Ben hasn't changed in the seven years that I have known him. And I don't expect he will either. If you some day have the privilege of visiting Charlottetown, Labrador, Ben and Effie will be as warm as ever in welcoming you into their home and sharing their fare, as they have with literally hundreds from all walks of life. But it takes more than a visit to get to know the lifestyle of the Labrador people. It takes years of living in a small community to understand the joys, hardships and background of tradition that have made these people the down-to-earth folk they are, generous beyond measure with hearts and homes open to the stranger's need. But even then, you will never totally comprehend their way of life; you just have to be born a Labradorian to do that.

If you fly into Charlottetown by single-engined Otter, you just may discover that your pilot on Labrador Airways is one of Ben's sons; he has three now who are licensed. After landing on the bay ice (if you travel there in the winter), you may not find Ben immediately at home, for he well could be on the trapline for the day. I have travelled with him twice by snowmobile back into God's silent wilderness, a trip of approximately fifty miles. He believes in starting early, generally around 6:00 a.m., so that he can be back to Charlottetown by mid-afternoon to tend to the paperwork in his small office at the back of his grocery store.

I have sat by the campfire at Big Lake with Ben in "April month" and enjoyed a meal of Labrador salmon which he cooked. He never fails to bow his head and thank his Maker for the food and many other blessings He has bestowed.

In 1978 Ben took Effie on a trip to Florida. Writing to me later he mentioned how very much she enjoyed the holiday, which made him most happy. Although Florida was not his land, he felt he had owed her that trip for a long time, after the many lonely days and nights she had spent, raising their family, while he trudged the trapline to earn money to put bread on the table.

On May 3, 1978 Ben travelled back into the country to strike up his traps for the season and came back with enough furs to pay all the expenses to Florida, with some to spare. A couple weeks later he wrote to me, "When I made my last trip on the trapline this spring, it was a beautiful morning. There in the quietness of the early hours I just stopped my snowmobile and had a word of prayer, thanking the dear Lord for caring for me over the trapline another winter. The Lord is real good to Trapper Ben."

It is a privilege to know Ben and to have a part in editing and introducing his book. You will get a true taste of Labrador in these pages, and you will love it, I'm sure.

— Joan Cartledge
Postville, Labrador 1978

1
A Boy in Carbonear, Newfoundland

Early Days

I was born in 1921 on the east coast of Newfoundland in the town of Carbonear, which had a population of 2,700 people at that time. The years 1933 to 1936 (the year I left Carbonear) were known as the years of depression. There was very little industry and very little money. We had a Responsible

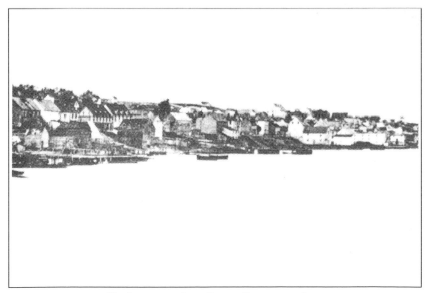

Carbonear when the author was a boy.

Government, but things went from bad to worse. Then a Commission Government took over and we thought things would improve, but we still had over 80,000 people in Newfoundland on able-bodied welfare getting six cents per person per day. Anybody who had a family of ten had to feed them on sixty cents per day.

Although I was born into a large family of five boys and four girls, we always managed somehow to stay off welfare. Many times it was a struggle from hand to mouth. I remember seeing Mother striking the old wooden flour barrel to knock down enough flour to make a little bread.

Father spent most of his life at sea. One of the old vessels he sailed on was the square rigger *Dorothy Duff*. In World War I she was torpedoed by the Germans and the crew was a long time getting home. So Father spent most of his time then in the United States working at construction and would stay away as long as two years at a time. We were still small boys and girls, but could help some with the hens, ducks, goat and gardens. Later when Father returned with some money, he bought a cow, a horse and a sheep, so we were almost self-supporting. We exchanged things such as fresh butter for rolled oats at the shops, as the storekeepers wouldn't give money.

Many people in our district found it much harder than we did to exist on that six cents per person per day. I remember one spring when all the people on able-bodied welfare got together and were going to demand a higher rate for their daily ration, as they called it in those days. So they marched the streets, rang the fire bell and church bells all night, and went to the homes of the business people, bringing them to the courthouse and demanding help from them. They then asked Captain George Windsor, the welfare officer for the district, to sign a higher rate on their welfare slips. Captain Windsor told them he could only go by the orders he had from St. John's. So they shoved his head through the glass windows in the old courthouse, but they soon saw that Captain Windsor would have died before he would have gone against his orders.

As a boy I well remember how the streets were still crowded with hungry people the next morning. I watched Allen

Cameron, who ran a grocery store, send his horse and driver up to the water tank with six barrels of hard bread for the hungry mob. The barrels were stuck up on their heads around the tank. Then Tom Clark, a big able man from Carbonear, walked up to them and with six smacks of his fist knocked out the six heads of the barrels! He started to pass around the hard bread, one cake to a person, but it couldn't reach around the great number of people that filled the waterfront. So the horse and driver came again with two more barrels, and as far as I know, all hands got a cake of hard bread.

When the train came in from St. John's, many of the ringleaders of the mob rushed to the station and put big poles across the train tracks so it couldn't move. Some of them got up where the engineer and fireman were and demanded them to show them how to operate the train. This went on for several days until at last the merchants and government helped the hungry with more food for awhile. The ringleaders of the mob were arrested and sentenced to time in jail, but there were so many of them that there was nowhere to put them; the jail was already full. Well, the old steamship *Meagile* was lying idle in St. John's harbour at the time. So they made a prison ship out of her and piled the men on board. But she was so filled that many of them crawled up through the smokestack and got away.

I followed on at school until I reached the third grade. I thought this was all I would ever need. To me it was more important to look for work and try to bring some food into our home. It was a good thing that education and intelligence didn't relate, or I never would have made it. By now I had reached the age of fourteen and I thought I could do a man's work. Although I was only small for my age, I was willing to work at anything to make some honest money.

That's when the first truck came to Carbonear. The owner was Eddie Janes, but he only lived a short time after he got the truck. When he died suddenly, Paddie Harrington, who operated a grocery store on Water Street, bought the truck and used it for freighting supplies around Conception Bay and Trinity Bay.

Paddie Harrington's grocery store where the author worked from 1934 to 1935.

These were mostly supplies from Saunders, Howell and Company Carpenter Shop.

I figured this would be a great opportunity for me to get a job on this new truck as a helper. So without waiting for him to ask me, I would be down in the mornings waiting for him to start it and I would help him load and unload. Sometimes we would be at it until three o'clock in the morning before we would get back from Trinity Bay or around the bay toward St. John's. This went on for several months and still he never offered to pay me or give me anything. Maybe he thought the ride back and forth was the payment.

Whenever the wind would blow from the east or southeast, I would be up at daybreak and down on the big, long beach to see what would have driven ashore. Sometimes I would pick up very valuable things, as I thought they were. Many times dead horses, cows, sheep, goats and hens would be driven up. I found this very interesting.

One morning I was there just at daybreak, and what did I see but a dead baby driven ashore! I thought this was different from all the other things I had seen, so I started downtown to look for a policeman. It was still too early for him to be on the front street, so I went to the courthouse. After awhile I got Sergeant Bursey to the front door and told him the story of the dead baby on the beach, a baby boy it was. So he and another officer went to the beach with a box and carried it back to the courthouse. I never heard anything else about the dead child.

The next day the wind was still on the land.[1] I was back again on the beach very early. Since a lot of driftwood had come in that night, I started to pick it up so I could later come down with a horse and pull it home for fire-wood. I was just stooping down to pick up the last stick when to my surprise there was a dollar bank-note which had washed ashore. I just grabbed it and squeezed it in my hand. I thought I was the richest boy in town! I stood there too excited to move and I looked toward the ocean where the strong breeze of the easterly wind struck my face. I believe tears came out of my eyes as I thought that somewhere over this great ocean there must be more opportunity for a young man starting out in life than on the beaches in Carbonear. At that very moment I made my first big decision in life – that I would leave my old hometown. I never knew what it was like to have money in my pocket, and now standing there with that one dollar bill squeezed in my hand, the whole world seemed to roll toward me. I thought about my oldest brother who had left home as a boy and had gone to Labrador, and had never so much as written home. But we did hear that he was living with his grandfather in St. Michaels Bay and was happy. This would be the answer: go and look for my oldest brother, Roland. That would be the land of milk and honey!

My biggest problem was to get some clothes, as I barely had more than what I stood in. Christmas was getting handy, so I spent my whole dollar on different things for Christmas. Soon after Christmas I started to prepare to earn some money. I thought I would give Mr. Harrington one more try and see if he would give me something for working with him. So I carried on with him for several days. Then one morning I went down really early, delivered all his groceries, carried bills to different people who owed him money, and got the work all done early.

[1] Blowing toward shore.

Still nothing happened.

I was feeling discouraged and started to turn for home. As I was passing the drug store, Mr. Burk was looking through the window and smiled at me. He was a very kind man, and all the boys liked him. He always had that smile for them and a kind word. He was a veteran of World War I and had a glass eye.

I decided to open the door and step in. I said, "Mr. Burk, can I use your phone just for a second?"

He said, "Go right ahead."

I stopped for a moment to think about the phone number of Mr. Harrington. When the number struck my mind I rang him.

He answered, "Hello!"

I said, "Mr. Harrington, are you looking for a grocery boy?"

He replied, "I have one."

But I said, "Is he pleasing you?"

He stopped for awhile, then he said, "There isn't much to do around here now, and the bit that there is to do is all done this morning."

I said, "Thank you, Sir," and hung up.

Mr. Burk looked at me with a sad face and said he was sorry Mr. Harrington had a boy already.

I said, "Sir, I am that boy."

Said Mr. Burk, "Well, why did you call him?"

I answered, "I have been working with him for a long time and he doesn't give me anything. So I thought I wasn't pleasing him. But after all, he is a nice man and I am only a boy, and he gives me a lot of rides in his truck, and maybe he thinks that's okay. So I can only call him a fine man." Then I told Mr. Burk I planned to leave home and I had to find work with some kind of returns for me to get clothes for my trip. As I walked toward the door I noticed he was walking toward the phone. I turned the corner to head for home when the thought struck me that I couldn't go home. I had to go east and look for work. I passed Mr. Fred Hawker's shop. He had a dry goods store filled with clothes. Marked in the window was a sign, "Boys' Clothes on Sale." I stopped for a moment and glanced at all the warm

Fred Hawker's dry goods store. To the left is Burk's drug store.

clothes. Before I had time to read the prices, Mr. Hawker came to the door and said, "You are the fellow I am looking for. Come right in." It appeared to me that Mr. Burk had phoned Mr. Hawker and told him my story. If he had anything to do, he would give me a chance.

I followed Mr. Hawker into the back of the building where we sat down by the side of a little coal stove. Mr. Hawker told me he had a job for me. He couldn't pay me any money, but he would give me a garment of clothes when the job was finished the next spring. I was happy. It sounded good. He told me to pick out the garment I'd like to have and he would put it aside for me. So I walked out and picked a brown windbreaker and looked at the price – $3.75. There was no tax. He told me my work would start the next day. "Come to the shop each morning, break up the boxes to light the fire, then go down to my home by the United Church and keep the snow shoveled away from the door and keep the water barrel filled with water," he said. It didn't seem too bad at all. But later I found that the water had to be wound up from a very deep well – about forty feet – which took a lot of time. But when there was no snow to be shoveled I could do all the work in about three hours. After a big batch of snow it would take me two days to get it cleared up. The water barrel was in the pantry at the far end of the house, and this meant I had to open and close about four doors. But I never complained, with that windbreaker in my mind.

It wasn't long before the news spread around our little neighbourhood that I was leaving home. Mr. Harold Maddock lived close to us and operated a general store downtown. He had a boy the same age as me, but he was very sickly. He had to be kept very warm. As soon as the wool began to wear off his underwear, his folks would buy new ones for him. He told his father that if I would bring him a few dozen hens' eggs he would give me two suits of his underwear. That sounded good to me. I was just waiting for the hens to lay their last eggs and then carried them to his home. I walked home with the underwear, which was carefully put away in my bag to wear up in the

Hobrock Hill overlooking Conception Bay where the author often went as a boy.

cold north that I had heard about and now longed to see.

Last Days

Things were shaping up good now. I had my underwear, and the windbreaker was in sight. Then one day, while coming home from work, I saw Mr. Harrington. He had just had a shipment of thigh rubbers come in and was hanging a pair over the door for display. I walked over to them and the name on them was "Super Excellent." The price was $3.70. Just what I needed for my trip, but I still had no money to buy anything. I started to walk away when I noticed a poster in the window, "Fresh Eggs Wanted. Will Pay 10¢ Per Dozen." So I went inside and asked Mrs. Harrington if I bought enough eggs could I get a pair of those thigh rubbers. She smiled and said yes, but the eggs must be good.

I made my regular trips with the eggs in a bucket, sometimes in the evenings and sometimes in the mornings. Mr. Harrington made out a little note each time and hung it over a long nail in the corner of the window which he used as a file. Every day I would watch the notes get higher, and as spring came more hens were laying and the notes were building up faster. I noticed the file was filled right to the top, so I asked Mrs. Harrington how many more eggs were needed. She got to work and figured it all out and said only one more dozen. That would make thirty-seven dozen eggs, so the next day I brought the one dozen eggs down to her on my way to work and got the rubbers. I was a very proud boy, since I had never been the owner of a pair of rubbers like that before. I was not fifteen years old.

By now I was wondering if Mr. Hawker would give me the windbreaker and if I could still work on until it was time to leave. I wanted to wear the windbreaker sometimes in the evenings, but I couldn't get up enough nerve to ask him because I still never had it earned.

The news got around that the outlook was really good for fresh salmon on the Labrador coast the coming summer, which was 1936. Monroe Export Company had already paid $2\frac{1}{2}$¢ per pound, and now with Mr. Lewis Dawe buying salmon on the coast that summer, the price could go as high as 5¢ per pound. The government was willing to help fishermen get on the coast to fish. Mr. Dawe, who lived in Bay Roberts and operated a fish room[1] at Fishing Ship's Harbour in Labrador, had already contacted my father and my brother, Max, and offered them salmon nets and some supplies to catch fresh salmon for him. They both decided to go north, but Father couldn't stay very long as he had to return in July to cut hay for the cattle and look after the gardens. By the middle of May things started to flourish on the water-front. The local merchants advanced the skippers and sharemen[2] a certain amount of clothes and other items for fishing. Many of the young men would dress up in their rubber boots, coveralls and jackets and go to church on Sunday. This was not unusual in the month of May. There were many other young men who wouldn't be able to get a berth to the Labrador

---

[1] A building where the fish-buyers collect fish from the fishermen.
[2] The crewmen who receive a portion of the income after the expenses have been taken out.

The author taking his last ride on the horse he loved, May 1936.

who walked the streets with naked feet.

By the 20th of May there was no more snow to shovel. I had to tell Mr. Hawker that I needed my windbreaker, as I would be leaving soon for Labrador. So he passed over the windbreaker. I thanked him and he thanked me for my winter's work with him. I thought the jacket was well-earned, but I don't know what he thought.

Last Hours

On May 27, 1936 I had my clothes packed. Right on top was a suit of yellow oil clothes that Mr. Harold Maddock had given me to pay for when I returned to Carbonear the next fall, as he thought I would. Early the next morning the motor vessel, *General Haig,* pulled into the wharf, bound for the Labrador. This ship was owned by Lewis Dawe and was at one time a Banking vessel[1] with a large raking bow. All hands had to hurry for she was only stopping a few hours. The price of the trip was

---

[1] A ship that had fished off the Grand Banks.

$3.00, but we didn't have to pay it until the fall when we got paid for our codfish and salmon. The skipper was a short, fat man. I didn't know his name. His voice was loud and very stern when he said, "Make it fast, boys. I want to get to Fishing Ship's Harbour before the drift ice moves back on the coast. That's about three hundred and sixty-five miles, and the remainder of our trip doesn't matter so much, as it's just salt cargo for ports farther north."

All hands rushed on board to try and get a bunk forward where there were twenty-four available. But those were filled in about two minutes. I was too late for one of them so about twenty of us lay on the forecastle floor on top of boxes and our bags. The main hold of the vessel was filled with freight, three parts up, and then the fishermen, women and girls lay on top of this freight. Most had straw beds to lie on. Each fishing crew had their own place to lunch so they could all be together. It didn't seem long before the skipper shouted to the crew, "Hold your bow line and slip your stern line." Then the motor went ahead and the ship's stern swung clear of the wharf. She went full speed astern, swung around, and headed eastward as we all waved to the crowd on the wharf behind. To most people it was a day like all others in May, but to me it was something new. As we passed Carbonear Island we ran into huge, long swells. I began to feel sick at once. I ran for my clothes bag down forward and lay on it. I could hear the pounding of water on the deck above and the noise of a chain striking.

The next day the motor broke down for a short while off Seldom, but it wasn't long before I heard the large Fairbank chugging again. I then fell asleep, and awoke to somebody shouting, "We're in Fishing Ship's Harbour!" I started to move around and struggled up top. I hadn't eaten since I left home, so I was very weak. The date was May 30. I had arrived in Labrador. I smelled the fresh air and viewed the dark waters from the snow melting off the high land and emptying into the ocean. I was to start a new life. I was to be a Labradorian by choice, not by birth.

2
Arrival in Labrador

As I moved on deck I heard the anchor drop. When I looked around I saw a group of buildings all together which made up Mr. Lewis Dawe's commercial fish room. Just around the point there was a little house and stage,[1] and farther out the harbour there was another little dark house and fishing stage. It wasn't long before the big motorboats began to come to our side. The captain said to Father, "This boat will take you and your supplies to your destination." That was a little harbour on the backside of Square Islands, known as Nowlan Harbour, about twelve miles north of where we were anchored. In less than an hour we had all the things aboard the boat and another crew was also coming along with us for Dead Islands, another mile farther north than Nowlan Harbour. The water was very calm as we moved through loose ice. A scattered seal would poke its head up and then draw down again, There were companies of eider ducks moving north. Strings of them would reach for miles. I thought it was really the land of the living. There were still spots of snow on the high land, but mostly in the deep valleys.

By midday we were entering the harbour, and the man who was at the tiller was called Frank, and the fellow who looked after the motor was called Joe. Joe was a happy man and was singing all the way along as it was Sunday. The last Sunday before leaving Carbonear I was at the Salvation Army, and the

---
[1] A small shed on a wharf where fish are split.

three back seats of the church were filled with fishermen going to the Labrador that week. They were all dressed up in coverall suits and rubber boots, and the preacher gave out the hymn to be sung, "Will Your Anchor Hold in the Storms of Life?" Those men in the back seats sang it right from their souls, and now this young man at the motor was singing the same hymn. Then Frank at the tiller shouted to Joe, "Go and watch for rocks." We were getting into shoal or shallow water now and I could see a very nice little place ahead. Soon the motor was shut off and we pulled right into the side of the rocks and started to land the freight.

There was one little shack in the harbour. The owner was not at home at the time, but there were eight big husky dogs there. Most of them were chained on and they were jumping and barking and the noise echoed up in the high hills. This was to be the place where Father and my brother Max would put up a little house in a few hours and fish there for the early part of the summer. The big trap boat then pulled out and I could still hear Joe singing. I learned later that this was Joe and Frank Ward from George's Cove who worked with Mr. Lewis Dawe.

Then a small rowboat came in the harbour with one man in it. This was the owner of the little shack, Tom Campbell. We had a lunch with him and I asked him what way could I find Square Islands Harbour. So he showed me a little foot-path and told me to keep on this and I would find Square Islands Harbour, about three miles away. There I would find my brother, Roland.

So with all my belongings on my back I said good-bye and good fishing to my father and Max. Sometimes I lost the little path, then I would find it again. I followed along by several little long ponds and then lost the path again. It was getting late. I never had anything to eat with me, so I went on to the highest hill I could see. There to me south about thirty-five miles away were some little islands. Looking to the east I could see about twelve miles and then no more land. I sat down and took a spell, then heard the sound of a motor. Right below me a boat was steaming through a narrow tickle[1] and I watched her go out of sight. I said, "This is Square Islands for sure." So I started to go that way, and soon I could see a lot of old weather-beaten houses. The closer I got, more houses I could see. This was it for sure. I then took a really deeply-worn footpath that headed to the nearest houses by the foot of a pond. As I walked over there several boys were there, and one older fellow with a big foxy whisker started to laugh when he saw me. His face was tanned with the sun, and when he laughed I could see the white wrinkles in his face. My brother Roland was only supposed to be about twenty-one years of age then, but this fellow with the whisker and the tanned face looked much older. Then he said, "You finally made it, Benny. Come right in and have a mug-up.[2] Aunt Maggie has supper ready."

As I walked toward the door I looked up at the house. It was about thirty-five feet long, the middle part much lower than the two ends and much older-looking. I then shook hands with Aunt Maggie, a white-headed woman with a long dress to the floor. In the middle of the house was a big old stove with a big round oven on it. Then Aunt Maggie opened the oven door and pulled out this big pan full of ducks, the full size of the oven. She said the lining in the oven was bad and it smoked up the birds. Then she put the pan on the table, and after she asked the blessing Roland said, "Help yourself." The smoke on the birds made them really taste good, and it was my first real meal for a week.

After lunch Roland said for me to come out in the post office and sit down. I walked out in the end of the house to the south which was the post office. There was a little space in the corner and one little box on the wall about 15" x 6" marked "Letter Box." I learned about Aunt Maggie later that she was the post-mistress.

Roland had been living with his grandfather who was John Campbell. Daniel, John's father, had come out from Scotland in

---

[1] A small strip of water between two pieces of land.
[2] A cup of tea or coffee.

the late nineteenth century and worked with the Hudson's Bay Company at North West River, Labrador, for five years. John married Martha Davis from Table Bay. After spending many years at Mulligan Bay near North West River, he decided to build a vessel and go to Nova Scotia. The vessel was called *Light of Home*. It was getting late in the fall when his little sailing vessel arrived in southern Labrador again and Aunt Martha was very seasick in the rough water. So he decided to turn back from Battle Harbour and go up in some bay for the winter. The bay he went up was St. Michaels Bay, which has three hundred and sixty-five islands. It was teeming with seals and ducks and all kinds of wildlife. The year was 1896, so they were among the first white settlers in this bay.

The first year they only built a log cabin, which was still there when I visited the head of St. Michaels Bay for the first time. It was eighteen miles from Square Islands. A few years later he built his new studded or clapboarded house, and this old house still stands today. They had a family of two boys, Alex and Tom, and five girls. Tom was dead before I arrived on the coast. One of the girls was my mother, who married a fisherman who at that time was fishing at Indian Bight in the mouth of Alexis Bay. Mother went back to Carbonear to live with Father where they raised a family of five boys and four girls. Great-grandfather Powell came out from England in the nineteenth century and spent his days at fishing and farming in Carbonear.

John Campbell was known as one of the outstanding men of the Labrador coast. He traded food for furs with the Indians on St. Michaels Bay, and the Indians always called him John the Baptist because they all liked him. John Campbell's children never went to school, but they all learned to read and write. My mother could read and write much better than I could. Mother told us in the long winter nights that they all would learn in front of the stove with birch bark lit, as they had to spare the oil in the lamps for other work.

John Campbell's log house. John's son, Alex, is on the right, and Ranger Rockwood is on the left.

3
Getting Ready for Fishing

On Sunday morning, May 31, 1936, Roland said to me, "We must get ready for salmon fishing." He had two salmon nets and a little rowboat fourteen feet long. The salmon struck on[1] about the tenth of June. While we were setting the nets in the water, the big Atlantic salmon were striking them. One net was set at the western point entering the harbour, and the other was set at Crab Gulch at the other end of the tickle. Those were supposed to be master places for salmon and were the places where Grandfather Campbell always fished his nets in the days when they salted their salmon in tierces.[2] But now we were to sell our salmon fresh, and were in hopes that we would get 5¢ per pound. This would bring a big return for our summer's work.

We used to row back and forth, just picking salmon from our nets, then row into the harbour and clean them. Each morning the salmon collector would come up from Fishing Ship's Harbour and weigh our salmon and give us a receipt for them. But there was no price marked on the receipt. This would be done later, we were told.

Sometimes we loaded our boat and would have to leave some salmon in the nets. Sometimes the icebergs would put our nets adrift, and more times the nets would drag ashore with the tide. Then we would have to haul up the anchor and row hard with the two sets of paddles until the net would get right straight. Then we'd throw the anchor over again. I called it real

---

[1] Began to get caught in the nets.
[2] Tubs where salmon were salted.

fun that we were going to get paid for. Plenty to eat and plenty to drink. Every Saturday we would row into the bay – a distance of eighteen miles from Square Islands to the head of St. Michaels Bay – or if the wind was right we would sail and then kill ducks for Sunday dinner or two or three seals, as those were very plentiful. Then we'd row back again and skin the seals and share them with all the Newfoundland fishermen who lived around the harbour. Sometimes they would give us potatoes for it that they had brought down[1] from Newfoundland.

The salmon fishery finished on the fifteenth day of July. Then we had a couple of weeks at the codfish. But with the very low price, and the fish had to be very dry and with the expense of salt and other items, there was no money in it. Most of the fishing crews that came from Newfoundland either had to get the government or the merchant who had outfitted them to pay their fares back to the island of Newfoundland.

So we shipped our fish, then picked a barrel of bakeapples[2] for the winter. By now Father, who had been with us for a time, had gone back home again to cut hay, and my brother Max decided to give us a hand to build our winter tilt[3] before he returned to the island. By the middle of September we had our tilt well underway. This was built on the south side of the head of St. Michaels Bay, one mile away from the three families that lived on the north side of the bay.

Many times people wonder why the native people scattered all over the place when they could have all lived in one or two little settlements. Well, this can be easily understood if you were to live on the coast. Only forty years ago, they lived "off the gun," as many people called it. Now we would say they lived off the wildlife resources. In order for all to have an equal share, they had to scatter about. There were three families in Campbell's Cove, one in New York, three or four in Newtown, one in Wild Bight, and now we were to build our little cabin,

---

[1] A common expression for going north.
[2] An orange-coloured fruit found in bogs and moist places, also known as cloudberry. It is delicious fresh or as jam.
[3] Log cabin.

8' x 10', in Nick's Cove on the north side of the bay. This was mainly because our trapline would run west to start with.

If all those people had lived in one of those places, it never would have brought the outside world any handier to us. The handiest nursing station was over forty miles away and the nearest doctor was over one hundred miles away. Yet those people in most cases were much happier than those I knew living in large cities.

By late September the log cabin was finished. Our floor was the ground and we only had felt over the rafters. My brother Max then boarded the next trip of the S.S. *Kyle* and went home. The next job was to go to Fishing Ship's Harbour to the merchant, Mr. Lewis Dawe, and get what the people called "settled up" for the summer's catch for salmon and cod. This included getting winter supplies; whatever we wanted for the winter we had to get then, as there were no shops at all in this area in the wintertime. So we went along with Mr. John Campbell in his motorboat. He only used this boat for shifting in the bay in the fall and again in the spring shifting their wood out. Then he used her in the fall to go up and get settled up and bring back the winter supplies. The boat was twenty-four feet long and was powered with a four-horsepower Acadia motor. It was far ahead of our rowboat.

The winter's supplies would be flour, butter, sugar, tea, molasses, baking powder, a little salt meat and salt pork, mittens, socks, and a few other items, such as candles and kerosene oil. There were no vegetables or fresh fruit. Then the man in the shop would run it up with his pencil and if you still had a good credit we would add on more beans, peas, some prunes or dried apples. My share was twenty-five dollars out of each hundred. So I thought I had a lot of money. When Mr. Dawe passed me my cheque, I put it in my pocket. This was the first money I had had since that one dollar note back in Carbonear. I don't know how much money my brother Roland had after he paid for his supplies, but he had been making good money each year.

After arriving back in Square Islands, one Newfoundland fisherman was selling his boat and motor, so Roland bought it for shifting in the bay. The boat was twenty-one feet long and was powered by a three-horsepower Acadia motor. We thought this was a really fast boat and a big one, and it sold for less than $100.00. By now it was time to get ready for the winter. We took our supplies on board and also Aunt Maggie, who we brought over into Campbell's Cove to live with her brother, Alex.

The S.S. *Kyle,* the coastal boat, was to arrive the next day, and all the Newfoundland families that were left in the harbour were to go on her. Now that we had the big boat, some of them asked us to come back out to Square Islands and put them and their freight on board. So the next day it was back to Square Islands again. We only took a lunch with us, because we hoped to get back to the cabin again that night. However, the *Kyle* arrived by noon and within an hour all hands were on board. Many of the young people whom I knew fished farther north were now on the boat going home for the winter. The boat was so crowded that she leaned to the side. All the people were on, waving to Roland and me as we were the only two to go ashore for the winter. As the old steamer pulled up her anchor and the crowd shouted once more, "Have a good winter!" a funny feel ing struck me, and I turned back on and wiped my eyes. Roland never noticed me.

We then went on shore to eat our lunch, which was all we had. We now had our stove moved into the bay eighteen miles away. Soon we were heading up there ourselves. At the best it would be late at night when we got there, if we made good time. After steaming nine miles out, our motor broke down and wouldn't start up again. The wind sprung up from the north-west, which was straight out the bay. So we put up the sail and thought we might beat to windward across the bay and back again. We were just making back and forth in the same place each time. It was no use. The boat was no good to sail. It had a small keel, and the propeller sticking out behind was a drag. We went ashore. It was getting dark. We picked a few red berries,[1] then got the boat in a little cove and moored up for the night.

The next morning, without any food, we put the sail on again. The wind was the same. It had blown all night, so we made one more try. It was no use, so Roland hauled her around before the wind and headed for Square Islands, thinking we might find some food out there or see someone. We arrived there by midday, and there was Mr. Barton Turnbull with some freight to ship on the steamer. He only learned then that the *Kyle* had gone south. She was to make one more trip for the season, but we would be on the trapline by that time.

The Barton Turnbull family was the only family that lived in New York Bay. He was a very clever man and could do almost anything. So he looked at the motor in our boat and found that the cylinder packing was gone, so he made a packing out of a skin boot and said it might last to get us home. He also gave us part of his food, and after we got going, he followed us along about six miles. Then the wind died down and veered in our favour. He waved us good-bye and headed back for New York to his wife and small children. They would spend most of their time alone while the breadwinner was out game-hunting on his winter trapline.

We made our little cabin shortly after dark. It was now the 28th of September 1936. In three more days we would be leaving for the trapline. So we hauled the boat up with block and tackle and shored her up,[2] draining the water out of the motor so she would be ready for the long winter, lying deep under the snow.

The next day I got the wood ready so we'd have some when we returned from the trapline. Roland packed the food for our trip. The next morning all that remained to be done was to take up the seal net which was in Salt Water Pond. So Roland told me to go up in the small boat and take up the nets and he would bake some cookies to take along with us. I thought this would

---

[1] Commonly called partridgeberry. Delicious in pies, breads, or as a jam to accompany chicken or turkey.
[2] Braced.

be fine. It would be a lot of fun if I had some seals in the net. There was a light breeze of wind from the west, so I put up the sail and tucked the rope in the risings of the boat and held it on with one hand in case a squall struck. I could see the dark clouds rising to the west. I started to bail the boat with the other hand when all of a sudden the squalls struck with a snow shower and the boat went bottom up and threw me some distance clear. I was a very poor swimmer, but I kept calm and swam back to the boat when another squall caught the top of the sail that was just sticking out of the water and threw it to the other side. I was only about one hundred yards from land, but was being driven away from it very fast. I pulled myself along by the side of the boat and tried to pull the mast out of the mast thwart, but it was there too solid and there was no slack in the wind. I looked again at the land and thought that if I was to swim ashore it had to be done right now. My body was getting numb, and the freezing sprays were flying over me.

I started to kick my thigh rubbers off my feet and almost had one off when the thought struck me that these were my first pair of thigh rubbers. It took a lot of hens' eggs to buy them. I just couldn't let them go to the bottom. Then the top of the sail came out of the water far enough for the wind to grab it again and I had another hard time trying to hold on. The last paddle that was hooked up in the sail broke loose, so I grabbed it, and with one leg on each side of the boat and with the paddle, I managed to keep the end of the sail under water.

I was almost to my armpits in the water, as the boat was going lower all the time. The way I was being driven by the wind, it would be two miles before I struck land. I thought I wouldn't last that long, as the wind was blowing fifty or sixty miles an hour. I would soon be out of sight of the two houses in Campbell's Cove. I knew there were only women home, as all the men were gone to their traplines. Then the wind seemed to slacken just a little, so I shouted to Roland three times and he heard me. I could see him between the showers. He had to rig up the block and tackle again and launch the boat that we had pulled up for the winter. Then he had to walk out in the water to his neck and put the anchor out for a backing. Then he hauled on the rope until he got the boat out. Back to the camp he went for the batteries and he was ready to start. On the first throw of the flywheel the motor caught, and he was heading for me. After he got alongside I thought I could hop on board, but I could not move my body. It was dead from my waist down, so Roland pulled me aboard and headed back for land. After a couple of days in the cabin I felt ready for the trapline.

4
Off on the Trapline

It was the first day of October before we left for the trapline in our sixteen-foot cedar canoe, piled high with food, the camp, the stove, and the traps. This was a canoe that Roland had bought from trapper Bill Davis of Cartwright. The year before, Bill and his brother, Theodore, trapped on Hawke's River, and when they were leaving Roland bought this canoe. It was still in very good shape, but the cedar was getting heavy from its long time in the water.

We headed up toward Salt Water Pond and hauled the seal net onto the land on the way along. There was one seal in it, a small doter.[1] This was the net I never reached when my boat turned over. After paddling along Salt Water Pond, we reached our first portage through the western valley about three miles. We had to walk about three hundred yards with our load of camp, stove, and food and then go back and get the canoe. The canoe was almost too much for me alone, so Roland did most of the canoe-carrying. I still wasn't all that strong for the bush.[2] I still had a lot to catch up with before I could manage the trapline alone.

After going through several ponds and short portages, we finally reached Big Gull Lake. Here we spent one week catching and shooting muskrats which were very plentiful in the grass. Some evenings we would shoot a dozen or more. We had three guns with us, two rifles and one twelve-gauge

---

[1] An old seal.
[2] Heavy woodland.

breechloader for the rats. After the week was up Roland said I had had spell enough and it was time to move toward the Southwest Feeder[1] of Hawke's River. We had to go on the north side of the White Hill Mountains, which meant a portage of about eight or nine miles. My, I thought, the western valley had been a long portage, and that was only three miles! We had taken our gear three hundred yards at a time, then had gone back for the canoe each time. But I was willing to keep up my end. So after paddling through several long lakes we reached the long portage. We moved slowly around the mountain-side, took a lot of spells, and lunched several times. We kept moving until one hour after dark, and at last I was too tired to go any farther. So we put up the camp and spent the night about one mile from the first pond on the Southwest Feeder of Hawke's River.

The next morning we didn't start too early. On the first trip we reached the pond with camp, stove and food. The next trip Roland took the canoe and I carried the three guns. This was supposed to be the master water for fur-bearing animals. After another couple of days we made camp, where we would stay until freeze-up time when we would return home to get our snowshoes and toboggan so we could haul more food and go right to the Hawke Mountains.

We did well with the furs, most of which were very good mink, very dark and valuable at that time. I don't think there were many mink farms then. We had otters, foxes, beavers, and only two lynx. My job was to look after the squirrels and weasels, and I was trying to make up one hundred of them on that trip. The red squirrels had a lot of fleas on them, and they used to bite me badly at nighttime, but this was all in the game, Roland said. While I couldn't skin the big furs, I just had to stick with the squirrels and put up with the fleas!

Time soon went, and the frost got colder each night. Soon the ponds were safe enough to walk across, so we crossed the big

---

[1] A tributary stream.

The author's first winter on the trapline. Bessie Campbell is in the middle, and Roland, the author's brother, is on the right.

lakes and looked at the Indian camping places. The Indians weren't long gone from the places where they camped. They had left a lot of wood cut up, and Roland said the women get the wood while the men went hunting. I said, "They sure aren't lazy." We looked at three different camping places of the Indians. Each place had the tent poles remaining where five camps had been set. The Indians were all moved on now.

After the first batch of snow we decided we would have to go toward home with our furs. One of Roland's mistakes was that he never took any spare pants or jacket. We had extra socks and mittens and now our clothes were torn up very badly in front from going through the bushes. The snow was piercing those holes, and without snowshoes we were sinking deep in some places. Going around the side of the mountains was the worst, as the land was higher and the snow was deeper. Sometimes I had all the pain I could stand, with the snow going in on my front and then melting. But three days later we finally made it. Then later Roland made two pairs of snowshoes and got the toboggan ready. In about a week we had the furs all done up and we were fitted out with new skin boots, new white dickies,[1] and pants. We had Aunt Maggie over to our cabin for a few days helping to get things ready for us.

The following Monday morning, the first of December, we started off again with our toboggan. It pulled ever so hard. We both had a rope with a loop in it that fit over our backs. I was to step in Roland's track. When he pulled up his snowshoe, mine would go down. It took me about three days before I could keep step with the leader. After that I was to take a lot of running lessons. When travelling was good it was nothing unusual to run half a mile at a time to make a tilt before dark. The average day's walk would be about twelve miles. This would give us time to get wood before dark. Once in awhile we walked up to fifty miles per day, or from 5:00 a.m. to 10:00 p.m. and sometimes until 12:00 midnight. Every limb in the old human body would be stiff and aching.

We kept at this pace most of the winter, going right to the Hawke Mountains. We saw plenty of cold days and nights, but we had lots of food at all times, mostly porcupines, partridges, and beaver meat. The caribou were very plentiful, but we never killed many as we had lots of meat without them, and we had no way to get them home from that far back in the woods.

---

[1] A hooded, winter parka that pulls on over the head.

Some herds were so large that we would get on their tracks and have a look for them. After spending hours we could see where they had come or if they were still in the woods. There would be tracks everywhere and caribou moss scattered all over the place where they had been eating.

Sometimes it would be too late to get back to the tilt for the night, so we would make a fire and spend the night in the bush. To me the nights seemed long before I got used to it. When it was ˉ25° or ˉ30° Fahrenheit, even a big fire wouldn't give too much heat in that kind of frost. This was the trapper's life, and one had to live with it. Take the good with the bad, and while there were pancakes nobody complained. We never had any bread. We used to mix up flour right in the flour bag and then roast it over the fire. Sometimes we would make doughboys in a paint can that had been thoroughly cleaned. Once in awhile, just as the water would come to a boil, down would come a knob of snow from a tree and you'd have soggy doughboys for that meal!

The best meat we could get to work on was the porcupine. One good meal of this and you wouldn't get hungry any more for the day. Rabbit would fill you up, but in a little while hunger would strike again. We only had the meat and salt, no vegetables. Until that time we had never heard too much about vitamins nor knew where to look for them.

By the middle of March the furs were very scarce, and with bad weather around, Roland said he would call off trapping for the season and would saw lumber for a house at Square Islands. This had to be done with the pit-saw. I found this harder work than pulling the old toboggan. A scaffold was rigged up, two long poles about eight feet high with a couple of cross sticks on them. Then, after cutting down the trees with the bucksaw and flattening the top and bottom with the axe, you'd roll them up on a high gallows, then you'd mark with a powder line where you were going to make each saw cut. Both the bottom and the top of the log had to be marked with a black line. In order to make the line black, we would put some gunpowder in a can with some snow, then with birch bark the fire would melt the snow. It was slow, but after awhile we would take the big pit-saw, about seven feet long, and one of us would get on top and the other under. I would always get under and Roland on top. He would haul the saw up and I would haul it back. You had to make sure to keep it on the black line, because one bad cut could spoil a board. It was slow work, but by the last of April we had the material cut and sawed to build a house 16' x 25'. As all this material was almost one mile from the salt water, we had to haul it to the landwash.[1] By the time this was done, we cut and sawed the makings of a new canoe. We hunted geese early and late in the evenings, and in the middle of the day we would be working at our new canoe for the following fall. We planned to start in September for the trapline.

The bay ice started to break up and the seals came in by the hundreds. We had plenty of seal meat and skins for our boots and mittens. We were both shooting them and catching them in our nets. Sometimes we would shoot those big square-flippered ones too large to get in over the side of the boat, so we would tow them all the way home. It was a lot of fun.

Then the sea birds started to lay, and we would get eggs for breakfast, ducks for dinner, and seal meat for supper. We lunched during the day on mussels. One could just live around the landwash anywhere without needing one cent in his pocket. Sure enough, this was the land of milk and honey!

Our way of life in those days could not hurt our wildlife resources. Man was only killing for food and not for sport. Times have changed, and man began to hunt for sport and often over-killed. With the change from rowboat or sailboat to the outboard motor, man could get around so fast and so easy even though there were three hundred and sixty-five islands in our bay. All those could be covered in a very short time, and soon man destroyed what his forefathers survived on. The same goes for our traplines. Man has invented the snowmobile, a unit that can lay down its track and very swiftly run over it. In this way

[1] The beach area between the low- and high-water mark.

it can get along in almost any kind of snow conditions, and any part of the most remote areas can be reached in a few hours without any hard work. Unless the government brings in new laws to protect our fur-bearing animals, in a few more years there will only be a few left.

On June 10 we started to move our lumber out the bay to Square Islands. The next chore was to get the firewood, cut it, and cleave it up for the summer. Then we mended up the salmon nets and did some hunting early in the morning. On June 8 Mr. Lewis Dawe, the local merchant, arrived at Fishing Ship's Harbour. We made the trip to Fishing Ship's Harbour for summer supplies, ropes, graplins, and six more salmon nets so we would be fitted out big for the salmon. By the time we got it all on board our little motorboat, we had a load. The biggest item was one barrel of gas. We got some potatoes and turnips which were a real treat after not having any for so long. There were hardly any tinned fruits or tinned meats to be had that early in the season. Later on in the summer, when the fishermen began to ship their salmon and cod, you could get some of this. I do remember once asking the old storekeeper for some tinned fruit, and he asked me if there was anyone sick at home.

In June we started setting our salmon nets. This was our first year with the motorboat for fishing, so we went across the bay with the six salmon nets that we set in three good berths. The nets were sixty fathoms long, so we joined them together and put two in a berth, then ran the nets about seventy-five fathoms straight, and the balance of the twine was used to make what we called "back and vee," a harpoon-like shape. The salmon would swim along the straight part of the net only to find themselves surrounded by twine. Then they would make a dash to get clear and end up all mashed in the net. While we were setting our nets, the big shiny salmon would be striking the twine. Every haul we made would bring salmon. When the wind would come on the land, this would drive the salmon in, and some of the nets would sink with salmon. Our best day for the summer was thirty-five quintals or thirty-five hundred pounds.

This was four hundred and twenty salmon, which would average out a little more than eight pounds per salmon. This was a lot of salmon to look at in the stage at one time! We ended up with one hundred and thirty-five quintals for the season, one hundred pounds per quintal. I don't recall what we got per pound as I never recorded it in my diary.

Everyone seemed to be happy whether they did well with the catch or not. Each evening after work the young people would get together and sing songs and play music. This would go on until eleven or twelve o'clock each night, whenever they didn't have to work late in the stages at the fish.

On Sunday nobody worked, unless it was to take ice out of their salmon nets. Most of the people would get in their motorboats, about two boats from each harbour, and go to the nearby harbours to talk with the fishermen there. We would go to Dead Islands, which was five miles north of Square Islands, and then on to Triangle, which was seven miles farther south. This was a lot of fun on Sundays.

There were only hymns sung on Sunday. The Rev. Lester L. Burry, the United Church minister, would make one trip along the coast each summer and hold services in someone's house. Many times it would be in a fish store or, if the day was fine, it would be held outdoors.

The salmon fishery would usually end the last week in July. Then the nets had to come up and be cleaned. Again we only did a little cod fishing. We dried it and moved into our little cabin for awhile. We built a new house for the winter. This was a studded one, caulked with moss. It was 18' x 10' with six-foot walls. We thought this was a really good house for a trapper, because we had a board floor in it and two little windows. Our first log cabin only had one little window in the door. We were sure moving into a much more modern house – one bedroom with two beds, one over the other, and we had a pantry and a kitchen. This was all we needed. In fact, we would only spend very little time home. We would be on the trapline most of the time, so you couldn't have anything in your home that would freeze.

After this we went back to Square Islands for awhile and framed up a new house for the summertime. This was out of our pit-saw lumber that we had sawed that spring. This was going to be quite a building, we thought, all sawed lumber. It was already late in September and people began to move back to the Island again on the S.S. *Kyle*. Very few would have any money to take with them.

5
Stormy Weather and Sickness

Roland took sick and wasn't getting any better. The nearest hospital was more than one hundred miles away and the Grenfell Mission boat, *Maraval,* had already gone south for the winter. The boat made two trips along the coast each summer and was doing a lot of good. The staff could pull teeth and take X-rays on board. There was always a doctor on her. But now it was too late. She had gone south where she would do work in northern Newfoundland. There was a nursing station at Mary's Harbour, only thirty miles south, so this was where we would have to go.

There was a storm of wind from the northwest and our little boat wasn't too seaworthy for the Atlantic Ocean in that kind of weather, so we decided to wait until the next day and see if the wind would drop out. But the next morning it was the same, a hard gale from the northwest blowing straight out the bays. We would have to cross Occasional Harbour, Ships' Harbour, Alexis Bay, and St. Lewis Bay, not to mention St. Michaels Bay which Square Islands is in. However, Roland said we would have to try it. We took food and plenty of gas for several days, but the hard wind and the choppy waves made our boat leak badly. It was my job to keep the water out. By the middle of the day, we were heading across Alexis Bay, but we just couldn't get any farther, so we went ashore on an island and had a lunch. Later the wind slackened a little, so we filled up our gas tank again and started off. We made Spear Point and Murray's Harbour, but as we rounded St. Lewis Cape the wind struck again with gale force. We kept punching at it[1] for hours and pulled into St. Mary's Harbour just after dark. It happened that the Mission boat was still there, storm-bound. The weather was too bad for it to cross the Strait of Belle Isle to Newfoundland. Roland got to the nursing station on his own while I bailed out the boat. I found that the boat was too leaky to stay afloat until daylight, so I put her right on the beach by the Grenfell Mission wharf and tied her on, so that when the water fell she would be dry and would not leak.

Mr. Acreman, who looked after the nursing station, told me to come over to his house and get something to eat and stop there for the night. I thanked him for his kindness, and after having my supper I took a rest. Then I went back to the boat and found she was dry on the beach and the wind was gone right calm. I went back to Mr. Acreman's house for the night.

I then got the word that Roland had to stop there for treatment and they didn't know what time he would be ready for home. Roland suggested I return home and move our supplies for the winter into our new house and get Aunt Maggie off Square Islands, because if all the Newfoundland people were gone, she would be there by herself on the island. Aunt Maggie was getting up in her seventieth year, but was still a very active woman. She was still doing a bit of trapping in the wintertime by herself. She was an expert on catching rabbits and trouting through the ice. She could find medicine in the forest for almost any kind of normal sickness and she almost always kept some kind of mixture on the stove ready for action. Her main medicine was lurch – juniper boiled in hot water. I often drank it and it gave me an appetite like a horse!

At the first sign of daylight I got up. I never waited for breakfast, but hurried to the boat. The tide had just begun to rise around the boat, and by the time I got gas in the tank and grease in the cups, I could push off into the water. I steamed out through the harbour, which was still calm, but as I crossed St.

---

[1] Driving against it.

Lewis Bay the wind slowly picked up. By the time I rounded St. Lewis Rock off St. Lewis Cape, there were about twenty miles of wind. This was not too bad, if it wouldn't get any worse. But it did. When I rounded Spear Point I could see that with the wind and tide in Alexis Bay I would never survive to reach the other side. It was now gale force and the water was drifting like snow. I hauled on my tiller ropes to head back for Spear Point and Harbour, but I couldn't get her head to move. There was only one way she could go there, and that was broadside. So there was no other choice but to live or die in Alexis Bay. I couldn't see any hope of ever reaching land again, but I was determined to keep my boat afloat as long as I could.

Then another problem occurred. My boat was so far on its side that the inlet that took the water to the motor was out of the water most of the time. The engine was beginning to get hot, crack and bang. So I hauled off my boots, then my socks, and dipped them into the water in the bilge hole and put them on the igniter of the motor. I was pretty busy with bare feet in the water, bailing it for all I was worth, and keeping the socks back and forth on the motor. But the boat was leaking worse all the time. I knew that some of the planks were beginning to come off. It looked as though there was little hope now. About halfway across this big bay I could see houses straight ahead. The way I was going, there was little hope of ever reaching them. The waves seemed to rise and break, so when one was going to break on my bow I would slow down and let it break on her stern. I would pull the throttle open and it would break just behind. I didn't know how much longer I could hold out under this pressure – throwing water, keeping the socks on the motor, working the throttle and the tiller, and then three big waves came, one after the other, and I thought this was it. For sure I'd be blown bottom up! But where the boat was on her side so much, most of the water was passing over her. The water I was bailing out was what the boat was leaking in. I raised my head for one second and another big lop struck me and almost washed me over the side. When I looked up, there were two big fishing vessels coming straight toward me. Those vessels had loads of salted codfish on board, were working their way south, and were caught in the storm. I thought they were coming to try and rescue me. As they got handy I saw that their sail was under double reef foresail and jumbo – this is storm canvas for the old sailing vessels. They may not have even seen me as they headed up under the land. They were trying to make Spear Harbour. Probably the captain was more concerned over his crew of many souls than he was over trying to save one. So I kept on with a hungry stomach, aching arms and cold feet. I was still moving toward those houses on the north side of the bay.

The tide seemed to slacken as I got handier to the entrance of the harbour, but the water still drifted like snow. I ran along by a big breaking shoal that had no marker to warn ships of its danger. I was now slowly entering this harbour, still bailing water for all I was worth and still keeping the socks full of water on the igniter. As I entered the tickle I could see houses on both sides of the harbour, so I steered for the ones on the north side. This would give me more shelter, as the boat had to go right for the beach. It wouldn't have stayed afloat, not thirty minutes, so I steered for a rocky beach by the side of a long stage and then shut off the motor. I ran forward and jumped ashore in my naked feet, holding the boat on as I saw a man coming toward me. As soon as he saw my condition and that of the boat, he shouted to some men who were on the flake[1] piling fish together. Those men hauled the boat out of the water right away. We could see that not less than six butts of the planking were off. The men told me this was Williams' Harbour and that the first man to come to my assistance was Mr. Bill Tom Russell. I can assure you, in the years that followed and my many trips to Williams' Harbour, this man was always the same. He was a man right through, not only a man in peaceful times, but a man in the time of need. He soon was back with a hammer, nails and oakum,[2] and before long had all the planks

[1] A frame for drying fish.
[2] A loose fibre of old ropes used for caulking the seams of boats.

back in place and tightened up. He told me that one hour before I arrived, Mr. Asaph Wentzell, Sr., had come in a big, housed-over boat that was now moored by the stage. He had his family aboard and was moving into Labrador to make it his home from Daniel's Harbour, Newfoundland. He said when he arrived that no small boat could ever live to make land. They had all they could do in their big boat. He then told me they had had fish that was spread on the flakes that morning and it almost all blew off. It was the first time he had ever seen this happen since he had been living in Williams' Harbour. We then put the boat back in the water and moored her by the stage. She was still leaking more than the average boat, but there was no problem to keep her afloat.

Mr. Russell then made me go up to his house and gave me dry socks while he dried mine behind the stove. His wife had supper ready for me. They had a big family there, but the children were all small. I then lay down and fell fast asleep and never awoke until daylight. I was just worn out. I learned after that Mr. Russell looked after my boat all night in case the water rose high enough to go over the batteries.

The next morning we had breakfast and there was very little wind. Mr. Wentzell's boat left just at daylight, so I was too late to go along with him. But there was another boat that was going to Fishing Ship's Harbour, so I followed this boat. She went on the back side of Williams' Harbour and we had smooth water until we got there. The boat then pulled into the wharf in Fishing Ship's Harbour and I pulled out and headed for Square Islands. I only had to go about nine miles along the coast and I would reach Square Islands. It was a nice day with just a light westerly wind. I was making good time and hoping it would keep this way until I reached home. I was just about one mile out of Fishing Ship's Harbour when the engine began to clack and bang and then stopped. The firing spring was broken, so there was no spring to open the breaker points. I thought there might be a spare one in the tool kit, but I was out of luck. There was a little too much wind for me to make the land with the sculling oar and I was driving off the land. No boat in sight anywhere. I was helpless in the ocean. Then it occurred to me that maybe there was a spring in the bottom of the boat that had fallen down, after all the jumping around I had yesterday. I started feeling around under the bedding of the boat and found all kinds of wrenches and springs, but they were all broken. I then put them all together on the firing pin and it looked as if it would work. I was happy it did, or this story never would have been written. For there were no other boats around that day, and the next day another gale came on, which would have taken me far out into the ocean. Not knowing how long those pieces of springs would last, I first made land and followed along the shore and went well into the bay before crossing over for Square Islands.

It was a fine day as I pulled into Square Islands. I tied the boat onto the stage and went for Aunt Maggie's house. I met John Campbell on the way. He said the Newfoundlanders all left a couple of nights ago and there was only his family on the island. He said there was a beaver up at the head of the pond cutting wood, so I walked over to the pond that came right close to the house, and looked up, and it was Aunt Maggie! She thought she might run out of wood and didn't know when we would be back, so with the hard wind blowing down the pond, she was cutting those small trees like a beaver would cut, then throwing them into the pond, and the wind would take them right to her house. Then she would haul them ashore and cut them up for firewood.

I told her the story about Roland and how he wanted to get off the island before it got too cold and before all hands had left, as they would on the first suitable day. While the weather was good, I put our winter supplies in the boat, which were for our new house in Nick's Cove, and I told Aunt Maggie to be ready to leave the next morning. I would take her to Campbell's Cove and stay with her and Uncle Alex and family until Roland came back. In the meantime, I got some parts from Mr. John Campbell, Jr., and put them on the engine. Within an hour I was on my way alone, about eighteen miles in the bay, and with about five hundred pounds of winter supplies on board.

I made it to our new studded shack, landed the freight, and headed back for Square Islands. It was dark now, but a very nice night. Three hours later I made it to Square Islands. Aunt Maggie had her belongings all packed up and ready to go. I had a good lunch of smoked trout and red berry jam, then lay down for a rest. It was a busy time, but once we got back in the bay we thought things would kind of level off for a few days.

Aunt Maggie had her little oil lamp lit long before daylight the next morning and had the fire going. Soon after breakfast I had all our belongings on board the boat, except the stove which had to be moved in two pieces. One part of it was the big round oven. I would have a job to manage this myself, so the Campbell boys – Daniel and Stanley – helped me put it aboard later on. By then they had all their things on board their own boat also, and before we turned the point of the harbour, I saw the other boat coming along behind. There would be nothing left on the island now, only dogs which would be picked up later on and carried into the bay.

Clouds began to move fast across the sky, and before we got half a mile it was blowing a storm from the northwest. Our boat started to take on water badly, and soon I couldn't keep the water from the flywheel. I looked behind and saw that the other boat had gone back to Square Islands. We were far enough ahead that it would be easier to try and get through Ship's Tickle and then make it up under White Fish Island. We would have it lund[1] until we got to Narrows Islands. But we had all we could take and couldn't keep the water from the wheel of the motor. As soon as we got through the tickle, I had to stop and bail out the boat, then got it going and moved slowly along the shore. The wind kept rising until it reached gale force, and we were forced to go ashore on Narrows Island. We moored the boat in a sandy cove as the wind was blowing right off this beach. We thought the wind would go down with the sun, but it

---

[1] Sheltered.

didn't. It howled all day and the water drifted like snow again.

I told Aunt Maggie there was very little hope of us getting off the island that day, and there was no need to worry. We had food, so I got to work picking up enough driftwood to frame up a little shelter. We took a roll of felt that we had in the boat and covered the shelter over, then put the big feather bed down and had plenty of bedclothes. After having a lunch over the fire, we both crawled in for the night. It was certainly much better than out in the cold. I will always remember Aunt Maggie keeping far away from me in the big feather bed. She was never married and never had a boyfriend in her life, and now to lie this handy to a man she felt out of place! But when it comes down to the struggle for survival, we have to make the best of things. The wind blew a storm all night, and by daylight there was no change. Aunt Maggie was out and had the fire going and the kettle on and was up on the hill picking berries before I was out. After a lunch I walked up the hill where I could see right to the head of the bay. It was feather-white. We wouldn't be able to make a move until the wind got better.

By dinnertime the wind started to go around with the sun, so I felt that by three o'clock it should start to get better. I got to work picking up driftwood along the beaches and built a frame all over the boat. Just left one hole for the motor and one behind for steering. Then I took the felt off our shelter and nailed it over the framing and stripped it all over. It was just like a decked boat. By three o'clock we heard a motorboat. By now the wind was still coming around with the sun, and the other side of the island would soon be the best shelter. We knew the boat we heard had to be John Campbell's now going in the bay, passing on the south side of the island, as this was the lundest side now and they could follow up the side of the bay when they crossed Dead Island Run which separated Square Islands from the mainland.

We were about ready to leave now. This time Aunt Maggie was to get to the motor and screw the grease cups and bail some water out. It would only be the water that the boat was leaking, as she was all housed over now. There were only two holes for our heads. I was to steer from behind. First, I had to give Aunt Maggie some lessons on how to screw the grease cups and be sure to keep her feet from the flywheel. We were about ready. Aunt Maggie was past her seventieth birthday now, but she had seen a lot of this kind of life in her day. She never complained. There was no animal in the forest that Aunt Maggie wouldn't tackle with her .22 rifle. In earlier years she used her muzzleloader. It was still on the rack in the old house.

We started across Dead Island Run, water flying over us, but none coming in our boat. We were making good time. The wind started to drop out fast, and as it got dark we seemed to go faster. When we got one mile from Campbell's Cove we met John Campbell's boat coming to look for us, since we had left two days ago. They came right in the bay that same evening the way we were supposed to go, and they saw no sign of us. They thought it was possible that it was the last of Aunt Maggie and little Benny, as they thought he never had the experience to survive!

Where the author and Aunt Maggie outlived the storm on an island facing the ocean.

6
Second Year on the Trapline and Christmas

It was early October when Roland arrived from the nursing station at Mary's Harbour. He really wasn't ready for home, but as it was the last trip of the coastal boat, the S.S. *Kyle,* going north, they let him go under the condition that he was to take it easy and by no means was he to get wet. His stomach was in bad shape. He was now twenty-three years old and had spent most of those on the trapline, eating food that most times was only partly cooked. He had eaten so much flour which had been roasted over the stove or fireplace that his stomach was badly damaged and needed the proper kind of treatment to be well again.

Once more we were ready for the trapline. Roland said he had to take it easy, and he thought he could, as we now had a new canoe that was only twelve feet long, built from balsam fir. We had made it that spring. From my first year's experience I knew there was no way to take it easy on any trapline. There is hardly a day that one is dry in the early part of the year. Just the water on the bushes would make you wet in a short while, and there would be days and sometimes weeks when you never knew what it was to be dry for one hour. Many times when you arrived at your tilt you would fall asleep in your wet clothes while the kettle was boiling. You had planned to dry out your clothes after lunch. The little tilts were so small that one could hardly straighten out or even sit up without bending your neck a little.

Within one week we were over the longest portage around

the north side of the mountains. I was more used to the job now
than I had been the first year, but I started to notice that Roland
was working in punishment. He was a fellow who would never
sit down to lunch. He always stood up by the fire and lunched,
while I was always tired enough to sit down on the boughs
close to the fire with my skin boots shoved down to my knees
to keep them warm in the snow. We were fitted out with supplies to stay in the bush until close to Christmas. We had our
snowshoes and some spare filling[1] for them. We spent quite
awhile on the South Feeder of Hawke River and did well with
the furs there, which were mostly otters and beavers. When
November came in, we started to catch mink, as they were getting prime then.

We left our canoe at the feeder, as the water was starting to
freeze up, and moved to the southern waters of Hawke River,
only a couple more days' walk. We still had no tilt built in that
far, so we used the canvas camp so we could move around in all
directions. The furs were average in there. Because mild weather prevented safe travelling we spent a week at the camp trapping beaver that were housed close by. We were living well on
beaver meat, and we dipped our damper dogs[2] in the beaver fat-
like butter.

Following the big mild we had a batch of snow. Our flour
was getting scarce, and the walking was very bad now, so
Roland decided we should head back home for more. I could
see that Roland was feeling the weight of the long trip back
through the deep snow. The first year he had done most of the
walking ahead, although we did take turns. The fellow behind
was only stepping in the track of the head fellow after the snow
was tramped down. But now Roland wasn't offering to take any
turn ahead, so I kept plugging at it all day while Roland carried
the biggest load on his back behind me. The heaviest were the
beaver pelts. I had the camp and he had the stove. We arrived
home a week before Christmas, and Roland said he would rest

[1] Network of rawhide within the frame.
[2] A dough patty fried directly on top of the stove.

a week and go back again after Christmas.

The weather turned very cold and windy. I spent most of my time getting wood, and it was always the rule among the people to have big dry juniper[1] for Christmas; I used to climb up by the side of the hill and cut down those big dry juniper trees, as big around as barrels, and cut them up in short chunks and drag them home. When Christmas Day finally came, we were invited to Uncle Alex and Aunt Maggie Campbell's. A long plate was in the middle of the table and this was filled with partridges, one for every person. I noticed they had the pile of white juniper wood behind the stove and another pile under the table that they used to put their water buckets on. After dinner Uncle Alex dressed in his Scotch suit with a little cap on his head and a feather in it. The suit, worn only on special occasions, was stored away in his homemade trunk. He would then sit down and play his violin and sing, and Aunt Maggie would sing the choruses in the background. After this we visited our neighbours, the Kippenhucks, who lived about three hundred yards to the northwest. We followed a footpath that led through heavy forest trees that no one was supposed to cut, because they were shelter for the houses. Uncle Sam Kippenhuck's father was a full-blooded Eskimo who shifted down on this part of the coast in the early days. Uncle Sam married a Carbonear woman who came down to fish in Labrador with her parents during the summer. She died when one of the children was born, so Uncle Sam had it very hard the rest of his life, raising his family and at the same time working for a living. Uncle Sam himself died many years later from a kidney disorder. He was a big man and there was no way to get him to a hospital. It was sad to watch this man dying when none of us could help him. It was also a very painful death, because there was nothing to give him to stop the pain. He died up in the loft of his house; the little stairway was so small that some floorboards had to be taken up from the loft to lower him down that way.

Uncle Sam and his boys were mostly barren-ground trappers,

---

[1] Tamarack or larch.

who trapped out close to the seacoast. They always got their share of foxes and were noted for their hospitality.

After leaving Uncle Sam's we would visit the house on the lower end of the footpath, which belonged to John Campbell II. John's father, Tommy Campbell, was now dead. Tommy was Uncle Alex's brother. John was in his late twenties and was in charge of the family. Sometimes after a bad fishery, they would move into the bay with only one month's food. Later they would go into the country, and as soon as they got enough furs, they would come back, get in the boat, and go to the Hudson's Bay Store at Frenchman's Island, about forty-eight miles away, and trade their furs for food. Mostly it would be flour, and with the bad weather in the fall, they would have some terrible times getting home with the food for the winter.

I remember one fall when they were coming in the bay. The ice began to make and they got their boat frozen in. They had just survived one storm on the trip and coming around Cock's Head a shoal broke on them and broke the keel off their motor-boat. They were forced back around the head in a cove where they spent a whole week before the storm died down enough to follow on their trip. Then coming in the bay they got stuck in the ice and we all got together and chopped out the boat and hauled it ashore for the winter. We rolled six barrels of flour into the woods and they later got it to their home by dog team. John stuck by the family and took the rough with the smooth; he lived long enough to see them all grown up and married before he died.

Christmas Day ended with boiling up one big meal for the husky dogs. They must have their Christmas dinner, too. This was always the rule of the Campbells. The feed was put into two half barrel tubs, and boiled on the stove with codfish heads in it or sometimes rabbits or caribou. The dogs would all sit around the tubs until the feed was cooled off with snow, then Uncle Alex would strike the tub with his stick and say "Go ahead," and the eight big husky dogs would bolt it down. The dog that was the leader had to have the last lick. Then he would usually make a howl that would be answered by the Kippenhuck dogs, then by John Campbell's dogs. After that everything would be quiet. I never ever learned what this howl meant in dog language, but at least they let each other know they were still around.

None of those teams of dogs could mix together. They had their limits to come toward each house. If they came any farther there would be a fight, and sometimes one dead dog left in the path.

L-R: John Campbell I, the author's mother, Grandmother Martha Campbell, Aunt Maggie, Tom Campbell I, dog-team driver for clergyman, and United Church minister.

Then we would go home to our little studded house for the night. We had presents to bring back, which were mostly mittens and socks, which would be the most needed. The following week we were to return to the trapline.

The home of John Campbell I. In front is a pit-saw scaffold built in the nineteenth century.

7
Return to the Trapline

We planned to go right into the Hawke Mountains which would be a three hundred mile trip, with all the different feeders to branch off on, back and forth. We had to haul more flour on this trip and the komatik,[1] which pulled easier than the toboggan.

We needed more traps for the new grounds, so the next day I was supposed to go out the bay ten miles and pick up some fox traps that we had out there. The morning was very cold – about -40° Fahrenheit – with very little wind. I had my dickie hauled over my sweater, which was all I wore back in the country.

This cabin was built in Campbell's Cove in the same spot where John Campbell had built his cabin one hundred years earlier, 1894-1994.

[1] Similar to a dogsled.

Back there you spent most of your time in heavy forest, which was warmer but now on the open bay it seemed plenty cold for me.

I made it down the bay all right, but when I turned to come back it was just too cold for me. But what could I do? I just had to make home, so I used to go about half a mile into the woods and jump and beat my hands until I would get a bit warm. Then I'd start again. There was just a low drift of snow blowing and it was very frosty. I knew it wasn't colder than 40° Fahrenheit as it doesn't blow then. It's always calm when it's that cold. I was only about halfway back when the sun began to drop behind the hill. It seemed to get colder than ever. Human flesh just couldn't take it the way I was dressed. Someone for sure would find me frozen to death on the bay if I tried to follow on this way.

There were still five miles to go. Sharp pains would strike the very marrow in my bones and make me jump and head for the woods again. This time I said I just must find the answer. I couldn't make it following the woods, because there were several big arms of water that ran to the southwest. It would take me about two days to follow around those and the walking was bad in the woods. On the bay it was just like the floor.

I started to look around and saw a big overgrown birch with the bark all hanging off it. At once I thought this was the answer. I started stripping off the birch bark. After I got all the loose bark off I took the axe and cut a long notch in there. Then it curled off in big strips. All that I could reach was off, so I started filling up my pants, starting at my skin boots. It fit around my legs like it was made for them. Then I got the biggest pieces around my body. I wasn't wearing my snowshoes, so I took the slings out of them and tied the bark around the lower part of my parka. It worked fine. I put both my axe and gun into my game bag and kept my hands behind me. I felt no wind blowing through my clothes. I was home about one hour after dark. Roland thought I had had a good idea. The bark kept me from freezing and it was also good for lighting fires in the mornings, as it burns like gas.

Roland had everything for the trapline, so the next day at dawn we were off, hauling our komatik behind instead of the toboggan that we had used the winter before. Travelling wasn't too bad. We made our tilt the first night on the Southwest Feeder about two hours after dark. While Roland did the cooking, I got the wood, which was my work mostly.

The next day Roland decided he would go across to the river and leave out the climbing going south around the mountains. This meant we would take the river twelve miles farther east. We made the river by dark, killed a porcupine close to our camp, cooked half of it that night and hung up the other half. We could need it coming back again.

We started up the river the next morning. Travelling on a river in the wintertime was generally bad, as a river usually is lower than the land and the snow lodges there. The wind cannot get at it to blow it away or make it hard. But we could keep moving slowly, and when there is plenty of food and a night's rest a fellow can work the short winter's day, even if it's hard.

Sometimes Roland would go some miles ahead with his rifle in his hand. He always carried his .44 rifle. I would dodge along behind in his track with the tow, miles behind him. Sometimes passing the little wooded islands in the river I would see something written in the snow. I would stop and read it, and it would read, "Go onto the island." After doing that I would find the island full of partridges, spruce ones. As Roland had the .44 rifle he couldn't waste his big cartridges on small game. And it would make so much noise that it would scare animals away. The little .22 rifle was the one for small game. I would kill about a dozen partridges and then move on. Too many would make my load heavy, and there was no need to kill more than were needed.

We camped at the Southern Feeder of Hawke River that night; the next night it was the mouth of Mountain Brook, under several large trees. The Indians had not long left the spot, but I learned something from them that day that I never forgot.

When we put up our stove, we always put it on four sticks, two on each side. However, I saw how the Indians only used three sticks, one on each side in the front and one in the middle behind, so that was the way I always did it after that. It worked fine and was a bit quicker. After the camp was up, Roland took a rest. He had been dry ever since leaving home. But I knew he was putting out his very best. Roland always wanted to take the hardest end and he still wanted to do this. But he was a sick man and wouldn't admit it.

I went across the river. White partridges were under the trees, and up in the trees were the spruce ones. There were porcupine tracks everywhere; all I killed was one very large porcupine. He was up in the top of a very tall tree. Roland told me never to shoot a porcupine in the stomach, but always in the head. But this one kept his head away all the time, so on the last of it I fired at his back and down he came. I then shot him in the head. He was a real old timer, so I dragged him over to the camp and Roland said he would skin him. When Roland discovered that he had a bullet in his paunch, he got awfully mad with me for doing that. He said he wouldn't eat any part of him, only his legs. It is believed the paunch is full of tapeworms, which flow through the body when the porcupine is shot there. So after things quieted down, we got the legs off the porcupine and into the cooking pot and had our good lunch.

One more day's walk in on the brook and it would be as far as we would go with our camp. We could then go one day's walk each way, and even if it meant getting home with the stars in the sky, it would be better than shifting the camp every day. On the trip the weather was fine and cold. It was ‾25° and ‾30° all the time, but was just nice weather when it was sunny. In the daytime we got a very dry frost inland, and it didn't seem to strike one the same way as out at the seacoast.

Time seemed to go fast. Furs were scarce. So far we only had two mink on the trip. A beaver house was there, but something or someone, maybe the Indians, had them all caught. So about dinnertime we decided to put on a big meal of porcupine. We filled up the stove with wood and decided to travel a ways on a little side brook that ran into Mountain Brook. It was only about a mile in where we had some mink traps. Roland said our flour was getting scarce, so next week we would move back toward home. After we got in on this little brook, Roland looked out to the eastward and said to me, "Do you see that big bank rising up?" I looked up and sure enough, all along to the eastward was a big blue bank which Roland said meant very bad weather, snow and maybe wind. So we took our traps and started to head toward the camp.

After we got to the camp Roland said we would eat what we could of the porcupine in the pot, but it was a very old animal and hardly cooked it all. So we tore off some meat with our teeth and I started to chew at one of the kidneys, but it was very tough. At last Roland said we had to go, so I swallowed the kidney and soon we had everything on our komatik and were moving down Mountain Brook. We'd walk one mile, then run a mile. It was good and dark when we arrived at the camping place in the mouth of Mountain Brook, where I learned a lesson from the Indians about putting up the stove. Roland slacked running and asked me if I thought I could hold out to make the next camping place, which was where the Southern Feeder emptied its waters into Hawke River. For a minute I couldn't speak. Roland thought maybe I wasn't sure I could hold out, but the trouble with me was that the old kidney I had swallowed all whole had come up and was stuck in my throat. I was trying to get it cleared up before I could answer, so I took it out in my hand and told him he should carry on to the next place.

The stars were still shining to the west, but to the east the weather was closing in slowly. There was no wind, so we followed on, running and walking. Just after twelve o'clock midnight we started to put up the camp. The first snow began to fall. We soon got the camp up and then got our wood. I took a candle to go look for water where the Southern Feeder emptied into the river. The ice was piled up about twenty feet high. I had to get down below it with my candle lit, and when I got to the bottom there would be running water. So I lit my candle and crawled until I found the water, then crawled back. Sometimes one doesn't think about the dangers involved until he gets back onto solid ice.

We had a good lunch, then fell fast asleep. It snowed all night, as big as flakes could be, and no wind. This kept up four days and four nights. All we could do was to clear out the camp door and get wood. The fifth day the snow lightened. We were all out of food now and the whole river was levelled off with snow just like feathers. We had a look at it, then tried it with our snowshoes on. There was little we could do, so Roland said for me to walk in on the brook about half a mile. We had a beaver house tailed up[1] in there. He was going to try and make a track toward our next camping place. There was no hope of getting very far the next day. I made it to my beaver house, but it took me all day to get in and out again and never had any luck with beaver. There were about five feet of snow everywhere. Sometimes you almost had to swim through it. Roland got down the river about two miles and got back. Now the serious thing was that we had very little food and the weather was too bad to go hunting. We had very little flour left and nothing else.

The next day we made an early start down the river. The first two miles were good where we had a track to follow. Then it was very slow, just one deep trench. However, it was all down-river which was a help. We made the next camping place by dark, and the half of the porcupine we had hung up there going in was still there. We soon cooked it up and spared the flour that was left. There was just enough left for about four little damper dogs; two would be for breakfast. Roland said we would have to leave our camp, stove and sled and only take one axe and one gun. I knew this was something unusual to do. It was now a battle between life and death, with only enough flour to make four damper dogs. Each would be about the size

[1] A trap was set there.

of a cookie and cooked on the tin stove.

The greatest barrier that stood between us and our hunting for food was a great layer of snow that didn't seem to settle in frosty weather. After lunch we headed for the little tilt on the Southwest Feeder. We made it by dark and crawled in, tired and hungry. We did find a couple of cakes of hard bread in a can that Roland had stowed away for rations, so we soaked them and ate the last two damper dogs. That was it. Fifteen miles to go, bad travelling, no food. I don't know what Roland thought about, but I thought about back home as a boy. Often if food wasn't like I thought it should be, I would leave it on my plate. If only I had this now, how I would eat it!

Nothing was said as we rubbed out our skin boots and started to put them on. Roland had saved my life last year in the boat accident. And I had saved his life once. We had come out of the country and found the ice very slippery. So that night we decided to go across to Uncle Alex's house and pick up some clothes they had washed for us. We decided to skate across. It was quite dark and Roland was skating ahead. Suddenly I heard this big splash. There had been a big crack in the bay ice and he had gone right under. I felt my way to the edge and then lay down. I could hear him swimming toward me, so he put up his hand and I grabbed it and pulled him to safety. It's very seldom that the best of swimmers ever gets back on the ice when he goes right under the water. A lot of people had died that way in our area over the years. Some were found frozen on top of the ice, but most were pulled from the bottom.

Now we were getting our dickies on and our game bags were very light. Only two mink skins on the trip. Roland had the gun and I had the axe; it was the lightest time we had ever returned from the bush. We headed down Three Mile Pond and the travelling got better after we got around the mountains. By three o'clock we arrived at Clifty Lake, which was halfway between our tilt and home. There could be a book written about this lake alone, but I won't go into the details as I want to speak a little about the trapline. Clifty Lake had only small timber. As we arrived we glanced at where we always lunched going and coming. But this time there would be no lunch. I watched Roland as he pushed his hunting knife farther back on his belt, then pulled his belt tight and looked at me as if to say, "Do the same. This will be our lunch this time." If we had had beaver pelts in our bag instead of these minks, we could have made some soup out of the fat that would still be left on them. But a mink would be the last thing that any human would be able to get down. Even a dog won't eat a mink, nor will a wolf when he is alone. But sometimes when they are in packs, and each is trying to grab from the others, they will steal mink from a trap and eat it.

From so many trappers lunching up at Clifty Lake the wood close to the lake was all cut down. We had used it many times for making fires and boiling the kettle. This was the lake where we always left our dogs when we went caribou hunting. In fact, all the trappers from White Bear Arm left them there when they went to the White Hill Mountains in the springtime, because if they brought the dogs any handier they would bark and frighten off the caribou. Or the caribou would smell them. We often cut down boughs for the dogs to lie on. For the past century this had been going on. So the trees were getting scarcer all the time.

We kept dodging along. The travelling was getting better. A lot of things were going through my mind, but never once did I think this would be my last trip to the Hawke Mountains with Roland. But if we survived, it would be a trip never to be forgotten. It appeared that the storm we had gone through inland had never struck the outer part of our trail, so we were able to make home early that night, where warm food soon brought more life to a hungry body.

8
Alone on the Trapline

We had a week of rest at home and plenty of food to eat. But one day Roland said to me, "I'm not strong enough to travel the country again this winter. In fact, I don't expect to live very long." It didn't surprise me at all, as I knew Roland was working under much pressure all the winter. The last trip was enough for any well man, not to mention a sick one. He told me it was up to me if I thought I could take over the trapline and make it on my own. He said he had plenty of food there for the spring and money to buy more when the merchants came on the coast again. But he didn't know if he would be around then.

I was now seventeen years old. I believed I could manage the trapline for that winter, as there could only be a couple more trips. The thought of going back in the bush didn't bother me, but the thought of coming home to our little cabin and finding Roland perhaps dead on the floor or in bed did bother me. Roland was aware of this, and he wanted to make it clear to me so that if it did happen it wouldn't be a surprise. It doesn't matter how big and brave you are. It would make you uneasy when you come to leave your closest friend behind in that state. I told Roland that if he thought he could look after himself at home, I would go back over the trapline and straighten out things once more, as we had traps all over the place. There were beaver houses that must be attended to or the furs would be spoiled as well as the place.

That night I went across the bay and talked to Uncle Alex about my plans of going over the trapline the next day by myself. He showed concern over the whole thing and said he would visit Roland each day he could cross the bay. The girls would be at home to look after things while he was gone. He was leaving the next day also to go over his trapline, and he said to make it easier for me, his third night he would camp at the foot of his beaver house pond where the two brooks meet, the one from Long Lake and the other from the beaver pond where they ran down in the southern water of Hawke River. This meant I didn't have to carry my camp on this trip. I knew just where this was since we always crossed close by on our way to the river. Our trapline went on the north side of the White Hill Mountains while Uncle Alex's went on the south side of the mountains. I would have to cover much more ground than Uncle Alex in those days, as I had to go down the Southwest Feeder of Hawke River. Under normal travelling conditions I could make it. I told Uncle Alex this was a good idea, and he would see me on the third day, weather permitting.

I went home to our little studded shack and started to get ready. Roland gave me advice on a lot of things and helped me to get ready. I was off the next morning. Roland walked out to the path end and said good-bye. "Take care of yourself, and good luck," he said. I told him, "So long. I'll see you when I return." I couldn't say any definite time, as I didn't know myself. If I said some date and never returned, then he would be uneasy.

As I crossed the trail where Uncle Alex was supposed to go, there was no sign of him, but he could be close behind. I made the tilt quite early that evening and lunched up. This was February, and the days were getting long, so I decided to go on down the feeder another three miles and hang my camp on the Indian tent poles as they were already up. A lot of wood was left there, so there would be nothing to it. This would also give me an early start for my next tilt farther up the feeder. But before dark I could see that the weather was setting in. It was getting very mild with no wind, and when it got dark it got as black as ink. The Indians had left a lot of different things there, and there were a lot of good files stuck in one tree. Roland told me never to meddle with anything the Indians had left.

There were a lot of rump bones of beaver and porcupine. This is what they called "good luck bones," so they always hung them up. At one time you could find a scattered one all over the country where the Indians would have meat for lunch. Then they'd hang the bone in a limb of a tree. There was one little skin bag hung up, so I was wondering what was in it. If Roland had been here he wouldn't have let me open it, but now I was on my own and I was going to see what was in the bag before it got too dark. So I got the bag out of the tree, and after opening it I almost got poisoned! It was little pieces of what the Indians called "tipsi," which are the cuttings of caribou hides that they use for making their snowshoes and moccasins. It was a bad smell now, so I hung it up again. I did put one file in my bag to take home to sharpen my skates. Then I had supper and lay down for a rest.

It was now as dark as pitch. I had just fallen asleep when I was awakened by an awful noise outside. It was the horned owls, which always make funny noises just before weather. One would hoot and another would answer, and this would go on and on. The ones that were doing it in the trees right over my head would send the sound right down the stovepipe so it would rattle on the stove. I looked out through the door. I was going to get my gun, but it was too dark. I just couldn't see anywhere. The owls made some awful noises all night over my head, my first night alone, so I sure had lots of company. I thought to myself that I wouldn't touch the Indians' belongings any more if the owls were going to make all this fuss over it. Maybe Roland was right when he said not to touch it.

Just before daylight the owls left. Then it started to snow, then to rain, and then misty rain all the next day. There was no chance of moving. So I stopped in camp and slept most of the day. The next day it was fine, so I travelled to the tilt on the turn of the mountains and had the night there. The next day I was supposed to meet Uncle Alex at the brookside, but I would

now be one day late. I thought Uncle Alex would understand
that, but that night we had a little batch of snow which would
slow me down the next day. As the sun rose, the wind rose and
was very high. I had to cross six different marshes and one
pond, so I was off at dawn. This was the last pond on the
Southwest Feeder waters. After crossing the marshes I would
be on the Southern Feeder of Hawke River that emptied into
the river twenty miles farther inland. I was about to take the
first one of the marshes which was the home of the caribou in
the early part of the year. But now they were starting to move
on to the mountains, where they would spend the spring on the
sunny side and have their young fawns. The first marsh was
small, and each one got bigger. The last was a very large one.
Before the snow in the fall, there would be a big path right
through those marshes, worn down with the caribou. Then all
the other animals would follow in their path, and this is where
we would snare the foxes and lynx, between each marsh where
the skirt of the woods was.

By the time I reached the big marsh, the sun was gone
behind the hill and it was getting very cold. Snow was drifting
in big squalls. I warmed my face with my fur mittens. I was
getting far enough across the big marsh that I could see where
the camp was supposed to be. I fancied I saw either the head of
a man or a caribou. I made no attempt to take the gun off my
shoulder, as it could be Uncle Alex trying to see if I was coming across this big open marsh. Sometimes I was sure it was
him, then the weather would close in and I wouldn't see anything for awhile. But as I got handier, sure enough, this was
him, just standing there watching for me. He knew the time was
up for me to arrive, and he was getting uneasy.

Uncle Alex had the wood cut for the night and supper
cooked. It was just like going into a hotel. We had a great night
in this little cotton camp. He had spent his lifetime on the
trapline. He was an old man now and could tell some very
interesting stories. He had notches worn into the flesh of his
shoulders from pulling his komatik year after year. He left his

camp set up there for me to stay in on my return trip, then he worked his way back home.

The next day I had a large beaver caught in my trap. It was half frozen in the ice and it took me all the next night to get him thawed out and skinned. However, I made the whole trip and didn't run into any trouble. There was plenty to eat and I enjoyed the trip. It was a real adventure.

9
Roland Takes Sick

As I arrived in sight of our little house I could see Roland looking through the woods at the path end. As I got closer, I could see he had a path worn right hard in the snow where he used to walk to the edge, to watch for me and then go back again. After I had left he worried about me, thinking he would be dead before I returned. It looked to me like he just wanted to keep living until I arrived. As I went through the door he said, "I was worried about you. Thought you might have had trouble. Weather wasn't all that good. Uncle Alex brought the news that you were gone to the end of the trapline." I told Roland I had a great trip, with no problems, and I did very well with the furs. He never made any remark.

I sat down by our little table and opened a book that was on it. Here I saw a note written on it, "To Ben Powell. After my death all I own belongs to you. Signed, R.E. Powell." I closed the book and Roland never even noticed me. I noticed the time. It was 4:30. Roland went to walk across the floor to get a drink of water and fell like a dead man. After telling me before that he wasn't going to live and now after reading his will one would really think he was dead. I took things calmly. There were no doctors, no nurses to call, not even liveyers[1] on that side of the bay. I stood and looked at him. I could hear him breathing, so I knew he wasn't dead. There was still hope. I decided to walk across the bay before it got dark and tell Uncle Alex that Roland was on the floor like dead. First, I picked up

---
[1] Newfoundlanders who moved to Labrador to live.

all our guns, as we always had those guns loaded since we lived by ourselves and were always ready when an animal came into sight. I thought it would be best to hide the guns away before leaving. Roland could come around and not be right in the head and think a person was an animal and use the guns. I hid them away in the woods, then went back once more and could still hear him breathing. It was only one mile across the bay. I thought of the many times I had crossed the bay, but I believe this was the fastest time on snowshoes. I never ran, just kept a good step.

I told Uncle Alex the story and he came back with me. Roland was still on the floor, so we got him up and straightened him out on the bench. For the next eight days he was unconscious. We took turns night and day tending the fire. The handiest nurse was at Mary's Harbour, nearly forty miles away, so I asked Uncle George Kippenhuck if he would go on his dog team and see if the nurse would come up to help Roland.

Uncle George started off the next morning. The weather was cold this last part of February. When he got to Rexon's Cove about halfway, he thought he would ask some of the Russell men to go from there to Mary's Harbour and bring the nurse to Rexon's Cove. His dogs would then take her from there back to the bay and would be fresher. There was a big dog team race going on at Port Hope Simpson in a few days. The Labrador Development Company had it every year, and Uncle George didn't feel like asking the Russells as they were keeping their dogs fresh for the race. However, Bill Tom Russell knew what George Kippenhuck had in his mind, and he knew this would be the right thing to do. He never waited to be asked, but got his dogs ready right away and brought the nurse back to Rexon's Cove where Uncle George took her right on with his waiting dogs. The next day when the race went off in Port Hope Simpson, Bill Tom Russell took first prize.

The nurse arrived at our little cabin about the middle of the day. She was Miss Cadwalder, an English woman. She came to the bench where Roland was straightened out like dead, but you could still hear him breathing. She said there was very little she could do for him, but when she got back to Mary's Harbour she would send back some medicine that would help. Most of the people from across the bay were over now to see what they thought was the last of Roland. So I called the nurse outdoors and we walked over by a little brook. She was going to leave right away again, so I asked her to tell me the truth, what she thought of Roland and did she think he would gain conscious-ness. She said he was warned not to get wet, but he had spent all fall in the country. He couldn't stand it, then he started to take his homemade medicine, which was good, but he took too much and had his body poisoned. But she said there were chances he would come around in a week or ten days. If this did happen, he must then have the proper food to get his stom-ach back to normal. She asked if we had any milk powders. I told her I was sure there was none in the neighbourhood. She said he would want milk of some kind and fruit juice and she mentioned a lot of other things. I never knew what they were. A trapper in those days didn't pick up his groceries from a super-market, but lived mainly from the wildlife resources.

On March 8 Roland opened his eyes and looked around. From that time he started to get on very well. In a little while he was able to get around, but was very weak. As soon as he was well enough, he got George Kippenhuck to take him to Battle Harbour on his dogs. This was where Baine Johnston Ltd. oper-ated a store that was earlier owned by an old English company. Baine Johnston's store had a lot of things that you wouldn't find in stores north of us. The trip was made in a few days. Roland was surprised to bring back some food that the nurse recommended. So before they left, I started out on my trapline again. They went to Battle Harbour and back again before I arrived home. By the time I got home, Roland had made quite a hole in his milk powders, orange juice, sweet biscuits, and a lot of other things. He was back to normal in a month or so.

After another busy summer fishing, Don Andrews and Erving Mercer, who operated a herring factory at Comfort

Bight, decided they needed someone to look after it in the wintertime. The old Hudson's Bay store at Frenchman's Island would now close down for the winter, and Andrews and Mercer would operate the store in one end of their herring factory for the winter. They needed a man to operate this for them, and as a lot of the business would be trading furs, they would have to get a man who knew good furs from bad furs. So they asked Roland to take the job, and Roland decided he would.

10
Roland Becomes a Shopkeeper

Roland's pay was very good. He was provided with food and another man to do the outside work. This man and his wife would live close by in another little house. He also had a cook sometimes, but these extra people often found it lonely and would leave in a short time.

The nearest settlement was Pollows Cove, five miles away, where five families lived. That winter five people died in that little place, and Roland read the burial to them all at the graveside. They were supposed to have died from different causes, but the main cause was hunger. The human body would weaken so that if one fell into the icy water and caught cold, the body would be too weak to stand it and it would be death every time.

Roland had no experience running a shop. He had left home in Carbonear when he was a small boy and had very little time in school. So now in the fall he had all kinds of books come in from Newfoundland. In the daytime he would be in the store, and every chance he got he would be catching minks and foxes not too far away from the house. Then on the long winter nights he would study his books and become self-educated. He had few problems in handling the business.

World War II was then on and Roland decided to join the merchant navy. He worked in the engine room of some of those large ships. He served his term, then went to Greenland on an American war site as supervisor over diesel motors that turned the generators that were used on the sites after the war was over. He said after that there was no place like the trapline!

I was married now and working the trapline alone. He told
me to give him back his prize gun that he had won in the shooting match at Port Hope Simpson and two dozen traps and he
would go to the bottom[1] of Gilbert's Bay and build a log cabin
and trap the outer part of Gilbert's River. No one else lived in
that bay at that time and he trapped it alone for two years. In
the spring of the second year Ron Bearings, who worked with
the Department of Mines and Resources, was doing some
forestry work in Labrador. He used to spend some nights at
Roland's cabin and made close friends with Roland. He offered
Roland a job in Port Blandford, Newfoundland, as a game warden for that area. They needed a man who knew the forest.
Roland spent some years at this and married in that place. He
ran a general store and had his own farm. His dwelling place
was built on his farm, where he had all kinds of ducks and
many kinds of wildlife, including beaver. This is where Roland
happily lives today.

For the next eighteen years I knew what the trapline had to
offer to one who was willing to put everything into it. I went
through almost every kind of hardship and ran into almost
every kind of disaster that could happen to a trapper on a
trapline, from falling through the ice and beating my way to
land with my hands to having my little canvas camp burnt in
the night, along with most of my clothes. I wrapped what I
could find around my body as I watched the stars shooting
overhead. I lost my axe another time through the ice sixty miles
from home. The trapper's axe is his only salvation that far from
home. I ran into storms on the far end of the trapline without a
crumb of food. I have crawled to my camp on my hands and
knees after knocking my ankle out of place. I fell on slippery
ice eighteen miles from camp and hurt my knee so badly that I
couldn't move that leg by myself. With a string tied to my
snowshoe, I would step ahead with my good leg, then pull the
other from behind on a string and finally made camp. Twice I
have passed out in my tilt, once with hunger and once with

---

[1] The place where a bay ends, the farthest point from the sea.

smoke. Somehow I have always awakened to see another day. It was really living one day at a time. Maybe to stick to the trapline you must have something in your blood that goes right back to your ancestors. From the very first trip I made, I never looked at it as another way to make a living, but as a way to make a living with a lot of excitement and great challenge. There was so much freedom. You were your own boss. You could go when you liked and stop when you liked. You just lived so close to nature itself. How much closer than to try to bring the paw of an animal into the jaw of a trap only four inches wide!

11
Organizing the Trapline and Hard Experiences

From the very first year I took over the trapline, it was my desire to get better organized. By this I meant to build more tilts, to have one every day's walk apart, so I wouldn't have to be carrying that canvas camp and stove any more than I had to. It took me three years to get organized, but after that I only had to carry or haul the camp and stove on the far end of the trail. This made things much easier.

The author and his girlfriend, Effie Campbell, in 1937.

It would be the last of September when we would leave Square Islands and move to Campbell's Cove in the bottom of St. Michaels Bay. I was married in September 1942 to Effie Campbell, and our little house made up the fifth house in the bottom of the bay. My first job was to get enough wood to last until I got back again from the trapline. There was plenty of wood around, so it wouldn't take too long. Then I had to get ready for the trail. The main thing I needed was flour. I sifted the baking powder through the flour so I wouldn't have to bother with the baking powder can sticking in my back when I travelled. We used to buy the baking powder in ten-pound cans. Then there would be sugar, butter and some baking soda to take in case you burned yourself, also pork, a little rice, and beans. I always took along spare mittens and socks. Then I'd have one water-tight can that kept the matches, ammunition, needle, thread, a few buttons, some white cloth in case you burned yourself, and the wife would always have a pan of molasses buns to go in on the very top of your bag. The last items would be a bundle of wax candles and a bag of tea. All this would have to be carried on your back before the snow came. So with your game bag full of food and a bundle of traps tied on the outside of it, your camp, stove, and a little strip of caribou skin to lie on at night, you would be about ready to strike the trail.

Then my wife would say to take care of myself. I mostly told her not to expect me until I arrived back. I'd put all my things in my little fourteen-foot boat that was on the landwash close to the house, including my axe and gun. Then I'd row toward Salt Water Pond, about one mile from the house. The tidewater ran in and out of this pond. If the tide was running in, there would be no problem. But if the tide was running out and was low, I would often have to jump out to my waist and pull the boat up the rapids and into the pond. On many trips I would reach this far with my clothes dry.

Once on the pond I would head to the part where my trapline started. There were three traplines there – the one I took, the one John Campbell II took farther down the shore from Salt

Water Pond, and the one Uncle Alex Campbell took, which was called the Middle Road, because it was between the other two. When I reached my path I would put the paddle under the boat and lift her out of the water. This was as far as I could get the boat myself. So then I would take the long painter[1] and put it around a tall tree as far to the top as I could get it. Then I'd get back in the boat and pull my best on the rope. The tree would bend right down toward the stem of the boat. This would be the same as if I had another man with the same strength as me. After walking around to the stern of the boat, I would lift her up on her keel and then she'd jump right ahead, as the tree would be pulling just as I was. Then I'd turn her bottom up to keep the snow out, as the pond would be all frozen up by the time I would return.

The trail ran three miles through what we called the Wester'd Lead, a very crooked trail. The first spell was only about three hundred yards. This was on a little round knob. I never minded going in this trail, but coming back it would mostly be after dark. If I was tired, sometimes I would trip down with my snowshoes in the underbrush. Many times I would have liked to lie there long enough to take a good spell, but there would always be the occasional wolf in this valley. A wolf is not that dangerous, as he lives mostly on crippled animals that are helpless. But if he happened to come up behind you, he could jump you when you were down. This little hill was only the start of the trail. Always when coming home, after being gone a long time, I would never pass this place without sitting down and listening to see if I could hear some sound of life from those in our little settlement. There would be no sound and no light. Many things could have happened to our little families while the men were out on the traplines. Usually all the men would be gone at the same time. After waiting for about five minutes, I'd hear the long howl of a wolf in the distance. My only light would be the reflection of the moon on the snowcovered trail.

But today it was different. I was going in the country and the

---

[1] A rope attached to the bow of a boat, used for tying up.

day was just starting. In a little more than an hour I would be through the Western Valley and then it would be Loon Lake. I had left my canoe at another lake farther in. Now I'd walk around the side of Loon Lake. In the very bottom were the remains of a little dory owned by John Campbell II, who a long time before my day used it to go up this lake. I saw that it was built from iron-cut nails; there were no more of those nails in my day. I could still see the old-time paint made from white lead, still stuck on the planks in places.

I was tailing my traps and snares now, all along one side of the lake. The next lake was called Tilt Lake, a beautiful spot where the big birches hung over the water and the ground was covered with the leaves. The air was so fresh! Everything seemed to be just right. I then passed a little spring of water coming out of the ground and running through the fallen birch leaves. I decided to lunch up there. That meant boiling the kettle, roasting some caplin over the fire, and having one big molasses bun. Then I was ready to go again.

After walking the full length of this lake, which was about two miles, I went down to where my canoe was at the end of Deer Lake. I had tied her about six feet up in the trees so the bears couldn't tear the canvas off her. I tailed my traps all along the trail between Tilt Lake and Deer Lake, then put off my load and walked up to my canoe. I was very disappointed when I found the bears had the entire nose torn off her. If I couldn't use her, I couldn't cross Gull Lake in one day, as my tilt was on the north side and I was on the south. It was a full day's walk to either go down around or up around this lake, as it was big and long, the home of muskrats and otters.

I took the canoe down and patched her up a little, but the entire head was gone off her. So I decided to put her in the water and have a look at it. She didn't look so bad to me, so I put all my load in the stern and then got right behind and decided to paddle all along the shore. If the wind dropped out, I could make it around the lake by early the next morning.

I was doing fine. I paddled through Deer Lake, then along

the shore of Big Gull Lake. Then I reached the Narrows. It was only a half mile from the Narrows to go straight across to the camp. To paddle all around would take me a long time. The wind was only about fifteen or twenty miles per hour, and it was only about four o'clock in the afternoon. So I thought I would take the chance to cross Gull Lake. But when I got out in the middle, I had it plenty rough. The little canoe started to take in water, so I kept it broadside and worked my way across. As I got in the middle of that lake I remember I had had a letter from my dad that fall telling me to be sure and take no chances. I thought maybe this wasn't so big a chance. Soon I was over at the camp and landed my heavy load. I went over to a marsh while the kettle was boiling and cut down enough wood for the night. I put it by my camp, then lunched up. I now had to make the very head of the lake before dark, then paddle back after dark. This ran up about four miles, narrow but calm now. Long grass was on both sides, and in the middle was the channel. I could paddle along pretty fast in the calm. There were muskrats eating the grass all along, but I had no time now for the rats. I had several traps to tail as I went along. The main stop would be the lucky place, which had several traps and snares. After leaving this, the next stop would be the head of the lake.

I passed along by Pearl Brook that ran from Pearl Lake. This was a beautiful spot. The water lilies were fading, but they were still sticking out of the water. As I paddled along, the sun started to sink. I began to daydream about my old home and the nights I had worked all night long for just a ride in a truck. Now I was all alone on this great lake. There was so much adventure; one could get from place to place without a cent in his pocket!

The calm water was broken all around me with something. I was no longer alone. All around me were big sea trout, Atlantic salmon, and char, some with their fins out of the water. They paid no attention to my paddle for they were heading for the spawning grounds in the lakes beyond. We went along together for more than a mile. The water was just teeming with those big fish!

As I reached the head of the lake, I had to go up the brook to Southwest Pond and tail up my traps there, then try to get back to the canoe before dark. When I started up the brook, I found it was almost dry. Salmon and trout, some of them about twenty pounds each, were dead there. The bears were living off them, and the birds. The whole length of the brook was the same. There were hundreds of barrels of them in that brook.

Several years later when I was at that brook, it was just the same, dry with fish. So I took my rifle and shot a big one to take back to the camp with me where I could take a picture of it. I used to carry a camera, one of the old type. I put him on a string on my gun and started down for the canoe. The fish was very heavy at first, but it seemed to get lighter as I went. I thought that was strange, for this big fish to get light. Sometimes when I would go over a bank his tail would strike, and when I took him off my back at the canoe, I noticed the big spawn was running out of him! I could track the spawn right back to where I had shot him. So this was what made him so light.

But on this trip I didn't need any fish and had no time to play with them. I had to paddle all the way back to my camp after dark, then light the candle and put it on the doorstep to give light while I got the wood for the night. After a day like that, you don't need any sleeping pills to get to sleep!

The next morning there was only a short portage with the canoe, and I was out in White Fox Lake. This lake was no good for furs. I never caught one single skin of fur there in all my years. It was just no use to tail traps or snares. The animals kept clear of the place. Then there was another short portage of a quarter mile and I paddled across a little pond. I don't know why we never gave this pond a name; we always called it the little pond between White Fox Lake and Clifty Lake. It was small, so soon I was across it. Then with only about fifty yards to portage, I was in Clifty Lake.

This was a remarkable lake under the White Hill Mountains, a very good place for fox, but nothing else. It was very chilly on the east side. As I paddled along that day, there was no wind, and the air was just cool for working. As I got to the far end, as usual it was boil-up time. This was the last water on the St. Michaels Bay watershed. It was then the long portage around the north side of the mountains, with no more water until I got to the Southwest Feeder of Hawke River, the master waters of the fur-bearing animals.

After sweat and toil and sore shoulders, I finally made it across this long portage in two days. The first water I reached was Three Mile Pond, a good place for lynx, mink and otter. Two-thirds of the way up the pond was where I had my tilt, very small but very cozy. This was the best tilt I had on the trapline. The ground was very dry, a spring of water was handy, and the forest was all red spruce, very thick and straight-grained, making it easy to clean. I liked this tilt very much, and I think I had come and gone from this tilt every hour of the day and night on my many trips, after I got married. If I arrived at the tilt by dark, I would make a lunch, then have a rest. If the weather was fine, I would wait until the moon rose, then put on my snowshoes and stroll home. The tilt was covered with birch bark; this keeps it dry and bears never touch it.

One time I was heading for the tilt shortly after dark. I crossed over the middle of the pond and didn't know there was a big spot of slob[1] there. I got into it before I knew what was happening. My snowshoes iced up and I fell in several times. Soon my clothes were frozen stiff, and it was almost impossible to move. After some time I crawled ashore. The trees were loaded with glitter and snow, and I was only a half mile from the tilt. So I thought it would be easier to try and make my tilt instead of trying to get a fire going in the woods that were covered with glitter. It was after dark anyway, so that would be a problem too. I crawled and walked, and late in the night I made my camp, but I was in such bad shape that I had to spend all the next day at the tilt to get back to normal.

In the fall of 1944 it rained most of the time. There was very

---

[1] Slush.

little frost. In early November there was still very little ice in
the ponds, so I decided to go back home and get more food
before going to the end of the trapline. I made it back to the tilt
at Three Mile Pond and spent the night, hoping it would freeze
before morning. But the next morning it was still the same. The
trees were loaded with sleet. I was fine and dry, as I'd just come
out of the camp, so I decided to follow along the side of the
pond as far as I could and keep dry. It was only two miles down
the pond, so I was doing all right. The ice was cracking and
breaking sometimes, but I was close to land. I was almost at the
end of the pond, and there was only one big arm bight to follow
around. So I tried the ice. It seemed strong and thick, so I
decided to cross. I was about fifty yards from shore when, without warning, everything gave away. As I was going down, I
threw my axe and gun toward land. Soon I was down to my

The author's tilt at Three Mile Pond, 1944. A trapper's home!

neck in the icy water. I started pounding away the surface ice
toward land. I had my thick skin mittens on, so this saved my
hands from the ice. Once or twice I felt my foot strike a big
boulder on the bottom, which was a help for me. After what

seemed like a long time, I beat my way to land, more dead than alive. I was just going to haul off some clothes and wring them out when I glanced out and saw that my axe had gone through the ice and all that was left was my gun. I knew that at this time of year, if the weather turned cold, I would freeze to death in one hour without an axe to cut wood. There was no second thought. I had to go back and get that axe from the water. When I got back to shore with my axe and gun, I had to make up my mind whether I should go back to the tilt where there was no food, or make a shortcut for home, fifteen miles away, where there was plenty of food. I decided to keep moving for home.

In a short while I was at the foot of the pond where I had to cross a long steady brook to reach the trail on the other side. There was a windfall across the brook which had been there long before we ever used that country. It was only a tree about eight inches in diameter, but it served the purpose well, both for me and the many animals that crossed on it over the years. So many had passed on over it that the top part was worn flat from their claws sticking in as they went back and forth. Now I stood on one side and looked across. Other times I would have walked right across, but now, loaded with water, I was too shaky. I might fall in the brook, which was deep but not very wide. So I cut a long stick to help myself to safety.

Once on the trail around the mountains, the woods became scattered. The ground was hard, and with a shortcut that took me to the Middle Road and to my boat at Salt Water Pond, I was home by dark.

Now the day was fine and the water was calm. I started down Big Brook from Three Mile Pond to the many ponds on the Southwest Feeder. Another two miles and I would put up my little canvas tent. I would stop here until the ponds froze up, then I would move on to the southern waters of Hawke River. But in order to go around the northwest end of the mountains, I had to travel a rough trail. I needed at least a week's rest after that long portage I had with the canoe. I arrived at the camping pond on the feeder about midday, and soon I had the little camp up and was settling down until the ponds froze up. However, things didn't turn out the way they were supposed to. Animals were scarce. I could paddle around four different ponds without any portages, tailing up every trap and snare I had. But things had never been so scarce as they were now. There was no meat to eat of any kind. I just had to live off the flour bag, and I had to go light on this, as this was only the start of the trapline. If the meat soon didn't pick up, I would have to keep plenty of flour for the trip back. So I used to make my rounds and come back to the camp without any more than a weasel. If it had been a red squirrel, I could have fried him up, but I wouldn't have eaten a weasel. That would be the last thing!

The ponds finally froze up, so I had to take up all the traps I had close to the water. There was still nothing in the others. I tailed up some rabbit snares, thinking I would catch some rabbits, but there wasn't even one rabbit to be caught. On the last of it I was getting too hungry at night to sleep, so I'd sit up by the stove for hours, wondering if it was worth it all.

One night I heard a very funny noise outside the camp. I listened to it for a long time, but never found out what it was. There was still no snow to see the tracks. So the next day I decided I would make up my mind what I would do, after I made another round trip to the traps.

This time I took the breachloader, twelve-gauge, so that if I came upon anything flying or pitched[1] I was going to have it! After making the round there was still nothing. I was only a quarter mile from camp and still hadn't made up my mind, whether to move on up the feeder or wait another day. As I looked up, there in a spot of gold willows was a white partridge! Just what I wanted! I already had the gun loaded with BB shot, so I fired, and blew that little bird to pieces. When a white partridge has eaten gold willows, he doesn't taste good, but now with the guts blown out of him, he might not be too bad. So I picked up what was left of him and headed for my camp. I was going to cook him right away. When I got back to

---
[1] Landed.

the camp, there was a spruce partridge sitting on the tent pole right over the camp door. It looked as though things were changing! I picked up the .22 rifle and shot him in the head. Soon I had both of them in the boiler and enjoyed a great meal!

I was ready to break camp the next morning and move up the feeder. That day I caught a beaver, which provided a lot of good meat. I still had a heavy load with my camp and stove, and the flour bag was still the heaviest item. The first half of the trail up the feeder was very good, as the Indians had it cleared out good, but the last half had never been cleared, and it was very rough close by the little river. If you left the edge of the river, you found yourself in deep holes in the woods.

I reached my little tilt by dark. This was about the coldest and dampest tilt on my whole trapline. It was high up on the north side of the mountains, and very seldom did the sun ever shine on it. There was no birch bark to get in that place for covering it, only damp moss to place on the roof. This made for dampness and dropping of water all the time, as soon as the fire was lit. The tilt started to rot after the third year.

Now the trail would be much easier to travel, just big open caribou country ahead. There was a year when I started to get older that I found it very hard to get to this little tilt. It was very bad travelling. The fast-moving water in the little river kept carrying away the snow from each side. It would break off quickly, and you didn't know what moment you might end up in the river. Then if I tried to keep in toward the woods, there would be those big knobs of snow coming off the trees as big as barrels. This was caused by the high land. When it rained on the low land, it would be glitter and then snow on the high land. After so much of it built up on the trees, it would fall off, which would make it difficult for travelling. I made it to the end of the path close by the tilt, but had to straighten right out and take a blow or rest. Then I took a pencil and paper out of my pocket and wrote down the date and my name. Then I wrote that I was getting older and my strength was failing and that I never planned to go this far again. After putting the note in a little

can, I took a fox snare and wired it up in a tree. But I went back
– and under the very same tree with the can in it, I made a new
trap house[1] and took many hundreds of dollars' worth of those
big silvery lynx from it.

On February 15, 1945 I was supposed to be found dead in
that little tilt. But somehow I awakened to see another day. I
had had a rough trip on the trapline. Every day it had snowed a
little, until there were about six inches or so of new snow. I was
hoping it would soon get better. I made the round to the very
last end of the trapline and got back to the tilt at the open tickle
on the southern waters of Hawke River. The next morning I
was supposed to head for home, but that night the wind came
up from the north and one of the worst storms struck. It kept up
day after day, until at last I had all my food eaten. All that was
left was one bag of pea beans and one piece of pork about two
inches square. So it was beans three times a day. All I could do
was to clear out the stovepipe and the door and get wood. I
would put the pork in the beans, and after the beans were
cooked I would put the pork on a log on the side of the tilt for
the next meal, because beans without grease don't taste good.
However, on the fourth day I ate the piece of pork without
thinking. So this was the end of the grease.

On Saturday morning the storm began to break, although
there were still very high winds. There was one terrible noise
from the bending of the trees. I remembered a short time before
daylight how everything seemed to be cracking and coming
across the roof of my camp. So I crawled out to have a look.
And here I discovered that a large herd of caribou had crossed
by my tilt that night. When they had struck on the back of the
tilt they split in two halves, and some of their horns had struck
the wood that I had stuck up in a tree close to the tilt. It was
knocked down onto the roof. They had been feeding on caribou
moss in the big open marshes north of my tilt. When the weather got bad they moved to the heavy woods south of my tilt
where they could feed off the trees. My little cabin was built on

---
[1] A sheltered nook of boughs which conceals a lynx trap.

the caribou trail right between those two big lakes. Now the venison was all gone south, and I was left still eating my beans! The snow had cleared and now it was only hard wind and drifting snow. So I decided I would try and make my tilt on the Southwest Feeder, as I had plenty of beaver meat and flour there. After leaving my tilt I had to go down the lake, then out a big brook about three miles. It was good travelling on the lake with the wind almost in my back. But when I got down to the brook where all the snow had lodged, there was a crust on top from hard wind. I just couldn't do anything with it. I had to haul my snowshoe back through the same hole that it went through, and this was deeper than my knees. After several hours I still hadn't moved more than a half mile, and I knew it would be impossible to ever make the tilt that night in that kind of travelling.

The woods were very thick on both sides of the brook, so I thought this would be the only chance I'd have – to take to the woods and perhaps find it more open as I went. After going a few hundred yards I struck good open leads that took me to the big caribou marsh. After five more marshes I would be at the pond where my tilt was. Then it would be beaver meat for me at night!

I was in good shape for walking after six days in the tilt eating beans. As I got to the big marsh the wind veered right from the northwest which was right in my back and a real storm. I just had to move along fast. I got to the tilt before dark and soon had the fire in and all my wood for the night. Then I looked forward to that big feed of beaver meat! I used to cook in a ten-pound Flako baking powder can. The cover used to push on, so I took the axe and cut up the meat and stowed it in the can. I filled it right to the top, so that when the frost came out of the meat it would only be half full. But even this would be a good feed for supper. What was left over would do for breakfast. So when I put the can of meat on the stove, the stove couldn't bear it up. That old stove was just about burned out; we had used it so much. We used to buy our kerosene in flour gallon tins, then use the empty tins to make camp stoves. The material in the tin was very light and wouldn't stand for one season. Now with the big can of meat on top, it was beginning to flatten down. So I took some fox snares and tied them around the can and onto the rafters. This did the job, so after filling the stove with wood I lay down for a rest while it boiled. The roof of the tilt started to leak as usual, so I threw my dickie over my head and turned back on to the stove. The heat at my back felt so good that soon I was asleep. Sometime later I was awakened by a loud bang. Then I knew nothing else. I passed out. The cover had been pushed tightly on the can of beaver meat. I thought it had been loose, but the meat got warm, then the gravy boiled and the steam couldn't escape with the cover so tight, so the can exploded. I would have been scalded to death if it hadn't been for my dickie that I had rolled over my head. But the gravy that had gone over the red-hot stove made smitch[1] enough to knock me out at the first blast. How long I was in that dying condition I don't know. The fire had gone out and the hole around the stovepipe was carrying away the smitch slowly. I began to dream about the old trappers I once knew. Most of them were gone now. Some had died by their camp-fires when they had no matches. Others froze when they were almost at their home, crawling on their hands and knees with broken ankles. Others died of cancer, and my turn had come. Someday someone would find me in my little log tilt and would never know the cause of my death.

I seemed to waken slowly. My brain still wasn't registering right. I knew I was in my tilt, but my tilt had no door, so I couldn't get out. Then I started to come around. I knew there was a door in my tilt, but I didn't know where to find it. Then I tried to raise my arm. I moved only a little. I could feel the logs above my head and something else. It was my hunting knife. I managed to get it out of the seam where it was stuck. I knew everything now, but I was too weak to get up. So with my knife I started to cut away the rotten seam in the tilt close by my

[1] Smoke.

head. I would cut so much away, then take a spell, then cut again. I could feel the knife going farther into the rotten log all the time, and after what seemed like an endless age, my knife broke through. The fresh air started to burst in, and as soon as I put my mouth to the little hole, I came right to life. I rushed for the door and pulled it down. I lit the candle and started to pick up the pieces of meat that were all over the ground inside the camp. My clothes were in a bad mess, so I cleaned them up a bit. I ate what I could of the meat, but I never got over that trip for a long time. Even today I am afraid to go to sleep in my camp with meat cooking on the stove.

12
Better Days

Well, I have been telling most of the hard times on the trapline, so I think I should mention some of the good times also. The reason I have mentioned some of the hard times is to show just how one can survive under such conditions working a trapline. There are good days and there are bad days. I should think you will find this in most walks of life. Sometimes you get all your furs the first day out on the trail; other times it's on the far end of the trail; and still other times it's right in the middle.

I recall one trip when I reached my third tilt on the high land and had caught nothing bigger than a red squirrel or a weasel. Something always seemed to go wrong and the big animals got away. I left my third camp at dawn on a beautiful day before the snow had come down. The ground was hard and it was just nice walking. My load was heavy. I rounded the first pond for the day, then had to go down over six marshes, each one a little bigger, until I got to the very large one. As soon as I took the path that ran the full length of the six marshes, there lying on the ground was a big lynx. This was in the war years, and it was very difficult to get snare wire that was suitable. So I was using a lot of picture frame cord. So the very place I had set a picture frame cord in a snare was the very place the lynx had gotten caught. He had gone over a windfall and broken the snare, but was lying there dead. This was luck. I wasn't that far from the tilt, but I hung this fellow up and would take him back to the tilt to be skinned on my return trip.

After doing this I followed on down the big deep path. There were many porcupines in my snares which I had to take out and throw to one side. As I got down to the third marsh I looked at my snare. It had been broken. Although it was a big brass wire snare, sometimes the hot sun in the summer would burn the snare, causing it to break easily. I looked at the hairs on the stick where the wire was attached and saw that a cross fox[1] had been in it but had gotten away. I was just going to put my load on my back again when I glanced into the woods and there was the cross fox, lying on the ground dead, the snare still tight around his neck. I also hung this one up in a tree to get on my return trip, as I still wasn't halfway between the two tilts.

I then went on to the big marsh where I had to leave the deep footpath. I was now down to my ankles in the white caribou moss with such a heavy load on my back. I didn't have as much flour as I had carried at other times, but it was still very heavy. I threw off my load, as I had to go down to Long Lake. I would only be setting my snares and traps once at this lake, as it was only good before freeze-up time. The animals would follow along the side of this big lake, and when they crossed on stepping stones, just as though they had been put there especially for the animals. So I would only go down a little way along the shore where there was an old beaver house. I would put a trap on this old house, but there was never a beaver in the house, while I passed along that trail at least. Then I would have a snare close by in a path, so all I would take down to this lake was my axe and gun. I would be taking up those traps now, as it would be freezing up soon, and once it froze up, the animals would walk around on the ice and wouldn't use the paths for the rest of the year. So I started down with only my axe and gun.

After being used to carrying the heavy load, I found myself almost going headlong with the first steps. Soon I was down at the stepping stones, and there at the end of the path was a beau-

---

[1] A variant of the red fox family with a premium-priced pelt. Distinguished by a more or less distinct dark cross formed on the back by a dorsal stripe and a band across the shoulders.

tiful cross fox, well-furred. More luck, I thought. But this time he was still in the snare. So all I had to check was one snare and one trap on the old beaver house. I left my gun and the fox on the ground, and just took my axe, as I would be back again in a few minutes. I got down to the old beaver house and took the snare in my hand to wind it around the stick. It would stay that way until another season. I was just turning for the trap, not more than two feet away from me, when all of a sudden there was a big overgrown lynx ready to spring on me, caught in the trap. He was the size of a small tiger. I sprang out of his way, and never could see how he missed clawing me to pieces. Those animals will usually look right into your eyes before they jump you, so I was back on to him and he was just waiting for me to turn around to look in my eyes. A lynx will use his claws before his teeth, but he can use both of them very fast. Any single wolf won't tackle a lynx, but a pack of wolves will jump on one in a trap and leave nothing of him but his claws. So now I had to kill this big monster and my gun was left behind. I walked back so far until I came across a good long dry stick and cut it with my axe. Then I went back toward that fellow, but I just couldn't strike him. He would spring back every time, his ears pinned right back on his head and his eyes sparkling and looking right into mine. I thought I would have to go and get the gun or he might get me after awhile. So on my way back for the gun I saw another dry stick like the one I had. So I decided to try another trick. I took the two sticks and held them over his head, then dropped one. He grabbed it in his paws, and before he could let go of it, I gave him a whack on the head with the other one and straightened him out. With a few more knocks I finished him off.

I was having a lot of fun all by myself, heading back to where the fox was, with the big lynx on my back, thinking this was a good day all right. Two lynx and two foxes so far. When I got the one fox on my back along with the old lynx, it was almost enough for me. There was no way I could manage with the big load I had left on the marsh – a game bag full of stuff, a camp, a stove, and a strip of deerskin to lie on, plus my traps. There was nothing to do but to sit right down and skin the lynx. I believe he was the biggest one I had ever caught, and I have caught a lot in forty years! Close to one hundred in three years, and those were my best three years. The one I was now skinning I sold later that winter to Mr. Massey of the Hudson's Bay Company in Cartwright. He paid eighty-five dollars for it. That was a lot of money for a lynx in those days, as he was really an overgrown one. After skinning him and leaving his fine carcass behind for the birds and foxes, I headed back for my load. When I got it all on my back, I had plenty to carry, with about eight miles to my next tilt down at the open tickle, as I called it.

I first had to go across a big marsh, the last one of the six, then crossed the brook and over another small marsh. This was the last of the open country. Before striking down through the woods to the southern waters of Hawke River, I checked a snare at the last end of the marsh. Here was another cross fox, only this one wasn't furred as good as the last one. He was what we called a part Samson fox. I just couldn't manage anything else, so I hung him up in a tree and would get him on my way back toward home. Just at dark I reached my little tilt. It was good to get that heavy load off my back. In awhile I got the fire going, and while the kettle was boiling I thought I would go out and check a snare I had just behind the tilt. Sure enough, here was another red fox. This definitely was a day of excitement and a big pay day!

This tilt was my last one on the trail. From here I had to move around with my canvas tent and stop where I found a beaver house. But I could do a lot of travelling away from and back to the tilt. I could go up to the river and back to the tilt, across to Gilbert's River and back to the tilt. This little cabin was built of dry juniper. Some years before I came to the coast, some kind of forest worm was going around. They called it an army worm, and it killed most of the juniper on coastal Labrador. Juniper gives lots of dry wood for fires, and it's about the hardest wood we have in Labrador. When I decided to build this tilt, I picked this spot because there was plenty of dry wood there, also lots of water, as the big open tickle ran right along by the camp. The water travelled too fast to freeze up, only in extremely cold weather, so I thought this would be a good spot. One spring, when I was going in for the last trip to strike up[1] my traps, I took my big axe and the bucksaw and in one half day I had enough logs cut up to log up the walls. Then I lay down on the snow and put a mark to my head and one to my feet to get my right size. The smaller the tilt the warmer it would be. I built the walls up on the snow, so that when it melted the cabin would settle down on the moss. And the next fall I planned to put the roof on.

When I came back to my tilt in the fall, I found that the spot was very damp, not as I thought it would be. Big, long yellow moss that only grows in wet places was there, not the short, dry brown kind that grows in the dry areas. But there was no time now to find fault, as I had to work fast before dark. So I got the gable ends up and then the rafters, about six on each side. I had some felt I had brought in the spring before, and I soon had that on, too. It was dark now. I still had no door, but that wouldn't matter. I would hang my dickie over the door until I could find time on some bad day when there was nothing else to do. I put the stove up by the light of the candle and there was plenty of wood around from the ends of the logs. I wouldn't have to cut any that night after dark. So I put on the kettle and leaned back for a rest.

It was just as cold in there as it was outdoors, because there was no caulking in the seams and many of the seams were large. Juniper logs usually aren't as straight as spruce or fir logs, so I thought I would have to start caulking the seams with the moss that was growing on the camp floor. It was the wrong kind, but it would do for now. The brown kind was what I mostly used, as it will stop[2] in the seams for years. But now there was no choice. The long green kind would have to do. By

---

[1] To take them up permanently for that trapping season.
[2] Stay there.

the time I got one end of the tilt caulked, the moss was all used. So I thought I could stog[1] the other seams with ground – anything to keep out the frost since I would need some rest after I got the caulking done. So I began to caulk with sandy ground. The moon rose and started to shine through the seams, and all the seams started to sparkle, and my fingers started to sparkle. Well, I thought, I must have struck a gold mine! I thought I should have claim on it as my tilt was built right over it! So I finished stogging all the cracks and soon I could find the heat all over the tilt. I looked between my fingers again and could still see the sparkles. I went out and washed my hands in the brook and could see the shiny sand fall from my fingers.

After a quick lunch, I soon fell asleep. The next morning I was up early and began to look around, thinking I might pick up a nugget of gold somewhere. Right behind the tilt there was a sandy beach, and here I could see a shiny vein that came right from my tilt and ran through the sandy beach and out into the open water. This shiny sand wouldn't mix with the other sand, so I thought maybe it was gold all right. But then I thought about what Roland had told me, that nobody ever got anything in this world, only what they worked for. Maybe he was right. I took a handful and went back to the tilt, got an empty matchbox and filled it up. The next summer I sent it to Montreal and found out it was fool's gold. But I wasn't disappointed one bit.

The next day I went up over the big lake. The ice was getting strong now, and it was good walking. There were strong signs of otters, so I went down to the river. I got back to my tilt in time to put four poles across the end of it for a bunk, then chopped some more for a door. The tilt was completed and was warm in normal frost conditions. But on really cold nights I had to keep the stove red in order to feel the heat. There was always that damp feeling from water draining underground between those two big lakes.

The next morning I was to go over the ridge to Jeffries' Pond, on the inside of Gilbert's River. The outside part is called

[1] Caulk.

Jeffries' after an old man Jeffries who had trapped there many years before I took over. At the first sign of daylight I took the kettle and headed for water. The green junipers that hung over the brook were all frosted over, a sure sign of weather. But it might not be until the following night. The stars were still dull, and I didn't think weather would strike that day. I soon had the kettle boiled. I took just enough lunch in my bag to boil up once. There was still no sign of snow, and I hoped there wouldn't be, as I had a big day's work ahead of me. I decided to leave my snowshoes too, figuring that if it did start to snow that night it wouldn't be all that much and I could make it to the tilt.

So I started off for Jeffries'. The head of that pond was the master spot for trapping. There was a big point that ran well down that pond from the head, and the river followed this point out – a very remarkable point. Animals following around the side of the pond would strike across the inside part of the neck and take the river, rather than following out to the big long point where the mouth of the river emptied out. Where the animals had crossed on the inside, there were paths worn down, some of them four feet deep, and this was where I would get them. Many times it would be an animal that wasn't worth much, as all kinds crossed there. Many times you'd end up with a red squirrel, while a big lynx passed by.

I would now leave the southern pond where the tilt was built and cross over a wooded ridge about three miles, one and a half miles up one side and the same down the other. This would take me an hour on the average when the walking was good, as it was then.

By the time I got to the top of the ridge, I could see that the overcast sky was going to bar the sun from shining. I made it to the pond on the other side and never felt better for walking. The ice was dry and hard. I planned to go to the foot of the pond and look for beaver houses. The pond was four miles long, then I had to go one mile over a marsh to the steady¹ where the beavers used to build their houses. If there was no house there,

¹ The wider part of a brook where the water remains quite calm.

I wouldn't bother to tall up any traps. I would work from the head of the pond in the river, as there were no other trappers in this area. The same animals that were using the food from the pond would make their rounds also to the head of the pond where I had traps all over the place.

By running and walking I soon reached the foot of the pond and went down to where the old beaver houses were. I soon discovered that there were no new houses built that summer. The beavers had moved inland, as they are used to shifting each year. Without losing any more time, I headed back again to the other end of the pond. Before tailing up my traps, I decided to boil up the kettle. The sky was getting blacker by the minute and the ceiling had lowered to about five hundred feet now. I had already walked and run about fourteen miles and was getting hungry. Soon I had the fire going and the kettle on. Then I thought it was time to look at my watch. I carried a wrist watch on a string in my pocket and was too busy that morning to stop and look at it. Now that I was waiting for the water to boil, I would have a look at it. The thought struck my mind that very often when the Newfoundlanders came on the coast in the spring they would say, "What were you doing all winter, sleeping?" I thought that if those fellows had one winter on a trapline, they wouldn't ask that question in the spring. I was so hungry that as soon as I got the tea in the kettle and started to eat, I ate everything I had with me. I never left one thing, only a bit of tea.

Then I started to set up the long trail of traps. Those traps had been in their places for years now, so sometimes it would only take me one minute to set the trap. The longest would take five minutes. I would keep doing this until I reached about eight miles down the river. There were a lot of open places on the ice, so I had to be careful. Each year I had a beaver house right on the bend of the river. After setting up this house, I was to strike north over what the Indians called the Blue Hill Marshes. Then after one hour I was to take a little dribbling brook and follow this right down to the pond close by my tilt.

To go back the way I had come would take too long, until late that night, and now the sky never looked more for weather! The ceiling was still dropping.

The river was winding like the figure "S" now, and at last I came to the beaver house. It looked very new and bigger than it had other years, but I only thought there would be about three beavers in the place. Soon I had the two runs to the house trapped. Now I was supposed to strike due north, but in my hurry because of the weather, I was not aware that last spring when the river burst out, it had carried away the old beaver house. When the beavers had built this new one, they built it on the next turn of the river. So instead of striking north, I was now striking northwest. I looked at my watch before leaving the beaver house; it was half past three, my time. I walked for one hour and found no sign of the little dribbling brook. I knew at once that something was wrong and that I was about four miles off course. In this big caribou country there are very few trees, just miles and miles of caribou moss, and now all the Blue Hills were closed in with the weather. At any moment the storm would strike. Without shelter one couldn't survive very long. If there was plenty of snow, you could crawl into a snow hole and weather out the storm.

I started to climb up some scattered dry juniper trees that were around, hoping to see in the distance the trees that grew on the riverbank, which was the only big timber in the whole area. After climbing two trees, a voice seemed to say to me, "Be careful. You have no food and a great storm is coming on. Your strength is limited. Your life depends on how you use your strength." So aloud I said, "Okay. I have your message, but I will climb one more tree." After doing this, I thought I could see the dark loom of green forest, but the ceiling was now about thirty-five feet above ground. I headed in the direction I thought would take me to the side of the river, and before dark I struck the big white spruces that grow on the riverbank, the full length of Jeffries' River. I was some happy to get my feet on solid ice! It was now almost dark and I had to find a suitable place to put up for the night. The ice was still bad, and at any moment I could fall through it and never be seen again.

I walked about one hundred yards and then decided I should make sure I was heading out the river and not in. So I broke off a dry limb and threw it into some open water, and I could see it went the other way. So I turned and went back a few hundred yards and saw what looked like a very good place to fight out a storm from an easterly wind. I got the fire going and was just going to boil the kettle for a drink of tea, which was all I had with me now. But before I got the water boiled, the storm broke full force from the southeast until midnight. Everything was wild. Those big spruce trees bent all around me. Many broke off and fell out on the river. I kept the fire burning as best I could. There were knobs of snow that came down out of those trees that almost knocked me to the ground. After midnight the wind veered to the south and came around southerly and blew harder than ever. It got milder, and with the wet snow falling out of the trees, I was soon soaked to the skin. My fire was getting blown all ways from the wind, but I managed to keep it burning. Several times I got the kettle on and warmed some tea and wished I only had a few crumbs to eat. I was very hungry and tired, but I had to keep my fire burning. The wind kept veering until it went southwest, and soon it was wester'd and still blowing. Now it was blowing right across the river at me. Awful squalls were coming. By four o'clock it started to get very frosty. I had to get my clothes dried before they froze on me. About six o'clock the wind started to drop some, and then I was able to get a good drying and another kettle of warm tea. I searched my bag, hoping I could find one crumb that I might be able to swallow, but there was nothing. I had been so hungry before that I had eaten everything. I tried to suck at my big jaw teeth that were hollowed out, hoping there would be crumbs there, but with no luck. I pulled my belt tight and this seemed to help. When the first sign of daylight broke, the wind had gone right down and it was getting very frosty. It was time to move on.

I figure this would be one of the most daring trips back to the tilt that I had ever tackled. There was bad ice everywhere in the river, and now with the snow on it, it all looked alike. You could step in a hole any minute, especially with the snow right to your knees and no snowshoes to depend on. I was living in hopes that once I got back to the beaver house I had trapped the evening before, I might have a beaver that I could roast over the fire. I was still about three miles out the river. From the beaver house out, I knew where the bad ice was, but now I was only taking a chance, muddling knee-deep in the snow. But there was a solid bottom beneath it which was a help.

Sometime that evening I made the path end. Then it would be two miles up the hill, if I could make it, then down the other side, which should be easier. So I kept humming to myself, "I will do it," and I kept this up until I made the top of the hill. Then I changed the hum to "I made it." I could see the lake right under me where the tilt was built. It was almost dark by now, but I kept dragging on, one step just a little ahead of the other. I wasn't taking either spell; I was moving slowly all the time.

It was dark when I made the lake, then headed across for the tilt. As I passed the open tickle, I got a kettle of water and crawled through the tilt door on my hands and knees. It was really frosty now. In one minute I had the fire going with dry brush and splits, then I fell back on the four dry sticks which were my bed and passed out. I had made it to the tilt just because I was living in hopes of the good meal I would have when I arrived. But the human body had all it could take and collapsed on arrival. I never found out how long I was lying in that tilt before I came around. It could have been a long time, because my watch had stopped and the water on the stove in the kettle was frozen to the bottom. So I lost count of the days. It was like I awoke out of a long slumber and I didn't feel hungry. I never touched the smoked trout, but just had soup and dough-boys for awhile. When I was in good shape again, I headed back home, none the worse for the trip.

For many years I kept going to the Jeffries'. This was a big spot for good furs. I had four different waters where I trapped altogether – the Gull Lake waters, the Southwest Feeder waters, the southern waters, and the Jeffries'. So it kept me busy with all those traps. I was most taken up with the Jeffries' Pond though, and thought this was where I was getting the most furs. But then, I always wasn't sure, because I was doing well at the feeders also. It was really hard to keep track of it all. One night as I lay on my little bunk in the tilt, I tried to figure out which trap took the most furs that winter. It was hard to be sure, so I thought of another plan. As I always had lots of small nails in the camp to use in spreading my furs, I would put a handful in my pocket, and each trap that I took a skin of fur from, I would put a nail in the tree close by. Each year I would start a new row. Then I could count up the nails and know what trap was leading, and each year I would know how many kinds of fur I got and which traps I had taken them from. Nothing was counted smaller than a mink, so it would only be a mink, otter, fox, lynx, beaver and wolf. So not only was the trapline one way to make a living, it was getting more interesting all the time.

This was one game I was probably playing alone – which of the four waters would come first and which trap on the four waters would take the lead. So every time you got a skin of fur, you'd count the nails. Sometimes there would be a tie between the waters; other times, between traps. But mostly each year one trap would always keep a little ahead by one skin of fur. Then the next year it would be on the other end of the trapline. So this was a game that went on right through the winter. As the years passed it became more interesting. The most I ever got from one trap in one season were six lynx. I did this four different years. Tried hard to beat it, but never did. Twenty-six lynx in one season was my best record, and the year before that one, I had twenty-five. I wanted to beat that tie at any cost, so I worked hard for that one extra lynx that finally came on the day the fur season closed. I had made up my twenty-six.

13
A Dislocated Ankle

One year I had quite a lot of beaver houses and I was doing very well with them. They were taking the lead for the first part of the year, then coming on toward spring the lynx took the lead by one nail in the tree. I still had one house over at Jeffries' Pond to check. There were at least two or three beavers in the house, but the water in the runs was awfully deep. The beavers were much quieter than I was, and I just couldn't catch them. They did everything to my traps.

Now it was about time to strike up my traps. Many trappers cut the top off a beaver house, but I didn't like this idea and very seldom did it. Only sometimes after the beavers were all trapped would I do this to catch an otter in a beaver house. It was a very cold day, and as I got close to the house I was planning to haul the stick up fast that the traps were tied to. I always used dry sticks, as these were harder for the beavers to bite off. Before they had time to bite them off, they were drowned, as those traps were tailed in about six feet of water and had to be lowered down with a string on each side of the trap. The water was too dark to even see the traps after they went to the bottom. So this was it – both traps were coming up for the season.

I knocked out the first of the dry sticks and noticed that the trap seemed to come very hard. Then it seemed to break loose, and I knew right away that I had a beaver. I could tell by his weight. As it broke water, I saw that he was a big one. The minute it struck the cold air and the snow along the side, it soon froze on. This would make him heavier to carry. Then I walked to the other beaver run and did the same thing. Up came another big beaver. Well, this was a real surprise! Two nails had to be driven in the big white spruce tree that grew right over the beaver house. The beavers were now taking the lead by one and the season was nearly closed. I looked at the two big beavers and both were what we call in trapper's language, two blankets. We have names for the whole family of beavers. The small one is the papoose, then the small middler, the middler, the large, and then the blanket, which would measure about eighty-eight inches when you measure the skin two ways and add the two fingers together. I doubted if I was man enough to get those two big fellows over the Saddle[1] on my back, about three miles, so I put one in my game bag and strapped the other one on my gun and axe and started off. I made the trail, but with every mile the load seemed to get heavier. If I were to take them off my back, I knew I would have a job to get them back on again. So I took a scattered blow by leaning against a tilted tree, then went on again.

I finally made the top of the hill, then descended down the other side. The trail was very rough because there had been a mild a few days before, and the big knobs of snow were in the trail, frozen like rocks. The load was getting almost too much for me, but I thought I would make the pond where my tilt was before I'd ever throw them off on the slippery ice where I could tow them across the pond. But on the very next step I struck one of those knobs of ice with my snowshoe and knocked my ankle right out of place. Down I went, rolling through the trees, one beaver still on my back, the other gone down out of sight in the snow. I had so much pain in my ankle that I was sick to the stomach. I had to get my ankle back in place as soon as I could. So I twisted and turned and soon it went back with a crack. But it wasn't long before it was swollen the full size of my skin boot, and there was no way I could stand on it. I was only in a little distance from the pond, and then it would be all hard ice across the pond. So I crawled, shoving one beaver ahead of me

---
[1] A high hill.

and pulling the other. After a little while I made the pond. I took a spell. The ankle still pained. Well, I thought, a fellow can put up a good battle in the woods when he has sound limbs, but now with a fractured ankle probably, it didn't seem so good. But then I thought it could have been worse. If the snow had been deep on the ponds, I would have had a real problem.

I crawled onto the bank again and broke off two big dry stumps, put my snowshoes across them, then my gun and axe, and then the two beavers. With the two strings from my snowshoes joined together, I started to crawl across the pond, not more than a half a mile. Then I had to cross a short neck[1] of woods, then a little steady, and then I would reach the camp. But a crawl was not like walking. Soon darkness set in, and it was almost like daylight. As long as the old wolf kept clear of me and my two beavers, I would make it. I had to get them to the camp. With all this meat I would be good for a long time, and I didn't know how long I would be there before I could stand on my ankle again. I hadn't seen any sign of the old wolf that was around all that fall, and I hoped he would keep away now.

When I had trapped the first beaver house over to Jeffries' Pond that winter, I caught all the beavers that were in that house. Then I cut the top off the house and was catching a scattered otter in the house. I was over there just before weather was coming on once and was just going to get down in the house when I looked up. Along the side of the little pond was a middle-sized wolf coming toward me. I didn't like the way he was acting, sneaking behind the willow beds and the trees. He was just about to my track, when I had come out to the beaver house. I hurried and tailed the trap, covered up the hole in the house, and then headed out around the point. I never went back on my own track. I never looked for trouble, if I could get away from it. It was a bad evening to go shooting at a wolf – weather was coming on and it was just before dark.

So now on my hands and knees I did hope that the old wolf

---

[1] A narrow strip of land between two bodies of water.

wouldn't bother me now with all my meat. Wolves are much bolder in the night than they are in the day. Sometime in the night I made the tilt and got the fire going. Then I got a piece of white cloth and tied it really tightly around my ankle. In a few days I thought I would be able to start for home, going from one tilt to another, but my ankle never got the same any more. It was easy to slip out of place.

Once I was on slippery ice on my way home when my ankle came out of place. I fell down and struck my knee so hard that all my leg went almost dead and I couldn't get it to move an inch. I was eighteen miles from home, and the only way I could do it was to tie a string on the snowshoe that had the bad leg. Then I would pull the injured leg behind me as I stepped forward with the good leg. I could walk a fair step like this and made home that night.

14
A Trip to Cartwright With a Patient

In April 1944 I was striking up my traps. This was the best winter for fur that I had to date. I had been over to Jeffries' Pond, and after striking up the last trap I came on the tracks of a big herd of caribou. I followed them so far, and I could see that they were heading for the White Hill Mountains. Those mountains served as the bread box for the few families in the bottom of St. Michaels Bay. Each spring we would hunt those mountains and usually get our caribou, which would last until the bay ice was gone. Then there would be lots of bird and seals to get.

I decided I would hurry home and get Uncle Alex Campbell to go with me to the mountains for the caribou. Uncle Alex was a top man for the caribou in his younger days. He could run a herd of caribou down and then shoot them, but now he was in his late sixties. After arriving home and telling Uncle Alex, he told me he would like to go but that he had had a problem last summer. A lump had come in his side, and the doctor who was on the Grenfell Mission boat, *Maravel,* told him that if the lump kept growing he would have to get it out at once. Right at that time it didn't seem to get any bigger. But after Uncle Alex had worked hard all winter trapping, the lump started to grow fast, and was now about the size of a hen's egg. The nearest hospital was over one hundred miles away but we had to get there. It was get him to either the St. Anthony hospital or the Cartwright nursing station. St. Anthony was out of the question because it was in Newfoundland. So it had to be Cartwright.

We got ready with the big husky dogs. Neither he, nor I had ever been to Cartwright before, but we thought we could find it. It was late the next morning before we got everything ready. We had new skin traces for the eight dogs and new bridles made of square flipper skin, plus three hundred pounds of dog feed tied to the komatik and some food for ourselves. We started off. The travelling was very good, but we were heavily loaded, because we also had the camp and stove. We were fitted out for both good and bad weather.

Our first stop was Norman's Bay, about twenty-five miles to the east. We had lunch there and then started off again. Darkness came upon us under Peter's Hills. The dogs smelled something, a fox or a polar bear or something, and took off at a stretch gallop. The komatik nosed right into a high snowbank. I watched the big skin bridle start to stretch as the dogs pulled. Then with a crack the little bit of whalebone that was on the end of the bridle went through the hole and all our dogs were gone. We were left sitting on the komatik. Uncle Alex yelled out to the leader dog and she came running back. Soon the others followed. Then we were on our way again.

Our next stop was Shoal Bay on the back of Frenchman's Island. Here were little piles of wood stuck up like wigwams all over the ice. This was wood the people had put on the ice to haul to their summer places at Seal Islands. Those people would have a busy winter cutting two lots of wood – one lot to burn in their winter stoves and the other to bring to their summer homes. It was remarkable how well the wood all stood together, and not one little stick had fallen down.

We moved on and soon we could see the houses of Shoal Bay and the good friendly people soon had us in for a cup of warm tea. Their name was Hopkins, two or three families of them. As soon as we had lunch we moved on again, and by dark we were entering Mussel Brook. There were quite a few houses there all along the side of the brook. Soon an old man came running down toward us and told us to come right in and have a cup of tea. His face was as wrinkly as the map of

Ireland! But we decided first to straighten away our dogs and put all their feed on the scaffold so the other dogs wouldn't eat it. Then we fed them for the night and went in for a lunch.

He told us his name was Uncle John Morris. He was living in a fair-sized house with a loft overhead. He had a wife and one little girl there. He told us the rest of his family was married. As we sat at the table, there was just bread, butter, sugar and tea. He told us he had to haul this welfare food from Cartwright, about forty miles north of us, and then he had to haul his dog feed from the whaling factory at Hawke Harbour, about forty miles south of us. The nearest firewood was five miles inland. This was so small that they almost had to dig it out of the snow after a big batch. He said he wasn't that well that winter, because he had had an accident that past summer. He was shipping herring on a vessel when one barrel fell out of the sling and struck him in the jaw, breaking it in nine places. But he said he only felt it at times. I watched as he used to bite those big slices of buttered bread, as if he never wished for anything more.

That night by the little oil lamp, Johnnie Morris told us many stories that passed the night very quickly – stories about the many times he came home in storms from the coast and his clothes would be packed with snow right to his naked skin. I believed every word of it. You could tell by the wrinkles on that weather-beaten old face that this human being had weathered many storms.

Around midnight we lay down for a night's rest. The next day I learned that the little girl was his granddaughter. She and the old lady went up in the loft. The night was very cold, and the wind blew around the old house and through the seams almost like it did outdoors. Before daylight there was a storm of snow, so we had to spend the next day there, too. We brought in some of the food that we had with us to share with the Morrises that day. I noticed that the little girl never moved off the bench. The old lady would give her a slice of bread and she would eat it and not move.

Before dark the storm cleared, and Efrom Dysom, who lived farther up the riverbank, came down and invited me up to supper. He said he knew my brother, Roland. We had a good supper of corned fish with pork fat over it. Later I returned to Mr. Morris' to see how Uncle Alex's side was. He said it was no problem, but I knew that's what he would say in any case. It would really have to be a hospital case before he would even mention it.

The next morning we were off at daylight. The dogs were fresh after a day sleeping. We passed through a little settlement called Bill's Brook in Rocky Bay. There were a number of little houses on both sides of the trail all built from round sticks. Many dogs were there lying around. It was still very early in the day and there weren't any men around to see.

Our next stop was Sandy Hill River. There were a few houses there, and Josiah Burdett had a very nice home that was painted. It was in a good spot by the side of the river that was heavily-wooded. People soon came out and asked us in for tea. We found everyone that we met very friendly, and the very first word would be, "Come and have tea." This makes it so easy to travel in strange places. In many places we just didn't know where to take the trail again after leaving a big open bay, but there was always something to mark it for us – sometimes an old iron kettle on a stump, at other times an old pan. There was always something, so we were doing as well as we could expect for strangers heading north. After lunch we shook hands again with those wonderful people and thanked them for the meal. Those people would probably give hundreds of cups of tea per month to people who were travelling this long Labrador trail, which was the winter highway of the north. The people who lived along the side of this trail had so little to offer anyone, yet the very language of their heart was, "Come, you are welcome to what we have." Yet many of them barely had enough to exist on.

Then we had the long drive up Table Bay and again we met several families living right at the head of the bay. We wanted to pass by those houses and go on to Cartwright, but there was no way to do this. They stopped us, and a little woman by the name of Purdy came out and took Uncle Alex by the arm and soon had him in the house. They got the stove very hot and then the little kettle was boiling. We had to have lunch again. In the big pond alongside the people were catching smelts through the ice, so we were made to stay until some of those smelts were fried for us. The old lady had a daughter she called Joyce. She was the smartest girl I ever saw, going back and forth to the table, getting more tea and smelts for us. Well, I thought to myself, just to visit this home alone was worth the trip to a trapper who was used to shacking for himself. Then they wanted us to stop all night. Maybe I would have, but after all, we were on our way to the hospital and we had no time to lose. It was getting late in April and the ice would soon be bad. So we started on again as those people waved us out of sight.

The next place was Goose Cove. We saw a number of houses there and the dogs went stretch gallop right on through the place. Only five more miles and we would be in Cartwright. We arrived by dark, and soon a man by the name of Donald Martin asked us to come to his house. It was now Saturday evening. We soon got the harnesses off the dogs and had our supper.

Later Uncle Alex went to the hospital where Dr. Forsyte met him and said he would have to have an operation on his side at once. This meant he would have to spend a few days there for it to heal up some before the long trip back over the rugged trail.

Donald Martin was a trapper who was not long home from his trapline. He ran his line from the headwaters of Paradise River to Burnt Wood Brook on Alexis River and hauled his sleigh all this distance. Only the strongest and most daring trappers could stand up under such trips, dragging such heavy loads such a distance.

A few days later I received the report from the hospital that Alex Campbell had his surgery and that he would have to rest at the hospital for five days. Then if I could get him home carefully, I could take his stitches out when they were ready to come out. The five days soon passed. In the meantime, I helped Mr. Martin haul his wood that he would cut up that spring to be used the following winter when he would be too busy on his trapline.

On April 22, 1944 we harnessed up the dogs and headed back for St. Michaels Bay. The travelling was good, and the dogs were well rested after laying up for almost a week. They were willing to put out their best on the homeward journey. The five miles to Goose Cove were soon covered. Then we headed out toward Table Bay Pond where a lot of people were smelting and had bough houses around the smelting holes. As we passed they waved their hands and we waved back. From there we went to the head of Table Bay. Our dogs never slacked a gallop. I thought they must be travelling faster than the train that ran from Carbonear to the north shore when I was a boy back in Newfoundland! The dogs made no attempt to go to the houses at Table Bay, but headed right down the bay. The land that seemed to look so far ahead of us soon got handier, but an over-cast sky appeared above, and we knew weather would come before dark. Perhaps we would make Bill's Brook before it got too bad, and there were people there who could put us up.

Uncle Alex had to be looked after now and couldn't get too cold and couldn't bend his side, as he might tear out the stitch-es, so we had to make shelter before the storm. We could do it all right in fine weather. But in stormy weather it would be dif-ferent. Most of the travelling was over barren country that was all strange to us. So we began to drive the dogs as fast as we could. They would trot for a few miles, then gallop. We were making good time and by midday we were at Bill's Brook.

We soon discovered that all the families had left their houses and had moved out to the seacoast for their fishing, as this was usually the practice of all the people along the coast. Then they would move back from the seacoast in the fall of the year where they would have more shelter and more fuel to burn. Then in the spring, around the last of April, they would move out to where they could get seals and birds to eat and also to get their fishing gear ready for the summer.

So I called the dogs to one side of the trail and put the drag[1] over the nose of the komatik to stop her. The first snow began to fall and the wind started to strike. The first house I went into had no stove; they must have taken it with them. The next one had an oil barrel stuck on its head but there was no wood around. I thought to myself that I would be a long time getting the kettle boiled in this one! Through the seams in the logs I could still see Uncle Alex sitting out on the komatik box, so I thought this was no place for a patient who needed care. In the third house was a big Waterloo stove, all lashed up with wire. The dampers were all gone and a piece of sheet iron was put over the top. Then ashes were piled on this to cover the seams in the stove. I was afraid to touch this, as I thought it might fall down in the night and burn the place down.

There was still another shack or two on the other side of the trail, and I started to go over to them. I could see that the storm was about to set in and the wind was starting to pick up. So I told Uncle Alex I thought we should try and make Mussel Brook. He said we had a good leader and we could depend on her as she would remember the trail from coming north the first time. The dog traces were all tangled up, but there was no time to straighten that out now. It was off with the drug and the dogs went stretch gallop. Soon Bill's Brook was out of sight, but when we got on the barrens everything closed in around us. The dogs all fell in line and I could only see the leader on times with her nose close to the snow and her tail straight. The other seven dogs had curls in their tails over their backs.

The storm was getting worse, and soon we could only see the leader, at times. It really made me uneasy with a patient on the komatik and I wasn't sure where we were going. We could go over a cliff or even pass Mussel Brook and go out into open water. We just had to take this chance. Sometimes I thought the komatik had stopped moving, because I couldn't see a thing for

---

[1] A heavy chain thrown over the runners of the komatik to slow it down and to stop it – commonly called a drag.

the snow that was driving. But when I put my foot down on the snow I soon found that we were going at a fair speed. We had a twelve-foot long komatik with whalebone shoes,[1] and now that it wasn't very frosty, it was almost running on its own. So we were making time very fast. But where we would end up remained to be seen!

This was one trying day for me. Soon I could see that darkness was setting in, and we now seemed to go faster than ever. The wind was starting to blow gale force, but it still wasn't very frosty out. Then we heard the barking of dogs and we stopped. As we looked around, there we were at the door of John Morris at Mussel Brook! I was never so glad in my life. I thought for sure my lead dog had done a better job than I could have done that day!

Uncle Johnnie was soon at the door and I recall the first words he said, "It's getting ever do dusty now." He helped us get the dogs unharnessed and then piled up all the skin traces and carried them in to hang close to the stove to melt the ice off them. We never boiled any feed for the dogs that night, but gave them some herring, just as they were, out of the bag. Before we had time to tie the rest of the dog feed up in a tree, all the dogs were lying down and were almost out of sight with the snow that was drifting over them. It was blowing around the house and then lodging in the lund on the house. We went inside and closed the door, and for the next two days that door was never opened.

We ate the last little bit of food we had. Then Uncle Johnnie kept giving us bread and butter. I was very concerned about his little granddaughter; I would say she was about five years old, and for two days this little girl just sat on the bench and never moved. On the third day I could see that the wood was all but gone, and once that happened we would be in trouble. The hard wind around the house seemed to slacken at times, so I told Uncle Johnnie that if we could get the door open I would try to

---

[1] A strip of whalebone on the sleigh's runners to receive the friction.

cut some wood which I had seen out by the door when we arrived. So we went to the door and hauled it open. There before us was one wall of snow! So we started to shovel the snow into the house, and almost had to fill the house in order to make a channel through the wall in front of us. As soon as this was done, we shoveled the snow that was in the house out through the hole we had made. Then I went out with the axe in my hand. I never saw a sign of my dogs, and I had all I could do to cut off enough food for that night. The old lady stood at the door and kept opening and closing it as I ran back and forth with the wood. Uncle Johnnie kept busy getting the last of the snow out of the kitchen. After getting a good pile of wood behind the stove, I came in and the old lady again put the latch down on the door.

All that night the storm kept up. By dinnertime the next day the weather started to clear fast. We could see several miles out the bay where it had drifted in high piles. Our dogs hadn't been fed since the first night, so we did that first. In no time we had our box and the dog feed lashed onto the komatik. As I went back for the dogs' harnesses, I took one more look at that little girl sitting there on the bench. I knew she was hungry, and there was no way I could help her. With a lack of vitamins and no energy, it would be hard for her to live on just bread and butter. No milk at all.

I thanked the old lady for her kindness to us and got Uncle Alex on the box at the back of the komatik. I put the drug over the nose of the komatik and set the nose against a dry old stump so the dogs wouldn't carry us away before we were ready. Uncle Johnnie was holding back on the nose of her too as the dogs were leaping the length of their traces. We still couldn't see very far because of the drifting snow. I pulled clear of the stump and jumped onto the komatik. Uncle Johnnie was still hanging on and couldn't get clear. The dogs went stretch gallop, and the next thing I knew we were going over a twenty-foot-high bank and down onto the brook. So I jumped off and gave Uncle Alex a shove. He went face down in the snow. I sang out to Mr. Morris, "Are you hurt?" but he never answered. When I looked again he was crawling out of the snow with the dogs all around him, so I shouted again, "Are you hurt?" He said he believed it was a hospital case, but I knew he wasn't hurt too badly in the soft snow. I first got Uncle Alex around the bank and got the komatik out of the snow and the dogs straightened out. I had no time to help Uncle Johnnie back to the house, as the dogs started once again at a gallop. But I wasn't worried about him. I was more worried about that little girl.

In the years that followed, I tried to find out if that little girl ever survived. It wasn't until April 30, 1977, when George Morris came to Charlottetown, Labrador, where I now live, that he told me the girl did survive. But many people didn't. They were bad times on the coast.

We headed out the bay at full gallop and soon we were passing the houses in Shoal Bay. The dogs didn't want to stop, so they went the shortcut across the point and took the trail on the bay. That night, as darkness set in, we were in Norman's Bay, only twenty-five miles from home. We had one meal of feed left for the dogs and none left for ourselves. At that time of year, no one had very much food. So Uncle Alex said we would take part of the dog feed for ourselves, as it wouldn't hurt us. The dogs would be home tomorrow and then have plenty to eat. So we shared the food. It was the first meal the dogs had had for four nights, but there was still plenty of strength in them. We stopped at Wilson Green's home there in Norman's Bay and they shared their food with us also. We found that people all along the coast were willing to share the very last slice of bread with a stranger.

The next day we made home! There was only one day left in April, and we had shot no caribou for the spring. I didn't think Uncle Alex was in shape to go on a caribou hunt with his side all sewn up. He was getting on in years now, and even if he hadn't had that operation, it was enough for a healthy man to climb those White Hill Mountains looking for caribou. But somehow he thought he was safe with me, and I thought I was safe with him. That was all we needed. I don't know why he trusted me so much since I was always getting into trouble. He used to get me to pull out his big jaw teeth. I thought this was dangerous, but when he would ask me to do something, I would always try and do it for him. He had some kind of a unit that was used for pulling teeth, but no doubt it was the old type. But I always managed to get the teeth out with no deadening at all. And he had some big teeth with three spears[1] on them!

He told his wife, "Lennie, girl," as he used to call her, "feed the dogs well tonight. We're going for caribou tomorrow." There wasn't much time left to get caribou meat for the spring, and he knew the caribou were in on the mountains. So he rested that night and his wife, Lennie, got everything ready for the next morning. Aunt Maggie had the medicine on the stove, all warm, and Uncle Alex had to take the second drink to please Aunt Maggie!

Uncle Alex was always like a father to me. When I first came on the coast I was quite young. I certainly hadn't spent much time with my own dad, because he was most always at sea when I was a small boy in Carbonear. Over the years Uncle Alex and myself had a lot of trips on dog team together. He had a family of seven girls and one baby boy along those years. The girls had to take the place of boys, so they went in and cut the wood, hauled it home with the dogs, and sawed it up. Uncle Alex was busy on the trapline most of the time.

The greatest randy[2] I ever had with him and his dogs was the first winter when our first baby was born. My wife, Effie, couldn't feed the child on her breast, and there was no milk to be had anywhere in our area. So Uncle Alex told me we would go to Battle Harbour and for sure there would be milk there. He had to get some paint too for his new boat that he had started to build. So the next morning we were off early. The trip was only about forty miles; this didn't seem too far when the weather and travelling were good.

[1] Roots.
[2] Exciting adventure.

We stopped at Rexon's Cove on the way along and had a lunch. Most of the men had gone in the woods, but Harry Shea was there. His home was at Battle Harbour, but he was at Rexon's Cove teaching school. The children were supposed to go into school at half past nine in the morning. I remember that Harry Shea didn't ring a bell, but stood by the school and gave one loud shout. It sounded through the village and echoed in the high hills that stood right over the houses. I watched children coming from every little house in the village, and I'm sure everyone was gathered in less than five minutes time. There was no other call, apart from the echo in the hills. I was very impressed with his way of getting the children to school, and whenever I hear a school bell today and watch the children linger as they go to school, I think of Mr. Shea's loud voice.

Soon we were crossing Alexis Bay on the ice. We were supposed to cross the neck of land and then come out in Fox Harbour, but before we took the path end across the neck, the dogs started picking up a scattered sea bird that was frozen in the ice; these were turrs and bull birds mostly. They took off at a stretch gallop and nothing would stop them. We were out on thin ice that was just as slippery as window glass. We put down the drugs, but they made no difference. They would take no hold. Uncle Alex had a new leader that year by the name of Diamond, so he shouted, trying to turn him for the land. But the more he shouted, the faster the dogs went. I don't know how thick the ice was, but it couldn't have been more than two or three inches. But at least saltwater ice is very tough. This would be plenty thick to hold us as long as we didn't strike any thinner spots. We were heading for Battle Harbour the same way the coastal boats went. We were right out in the Atlantic Ocean!

Very often the ocean will catch over as far as your eye can see, if winds are calm for several nights and it is frosty. But a very small wind or a big sea will easily break it up again. We went through the two islands at Spear Point and then headed for Lewis Rock off Lewis Cape. I believe it was the fastest time I ever went to Battle Harbour!

We did our trading there and came back across the neck of land on the back of Fox Harbour. We made sure the dogs didn't carry us out on the ice going back. It snowed that night and it took us two more days to get home in the bad travelling.

15
The Caribou Hunt

Everything was ready for the caribou hunt. We were off early on Saturday morning, April 30. The day was going to be hot, as we could see the sun rising in the clear bright sky as we passed the first trapper's trail, which was John Campbell II's. Then we took the Middle Trail which was Uncle Alex Campbell's, and soon we were on Big Middle Lake. Then we went across the short neck and out onto Little Middle Lake. In another hour we were on Clifty Lake. This was as far as the dogs would go unless we killed a caribou farther on. Then we'd need the dogs to haul it out. So we cut down a bed of boughs for the eight dogs to keep them as still as we could. We then took our rifles and game bags with our lunch in them and crossed a short neck to Pearl Lake.

The sun began to blast down; the snow was soft and sticky for our snowshoes. I could see that Uncle Alex was working hard, but he wouldn't give in. We went three miles up Pearl Lake, then across another neck of land and there was White Hill Lake, right under the White Hill Mountains. Those mountains just glittered in the sun. We had to go across the lake about two miles and then we would take the Deer Lead – this was the main trail where the caribou went up and down the mountains. Farther to the east was a sort of round valley that was called the Deer House where the caribou would spend much of their time when the weather was bad on the mountains. But we knew the caribou wouldn't be there on this beautiful day.

We were only about halfway up through the Deer Lead when we came on the track of what looked like the same herd I saw going toward the White Hill Mountains when I was striking up my trapline about three weeks earlier. We followed the track for miles. There was no wind and it was very mild. We saw where the caribou had been feeding and spending the night. Then we followed their track to where they had made a big round and headed for the head of White Hill Lake. They would only be able to get back off the mountains from the western end, the way they were heading. A little light wind started to blow from the southeast, so Uncle Alex said we must get off the mountains before they smelled us. He thought they would be around the head of White Hill Lake. So we started down again and soon were on White Hill Lake. When we got to the cliff that ran most of the length of the lake, we could see a little island out in the lake. To me it looked like big rocks all over it. Uncle Alex said it was the caribou, resting in the sun. It was a very hard spot to work in a shot at them. So he sat down and took a spell and looked at his watch. He figured those caribou would soon be looking for their evening meal. He told me he would have to go about one mile around the cliff so they wouldn't smell him, and he told me to stay on the point because if they started to run they would come for the Deer Lead for sure. While he was going along by the cliff he wouldn't even know if they had started to run until he got out on the other side.

He opened his game bag and got out a big molasses bun. Then he melted a little snow in a can and with his white kerchief washed out his eyes. I thought to myself, "This is not the first time I've seen him do this when we've been caribou hunting." But this was the warmest day I had ever seen this done. Mostly he did this in camp, before leaving on a hunt, his can on the stove. We had made a lot of caribou hunts together; most, if not all of them, were in the spring, after I was finished on the trapline.

Now he started off around the cliffs. His side was still full of stitches from the operation. I was in sight of the caribou all the time. I waited for what seemed like a long time, almost an hour. At last I wondered if he had fainted under the scorching sun, going around those cliffs. I soon would have to follow his track to see. But then I saw one caribou stand to its feet. I went a little farther out on the point and I could see Uncle Alex as he raised his rifle. I heard the crack and the leader fell back dead. I knew this must have been the leader getting ready to go and feed. Now with the leader down, this would make the others more bewildered and would slow them down. The next one rose, and before I saw anything else, Uncle Alex fell to the ground. The tramp in the heat was too much for him. Five caribou were now on their feet, and Uncle Alex was down. I watched him get to his knees and lean on one elbow to shoot. One caribou after the other fell. He had five on the ice and one left on the island. There were all the cartridges that were in his magazine. Then he fell back again. The rest of the herd turned and went back north around the mountains. We had six caribou, enough meat for the spring.

Soon I was up to where Uncle Alex was. He told me he took a cramp in his side that knocked him down with the pain. Soon I had a fire going and the kettle boiled and he was fine again. After lunch he paunched the caribou and I went to Clifty Lake to get the dogs. By the time we got back to Clifty Lake with three caribou on the komatik and put up our camp and got wood, it was a little after midnight. This would try any sound man. The next morning was Sunday, and we were home early with the caribou. On Monday I took the dogs myself and went back to pull home the other three caribou we had left. We shared the meat with all the families in the bay.

The following Tuesday I took the stitches out of Uncle Alex's side, and Aunt Lennie talked him into resting a few days while she cooked the venison. In the years that followed that trip, we made a lot of caribou hunts, all in the spring of the year. We had some exciting times, and never ran into any more difficulties.

Alex Campbell with two otters he got with one shot, 1949.

Some of Alex Campbell's daughters proudly holding some furs their father had trapped.

As food got scarce in late April, Uncle Alex arrived with a stag caribou from the White Hill Mountains.

Most of the population of Campbell's Cove had been after this polar bear. One shot from Alex Campbell's .30-.30 rifle killed it. Alex is in the white dickie.

16
A Trip for a Christmas Box

Shortly after that caribou hunt, Uncle Alex adopted a little Marshall boy from Norman's Bay. But later the dogs bit him in the privates and he died. Mr. Campbell found this a hard blow, and it took a long time before he could get over it.

The following Christmas I came out of the country to spend Christmas at home. Somehow Uncle Alex learned there was a Christmas box down at Mr. Turnbull's at New York Bay, so he asked me if I would go along with him to get the box, as there was very little for the children for Christmas.

There was a lady doctor from the United States of America who had been on the Grenfell Mission hospital boat that past summer who had made friends with Uncle Alex and Aunt Lennie. Later that summer she sent the box. When the coastal boat went north early in October the package was carried too far and went north. By the time the boat came south again, the head of the bay was frozen up and nobody went out to meet the boat. They weren't expecting anything on the boat returning south. So Barton Turnbull from New York, in the mouth of the bay, was out at his fox traps when the coastal boat blasted her horn. He went out to her and this was what the boat had, a small package for Alex Campbell. So Mr. Turnbull carried it back to New York and later met the Kippenhuck trappers who ran a trapline not too far from New York. He told them about the box.

So we got the dogs to haul a small boat about three miles out the bay until we struck open water. We put the boat in and one of Uncle Alex's girls, Margaret, drove the dog team back again. It was a very calm day and not too cold, so we started to row our fourteen-foot boat out the bay. It was only about ten miles to New York, as we already had three miles covered on ice. We killed a few sea birds as we went along, figuring that if we didn't make it that day we had the camp and stove in the boat and could cook the birds. When we got down to Kelly's Cove we thought we had enough birds, so we thought we'd go ashore and boil the kettle. After lunch the weather was still good and the wind calm, so we crossed the bay at Salt Pond Head. Then we were supposed to go on the inside of the islands which was called Cross Fox Island, but when we got there the tickles were all frozen up. So Uncle Alex said this looked bad. We would probably have to go around Lewis Island, and with nothing but the ocean outside of us, it could be bad. But if there was no sea on[1] and no wind, we could get to New York by dark.

We started to row and it wasn't too long before the wind began to blow from the northwest and it started to get cold. The wind was now almost in our favour, but when we had to turn around Lewis Island we would have to face the wind in our little boat. Soon the wind was very heavy, and there was nothing to do about it. No coves to get into and every tickle was frozen as we came to it. We were out in rough water. Mountains of sea were being thrown in from the ocean. Uncle Alex said our only chance was if we could make White Fish House on Lewis Island. This was a small cove on the outside of the island with a rock in the tickle that stuck out of the water at low tide. Now with this sea on, it would be a breaking rock, and there would only be one chance out of a hundred that we might make it. Outside of us was the ocean.

We kept rowing. I was forward hauling on the paddles. Uncle Alex was behind, shoving on his paddles so he could see what was a little distance ahead. But I had to turn my neck to see ahead. Soon our boat was icing up and it was almost impossible

[1] Meaning no large waves.

to move our oars. They were just like cakes of ice. The snow was blowing over the water from off the land. We turned the point and only had about a half mile to go to be in a sheltered cove. This would depend on whether or not we could make it over this shoal. We kept beating the ice off our oars, but our little boat was just like a pan of ice. It was hard to tell if we were moving or not. Soon it was dark. We could see that the stars were shining brightly, but all around us was the drift of snow and vapour off the water. It almost took our breath away. We were slow moving under the high land. The wind was more in squalls now, and between the squalls we would move ahead a little. Once in the squalls we 'would barely hold out. Nobody spoke for at least two hours. We just kept bending on the paddles. We took turns knocking the ice off the other's paddle. We were no longer knocking away at the boat. We had reached a point between life and death, and it was just straight ahead, taking whatever happened.

We soon heard the pounding of the sea on the rock right ahead of us. We could hear the little tickle breaking right across. We could count the big seas – there would be three breakers, and then there'd be a slack, then three more breakers and a slack for what seemed like three minutes. I knew just what Uncle Alex was thinking; it was the same as I had been thinking. If we could reach the rock just as the third wave struck, there would be a chance we might survive. We just couldn't row any faster. We had been rowing for our lives now for more than three hours. Our mittens were frozen to the paddles. We were both just like ice men, frozen in that little boat that was now only floating above water.

Once again we counted the breakers. It broke three times and then we moved in over the rock. Still neither of us spoke. We were now out of the breakers. Another hundred yards and we would be at the bottom of the cove. We kept the same stroke until we heard the nose of the boat strike the wall of ice that had formed around the cove. I soon tore my hands out of my mittens and my trousers off the seat of the boat and reached over the nose to hold on for awhile. Uncle Alex still never spoke. I then got ashore and pulled the frozen rope out of the nose of the boat and beat it around to get the ice off. I tied the boat to a stump that was sticking out of the ice, then jumped around and beat myself to get the blood circulating again. We were still alive. Then I asked Uncle Alex how he felt. The first words he said were, "It was a good job that the shoal had broken at the right time." Then he asked me to get some molasses buns out of my bag and he'd try to get ashore after he had something to eat. He was still too weak to move. I beat the ice off the game bag and soon got his bag of molasses buns out. They were full of pork which made them strengthening to eat. He started to eat his buns. The drifting snow coming off the barren land was just like smoke. I had never liked the seacoast in the winter. After this trip I would like it less! I was used to the trapline where there was lots of forest. The coast was only meant for the Eskimos, I thought.

I then went ashore and started to dig a snow hole for the night. This would be the only thing I could do, so with my snowshoes I dug a large one, just as big as our canvas tent. The snow was dry right to the blackberry bushes. Then I went back to the boat and helped Uncle Alex ashore. He said he was feeling A-1; that was the very word he used often. So we got in the snow hole for awhile, but the drifting snow was still bad as it baffled around and came in the hole. It was severely frosty, so Uncle Alex told me to go aboard the boat again and get the camp and stove and bring them back in the hole with the pipes. It wasn't long before we had the tent up in the snow hole with the paddles and some old stumps to hold it up. We got it up enough to crawl in, then we got the stove up and the dry blackberry bushes burned like everything. So it wasn't long before we got some snow melted in the kettle and had some tea. This put the life right back in a half dead fellow! Both of us then dug out enough stumps to keep the fire going until sometime in the early hours of the morning. By then the wind had gone down some, but it was still bitterly cold. The stars were still shining, so I told Uncle Alex I would go back over the island and see if I could find a stick of dry wood. After beating the ice off my axe, I took my snowshoes and went over the island. I heard Uncle Alex shout, "Don't go very far."

It was still drifting. The cold wind struck my face like a knife. I found three sticks of wood, got them on my back, and before I got back to the camp, I ran into Uncle Alex coming to look for me. He thought I must have fallen into the water. Soon I had the sticks all cut up and a good heat on. We were ready for one good nap before daylight. As I leaned back I thought we never could have gotten that camp up under such conditions in that snow hole and in such a blizzard. But after all, I had to give Uncle Alex the credit for this; it was his idea.

Uncle Alex was in his sixties now, and this was the kind of life he lived. It was only one incident of hundreds he had experienced over the years. He lived through so many of those storms that he could face death calmly and never get excited. If I was to survive on my trapline, I had to learn from his ways of life.

We both had several hours of rest before daylight. When daylight broke I looked through the camp door and the first thing that looked into my face was a big harp seal. The harp seals were now going south, and the ocean was full of them. One big school came right close to our camp, but by the time we got the ice beaten off our gun coats, they were gone out the cove again. So we melted some snow and got ourselves a lunch. The wind was still a fair breeze, blowing right out of New York. As soon as we got the camp down, we chopped all the ice off the boats and paddles. This was a big job. Then we started across New York Bay, and with the wind broadside we made it across. We then went ashore again and chopped the ice off the boat and our paddles. Another half mile to go along the shore and we would be at Barton Turnbull's house in the bottom of New York. Soon we were there. He and his big family lived there all alone. He helped us haul up the boat and then we went into the house for a lunch. Mr. Turnbull was a clever man. He was the one who had made the packing for our motor out of an old skin boot. He had to find ways to meet most of his wants in life by his own talents. Many people in Labrador couldn't have done it, but Barton Turnbull was about the most clever man I ever met to do things for himself; I could tell by his home.

The wash basin had worn out in the bottom so he had a wooden bottom in it. His bread pan had a wooden bottom in it. He could turn snowshoes just as good as the Indians; you could hardly see where the bow was joined. He used to saw lumber with his pit-saw with a weight on one end and he would be on the other. That fall he had carried a small caribou home on his back to his family who were in need.

We took a rest that day, a badly-needed one. The next morning Mr. Turnbull harnessed the dogs and took the Christmas box for us up to our homes in the bottom of St. Michael's Bay. We could ride sometimes, but other times we had to walk ahead of the dogs. We made it home that night, and the few things that were in the Christmas box were enjoyed by all the children. They had never been used to much in their stockings, but we had a very happy Christmas. Just to see the children happy on Christmas Day paid for our trip.

The author breaks camp and heads for home with his furs, New Year's Day 1945.

17
Two Trappers Meet and Plan Their Future

By 1950 I had my trapline well-organized. I was covering several hundred square miles of what I thought were choice trapping grounds. I had plenty of traps and snares to look after the whole area. I had long ago given up hauling the toboggan, as I had enough tilts to serve my trapping line. Only on the very far end of the trail would I have to use the canvas tent at all.

My ankle was giving me trouble that fall, and also my knee when snowshoe walking was bad. But I could still make a good day's walk. Somehow I had gotten a porcupine quill under the cap of my knee, and this was the same knee I had hurt years before. Porcupines often drop their quills in the summertime and I think I must have knelt on one sometime getting into my tilt after dark.

On the last trip in the spring we would always take down the tilt door and stick it up by the side of the tilt. Then when we returned in the fall on the first trip of the trapline, should it be after dark when I arrived at the tilt, I would always light a match to see if there was a bear in there. He could have used it for a cave in the winter. If he wasn't asleep, he probably would embarrass you and jump in your face. Many trappers have found them in their tilts.

Uncle Alex arrived at his tilt one time after dark and crawled in without lighting a match. After he got in and lit his candle he spotted a big black bear lying in his bunk! The bear had eaten a bag of tea that was left in the tilt and it made him very stupid. As it was already dark, Uncle Alex wouldn't shoot him, thinking he might only cripple him, so he left the bear in the tilt all night and stopped in the bush until daylight. Then he went back and shot the bear. After cutting him open he discovered that he was doped with the tea that was lying dry in his stomach.

So I must have picked up the quill sometime crawling into my tilt after dark and didn't notice it with just a match lit. For several days I felt something sticking in my knee, but it wasn't paining all that much. I planned to have a look at it sometime when I would have to spend a day in the camp because of bad weather. So when the bad day came, it was too late. There was only a very small end sticking out, and when I tried to haul it back, it just slipped in out of sight. There was nothing I could do about it, and it is still under my cap bone today.

I believe that porcupine quills kill more animals in the country than anything else I know of. When you look at a quill with a magnifying glass, you see it has a barb on it like a screw nail. The very moment it touches your flesh, even the top of it, it will keep moving in until it goes out of sight. So if it strikes in the killing part of an animal, it will slowly kill it. I have seen wolves full of quills, and they were so stupid from them that you could run them down. Porcupines seem to be such harmless things that most animals will stick their noses in their long black hair to take a bite of their flesh. But along this black hair is their armour, the only thing they have to defend themselves with. So when the needle-like quill sticks in their noses, the animal gets angry and makes more bites. At last their noses are just covered with quills, and sometimes their paws, so they go away in a great rage and many of them die after awhile. Often we have had to tie up our dogs when they get full of those quills and pull them out with a pair of pliers. They are really hard to get out. I have found horned owls full of quills, sitting on a dry stump just about dead. I have caught weasels in my trap with one big quill sticking right out of its nose like a narwhal, and the quill would be about three inches long. Animals really do have a hard time when this happens.

On the first day of March 1950 I arrived at my little tilt on

the southern waters of Hawke River. One more day and I would
have my trapline covered, then I'd be heading home. Furs were
scarce this trap, but I had done really well all winter. The next
morning I planned to go down to Hawke River. I was up at
dawn, took my kettle and ran in my stocking feet to the open
tickle for water. I took a glance at the green juniper trees that
hung over the tickle; there was no frost on them, so this meant
no bad weather for that day at least. I came back and put the
kettle on the stove. Then I began to rub out my skin boots[1]
while the kettle was boiling. I got some meat out of the pot that
had been left over from supper the night before. After breakfast
I threw all my clothes outdoors to put on, as the little tilt was
almost too small to get your clothes on properly. You couldn't
sit up on the bunk without bending your head a little.

Soon I was heading up Big Lake, about four miles long, and
then I had to go down a very rattling brook about one mile
where the water emptied into the river. Mostly I would keep in
clear of the brook a distance and strike out to each trap, then
strike back again. It takes a little bit of experience to do this. In
fact, I wasn't that good at it when I first got on the trapline.
There is so much to learn, and the first thing you must learn is
the whole watershed of the area where your trapline is to run.
You must know that all water must run into the ocean – all
small brooks run into bigger ones and many into rivers which
empty into the ocean. So it's possible for you to miss the trail at
times, but when you know the watershed you very soon will
pick yourself up again. You learn the valleys between each
water, so you can strike out anywhere you feel you would like
to go without worrying anything about getting lost in the country.

Soon I was going down the brook to look at my last traps. I
had had nothing more than a mink or two. I had to go down the
river to what I called the Three Islands that stood in the river,
one close behind the other. These were my last traps. I had one
lucky place alongside a big cliff. There was a hole in the cliff

---

[1]Knead them to soften them.

where the animals would go in and follow along the river and come out in another place which would bypass the rough, rattling waters. I had a lot of furs from this hole, mostly lynx. But this time there was only a red squirrel in the trap, which I threw onto the river.

Soon I was down to the islands, a very dangerous part of the river. Fast-moving water kept it from freezing up as early as the slower water of the river. The only way this fast water can freeze up is from the bottom first. We call this anchor ice; it will keep coming up and sometimes raise the river as much as eight feet. Then it will make a smooth surface on top. As soon as this happens and maybe gets two or three inches thick, it stops the cold air from getting at the ice that is frozen from the bottom. So the anchor ice lets go and all clears out, leaving the top ice only like a bridge across the river. This is a real death-trap to anyone going over it. After a bit of experience, you will have some knowledge of those bad places and can keep clear of most of them. I have gone down many times in those places, but in most cases the water wasn't too deep for me to get out. But I did save the life of another trapper once who was hanging by the tops of his fingers in one of these spots. He would have lasted only about one more minute and then would have been carried away with the mighty waters of the river.

I was now on my way back, following my track. I would soon come to another lucky trap I had tailed under a big white spruce tree. This place almost always had a lynx. The old rusty trap would have a shiny chain from so much beating around these years. After carrying those big lynx around on my back time after time in the winter, sometimes I would be getting tired about March. If I was able to catch them in the traps close by my tilt it seemed a lot better. But the long carry was hard when the snowshoe walking was bad. This time I sort of glanced at the trap under the big tree. There was only a rabbit in it, so I took it out of the trap and put it back again in the trap house for bait. I wasn't one bit sorry that a lynx wasn't there, for I had had a good winter, and the ones that wouldn't be caught now would breed for another season.

From the big tree I would make a shortcut back to Big Lake and now follow my track all the way back up the river. Only about one mile into the valley and I would be halfway down the lake. This was a blind valley – all red spruce about the same size. I took a dead reckoning and hoped to strike the same tree each trip. When I reached the lake, then I would haul my axe across, making a scratch in the tree only like a saw would make. Then at the end of the season I would count the marks on the tree and by doing this I would know just how many trips I had made into that valley that winter. But if I struck about fifty yards to one side of the tree, then I wouldn't put either mark on the tree. This would be out of the game.

However, this trip I was about halfway into the valley when all of a sudden I ran into a big company of spruce partridges. The trees were just full of them, from the top limb to the bottom. Anyone who knew about spruce grouse knew they are a quiet bird. I have often killed them with a stick, and over the years I have snared hundreds by putting a rabbit snare on the end of a stick and slipping it over their necks, hauling them out of the trees. Now I thought I would kill some. I didn't really need any at the camp; I had lots of meat there, but it was always our practice to keep enough meat around for the bad weather. I had no cartridge in my magazine, so I opened my game bag and took out one box of .22 cartridges. I filled up the magazine and lay the box on a stump. There were supposed to be fifty cartridges in the box. So I started shooting the lower partridges out of the tree first so the ones on the top of the tree wouldn't see them and be frightened. If I shot the top ones first, they would fall down and scare the lower ones. When I had fired the whole box of cartridges, I said to myself, "That's enough." The trees were still full of them, but I started to pick them up and put them in my bag. I counted forty-nine altogether. So whether there were only forty-nine cartridges in the box or whether there was one partridge dead that I couldn't find, I'll never know. I put the load on my back and started in through the valley and stuck very close to the tree with the marks on it. I put another mark on it, and I hoped some day to count all the marks I had on the tree, but it wouldn't be this time as my load was heavy. I would try to make my tilt without taking the bag off my back.

Very soon I was getting close to my little tilt by the open tickle. I was coming in the trail from the north, and there was another trail that came to the tilt from the south. As I got handy, I was kind of bending over with the weight of my back. I was just about ready to throw off my load by the door of the tilt when I straightened up and looked right into the face of another human being. This was a strange happening on any trapline to ever meet another trapper. Only once before do I remember in all my years meeting anyone, and that was in 1948. I was over at Jeffries' Pond one year in March. I was heading across to where I had a trap on an old beaver house when I heard someone shout out. I looked around and saw nothing, so I kept going, when I heard another shout. So that time when I looked, I saw a man up in the bottom of the pond. I headed up that way and saw three other men there. They had two camps put up; one told me he was a Pardy from Cartwright, and the other two were Lethbridge. The other fellow who did the yelling said his name was Ronald and that he was on a beaver hunt. The Lethbridges were from Paradise River. They told me they were getting short on food and asked me if I thought they would get any at St. Michaels Bay if they came out with me. I told them I was sure they would get some flour, but couldn't promise anything else. My tilt was only three miles away, so they said they would meet me at my tilt in the morning and we would go along together back to the coast. One came along with me a little way, thinking he might get a porcupine for supper. In passing my first trap on the beaver house, there was an otter that had been in my trap and broken the chain. He had gone off in the river with the trap still on him. We followed the tracks so far, then the otter went through a hole and got into the river. So Ronald saw the track of a porcupine and killed him. As he was skinning him I left and went to my other traps, then back to the tilt.

That night we had a batch of snow, so the trappers never turned up the next morning. With the bad travelling, they must have thought it would be the best idea for them to head to Paradise River.

So now at my little tilt I found that the trapper I almost ran into was Clarence Perry, another trapper from White Bear Arm and a brother-in-law of mine. He and another trapper by the name of Ralph House and I were all brothers-in-law; the three of us had married Alex Campbell's daughters, and Perry and House lived in Daniel's Harbour, Newfoundland. Both of them were trappers in Newfoundland, but wanted a winter on a trapline in Labrador. So the trapline they worked ran to the south of mine, and at one point was less than a day's walk from mine.

Now on this trip Ralph House had a bad back and couldn't make the trip. So Clarence knew I was supposed to be at my little tilt at that time, so he came to spend the night with me. It was certainly great to have someone there. He told me he had killed a porcupine out on the brook, thinking I might not have any meat for the night. I told him we'd have it for supper, but there was sure no shortage of meat. I had a bag full of partridges, and over our heads in the tree was part of that old stag caribou I had killed in October on the big marsh. It would soon be dark, so there was no time to tell trappers' stories until we first got the wood.

There was plenty of dry wood close by the camp I had left, but it was too big to cut. I used to go across the brook and cut small wood that was easier to cleave. Clarence asked me to loan him my snowshoes, as his were filled with thin caribou skin and would break under a heavy load. Mine were filled with thicker hide and were good to use in frosty weather. Soon Clarence was cutting down juniper trees and carrying them over and throwing them off by the door. I could hardly lift the big end of them. Clarence was a very powerful man and was used to the lumber woods as well as trapping. It wasn't long before we had wood enough in the tilt for the night, and enough left outdoors for another two nights.

Then it was time to prepare supper, so we got the porcupine ready. It was a small one, so we put the whole thing in the pot. While it was cooking, Clarence went outside again and came back with his arms full of green brush to put on the floor. This

Clarence and Margaret Perry enjoying a holiday in Bermuda.

was his bed for the night. I told him he could have my bunk – it was only made from four round sticks that didn't even have the bark off them, but it was good to lie on. After you moved around a few times, the knots sort of cleared.

When two trappers get together, they talk about trapping, never about farming or fishing or truck driving. But maybe the language of a trapper would be hard for those fellows to understand. We talk about otter rubs[1] that are worn as smooth as the floor; the big beaver houses that were as large as grandfather's old house back home; the big dams that had all the water backed up and the marshes flooded; the big lynx that broke the

[1]Snow-covered ground where otters play.

trap chain and got away, leaving a track as big as a bear. So our stories are just like those of the fishermen – the big ones always get away!

Clarence then wanted to know if there were any more caribou where I had killed that stag. I told him the stag was by himself and I really didn't want to kill him. All October had been rainy. I was wet every day. I know this old stag was working the southern lake back to the big marsh. I never saw him, but his fresh tracks were there every time I made my round. The rain kept coming and the lakes kept rising; I knew if this kept up for another week the lowland where my tilt was would go below water. So I decided I would have to move my tilt to the White Hill Mountains.

The next morning the tickle had risen about three feet overnight, so I took off all my clothes and tied them on my head and waded across. My clothes would be dry for awhile at least. For three miles I walked until I struck the big woods at the lower end of the lake. By the time I got to the first marsh I was as wet as could be. Then I ran into a company of partridges, so I thought I would shoot a meal for supper. I took the coat off my gun and killed six; this was all the cartridges I had in my magazine and it was plenty of birds for me. I put those in my bag and started across the big marsh, when all of a sudden, out of the woods popped this big stag. He was one of the largest I had seen and he started to walk along broadside with me, only a few yards away. I didn't want to kill him; I had no use for him because I had lots of meat. I was soaked to the skin with water and my camp was still ten miles away. So we walked together broadside for a time. Then we came to a little swampy pond in the marsh. He was on one side of the marsh and I was on the other, maybe ten yards away. Well, he began to blow steam out of his nostrils and shake his head and I didn't like the look of him. I had no cartridges in my gun; they were all in a can in the bottom of my game bag. I wondered what he would do when we got to the other end of this little swamp. We would probably meet together and I wasn't planning to take any more chances. I hauled off my game bag and came out with the can, off with the gun coat, and reached for a cartridge. The first one that came to my hand was a long one; normally it would be an extra long one I'd use on a caribou. But now I would try this one. I took aim behind his fore-shoulder and he went away stretch gallop as I fired. It looked as though he wasn't hurt, until he was almost out of sight. Then I saw him go all a-tremble and drop out of sight. I ran across and there he was, trying to get up on his legs. I could see he was done, so I walked up and gave him a blow on the head with my axe, then took the knife and slit him up the middle. Then I paunched him and took his heart along with me for a fry that night. I found the bullet that had entered between his rigs; it went through his heart and then broke a rib on the other side, stopping in the skin. After putting a bough in his belly to keep the flesh from coming together and spoiling, I went on to my tilt. So that was the story of the stag.

Then with the little candle lit, Clarence and I ate our supper. Then Clarence asked me how long I expected to follow the trapline. I thought to myself that this would be a hard one to answer. I told him I loved the trapline and was never used to working under a boss. There was such freedom and challenge out here. It seemed to get into my very blood and I just craved for it when the fall of the year came around. I felt itchy all over. I wanted to get back to the big otter rubs and the big beaver houses that had lots of tracks around them when I struck up my traps the spring before. This made you feel there would be lots of furs again when you started setting traps in the fall.

But then I told him there was something that made all the difference. After you are married, you must consider the future of your children. Things were different than before I was married. We have heard of the progress all over the world. We read about it in books how World War II ended with war-torn cities which were rebuilt, while we were up here on the Labrador hardly holding our own. I hadn't seen one improvement over all the years I had spent in Labrador. I thought we must be living in the Stone Age. I told Clarence I didn't think our children

would ever settle for the lives we lived on those traplines, but
they would move out to where life looked brighter. When we
older ones passed on, the little oil lamps would no longer shine
from the many little homes around our bay.

Then we talked abut education. I thought it looked very grim.
The Rev. Lester L. Burry from North West River was trying
hard to get a teacher to come into the homes and teach. He did
get one the past fall to come on the boat for the north. But when
the boat returned south, the teacher left again because he was so
lonesome. The men had all been out on the trapline and only
the women and children were at home; he just couldn't stick it.
Then Rev. Burry got another teacher, Archie Simms from St.
Anthony, Newfoundland, who was supposed to spend part of
his time at St. Michael's Bay and the remainder of the winter at
Sandy Hill River where there were a few families living. This
would only be very little help to the children. That winter, after
Archie went to Sandy Hill River, he got the measles and there
was no way to get him to the hospital. When they did get him
there finally, it was too late. He died. So this made things even
worse for getting teachers to come to little places where there

**Effie Campbell and Archie Simms in front of John Campbell's shop
where he traded furs with the Indians.**

were only two or three families living. We seemed to be living in one of the most isolated places on the coast, as far as education went. If you went right up north you would find that the Moravian missionaries have been there with schools for over one hundred years. And all the way down the coast from there the Grenfell Mission had nursing stations. Where those stations were, there were schools for the children.

I then told Clarence the story that had happened a few years before he came on the coast. It was always the practice down through the years to try and get caribou in the spring of the year to last until breakup time was over, as there would be several weeks in the spring when the bay ice would be too thin to travel on to hunt and the snow would be too rotten[1] to get into the woods. With caribou on hand for meat, we would make out all right until the bay ice was gone and then we could get seals and ducks. But this year the caribou never stopped on the White Hill Mountains; they left and went to the big marshes. So several men decided to go farther north – Tom Penner, George Penner, Barton Turnbull and John Campbell II. All of them started off for Hawke River where there was a tilt. They could spend some of their time overnight there, and at the same tilt would be other trappers who would also be caribou hunting from the Cartwright area – Bill Davis and Theodore Davis. The party from St. Michaels Bay hunted the whole area and saw quite a few tracks, but in the bad weather they weren't able to hunt them down. When their food started to get scarce, they had to return home. When they reached the tilt on Hawke River, they found a note on the table, but no one could read it. They looked it over and over, then put it back on the table. Then they returned home. All of those men were breadwinners with big families, and all they had to bring home were some porcupine paws. They had eaten the porcupines on the trip and brought home the little paws for the women to skin out, as it would be a little bit of food for them.

---

[1]Much too soft to use a dog team, and where it had melted there would be too many stumps for snowshoes to be used effectively.

However, later on that summer, they met Mr. Davis from Cartwright, and he asked them how they made out with the caribou he had killed and left behind on the marsh in the back of their camp. The men said they knew nothing about this. "Well," Mr. Davis said, "didn't you see the note I left on the table in your camp?" They told him they had seen it, but that nobody could read it. The note read, "Five caribou left on big marsh behind camp for you."

Clarence filled the stove up with wood at this point. "Well," he said, "that was tough all right." Then I told him about the mail service. He never really complained about it, but after all, everyone liked to hear from their friends once in a while. The mailman would come from Seven Islands by dog team the full length of the coast, but wouldn't come in our bay to deliver ours. If there was ever a letter for St. Michaels Bay, it was dropped off at Mr. Turnbull's house at New York. There was only one little bag that was carried, called the nunny bag. Billy Murphy would carry the mail from Battle Harbour to Comfort Bight, Rocky Bay on dog team, something like a distance of fifty miles. In bad weather it could take him sixteen days to make this trip. He would have to spend many nights in snow holes. So the mail in between this distance was put in the nunny bag and then for the next fifty miles it was sorted and the same thing was repeated. The mailman couldn't read or write, so when he came to New York he would pick out the nunny bag and give it to Mrs. Turnbull to pick out the mail for New York and also for the head of St. Michaels Bay.

I came out of the country in March, and I thought it would be nice to hear from the old folks back in Carbonear. So I said I would go to New York and see if there was any mail out there for us. I wore my snowshoes, because it was a twelve-mile walk. Twenty-four miles round trip. This didn't seem like much to a fellow who was walking every day that the weather was fit to walk. I reached the Turnbull home before dinner, and the first thing I had was a lunch. Then I told Mrs. Turnbull I had come to see if there was any mail for us. With a smile she said the mailman had gone north yesterday and there was a Christmas card left for me. Well, I thought it was a paying trip after all. It was good to have a Christmas card from home. When she passed the card I knew the writing – it was from my dad in Carbonear. This was sometime in March that it arrived; Christmas was long ago. If there were any newspapers to come, they wouldn't arrive until June or July. The mailman didn't haul papers. These had to wait until the coastal boats started on their summer service.

As far as communications went, we had none. There was a Marconi station at Battle Harbour, more than thirty miles away. The hospital services were as good as the Grenfell Mission could do under the conditions, with such a big area to cover and so little to serve it with. They made one or two trips each winter on dog team with a doctor; in the summer the hospital boat, *Maraval*, visited every harbour along the coast at least twice. We found those nurses and doctors to be the very best and very kind. I am sure no better could be found anywhere in the world.

When midnight came in our little tilt, it was time to get the kettle on again. I was doing all the talking. Clarence was just listening. I had told him how most of the conditions were in the days past, and he knew from his first winter on the coast that there was still no change. I hadn't mentioned anything about hunger, because anyone who has experienced hunger doesn't talk about it. In all my years on the coast, talking to many old-timers, they would tell me the stories of long ago with a sense of pride in their voices – how they pulled through the storms and lived in snow holes, but never did I hear them mention the fact of hunger. Nobody wanted to talk about it. But now there was no way to get away from it. There were times when we had to face it. I knew for myself that I had made several decisions in my life that could easily be forgotten, but one that I made on my trapline would never be forgotten.

I had been out on the far end of my trapline when the weather turned bad. There was one storm after another, and it was too bad to hunt for food. I was heading for home slowly. My flour had to be rationed, and at last I could now have one little damper dog per meal. When I reached Clifty Lake, only ten miles from home, it was Christmas Eve. I hoped to get home for Christmas. I was down to the last damper dog, so this would be the spot for lunching. I tried to make it a bit farther on, but this had to be it. I went as far as where the trail left the lake, then got a fire going. Soon the kettle was boiling and I held the last little bit of food in my hand. The decision I had to make was whether or not I could afford to eat it all then. I could have shoved it all into my mouth at one time, but then there was no more after that and ten miles remaining to travel with bad snowshoe walking. I made the decision to eat it, but that will never be forgotten. I have never told this to anyone, not even my family. How I staggered home that Christmas Eve, not from drinking, but from hunger!

The author standing behind the coffin of his first baby girl who had died. To the right is Uncle Sam Kippenhuck.

That same year was when our first baby was born. It died shortly after we were supposed to shift from the head of the bay to Square Islands on dog team. My wife, Effie, still wasn't very well, so her mother, Aunt Lennie Campbell, said she would come out to Square Islands and look after her for awhile. After we got there, several families of us, we knew we all had enough flour for the spring. With the meat we could kill, there should be no food shortage until the local merchants arrived in June. But shortly after we got on the islands, the Arctic ice surrounded us, making it impossible to hunt on the water. There wasn't a drop of water anywhere. The flour started to get scarce; one person started to share with another, and soon nobody had very much. The little bit we had left I carried up and put in the bedroom. Still there was no change in the icy conditions. To get out for milk or sugar wouldn't even be mentioned. As long as there were molasses and flour, that was all we needed. Soon there was no more flour and nowhere to get any. We were just stranded on the islands, surrounded by ice. The little flour I had in the bedroom wasn't enough for all hands for one week, even on rations. My wife was still sick in bed. Some of the young women, about sixteen years old, who came to visit her, would pick up crumbs dropped on the bed clothes as Effie was eating, and they would eat them. This was real hunger. But all hands survived since the next day the wind came off the land and the ice moved off with it.

As I write this story now, thirty-two years later, it brings back memories fresh to my mind and I dream about them at night. Often my wife will ask me what's wrong because I don't seem to be sleeping. It's because I dream about those days. Most people who read this book awake in the morning and are glad they have only dreamed an event at night. But I wake knowing I have had a true dream, and I'm glad those days are past.

It was now the early hours of the morning in our little tilt. I told Clarence that if we could find something else to do to earn a living, I was willing to hang up the traps on the trapline. He then told me he was always used to working in the woods logging since he was a small boy. He knew all about the sawmill business, and he said if I could find the suitable timber and get a sawmill and supplies for the winter, then he would be willing to do what he could. Clarence said it wasn't the same living in Labrador as in Newfoundland; we would run into many problems and it would be hard work, but he felt we could manage it and it was worth a try.

I was getting pretty sleepy as daylight approached. We needed some rest for the next day on the trail. I was just about to close my eyes when Clarence said, "I'd like to know what happened to all the Eskimos who once lived in this bay." I told him I didn't know. There were three hundred and sixty-five islands in our bay, but the only one to find Eskimo graves on was Yellow Fox Island. This was one of the nearest islands to the ocean and was the real home of the seals. After I came to the coast as a boy, we used to always go to this island on weekends and kill several seals to take home and share with the Newfoundland families that were fishing at Square Islands.

I tried to find out about the last of the Eskimos who lived on that island, and I thought the old Kippenhucks would know, as Uncle Sam Kippenhuck's father was a full-blooded Eskimo. But Uncle Sam never talked much about his father. I recall one of the first springs I was on the coast. Roland and myself took our map and went down on Yellow Fox Island to do some bird hunting. After we were there a little while we learned that Uncle Sam Kippenhuck and his son, George, were camped on the other end of the island, since they were cutting some wood for the summer. So just before dark I thought I would walk across the island and visit Uncle Sam and hear some of his stories about the days long ago. He could tell some wonderful stories and laugh so hard at them! He was old then but still a strong man. I wasn't there very long before dark, and Uncle Sam got the little lantern lit and started telling his stories. Uncle Sam was a very honest man and made sure not to tell any lies. But he could tell it to sound funny enough that we'd all be laughing!

There were several Eskimo graves on the islands. The Eskimos buried their dead by laying them on the ground and then putting rocks all around them and then one or two big flat rocks on top. I often went to the graves and looked at their beads and some other things that were put on their graves. Uncie Sam told me that night that he could remember that when he was a boy one of the graves had cobbler's tools in it. One of the families that lived ashore from Yellow Fox Island, by the name of Batten, from Conception Bay, Newfoundland, sometimes would take a loan of the old tools to fix up their leather boats. But if the tools weren't back on the grave by dark, they would hear some funny noises. So they always made sure the tools were returned. Uncle Sam told so many old ghost stories that night that when I put my head out through the tent door to go back to my camp, I wondered if I would see some of those ghosts as I passed along not far from the graves. However, I never saw any ghosts on my way back. Some of the big leg bones in those graves showed that some of the men were tall.

Clarence and I were both settling down for a nap now. It wouldn't be too long before daylight would shine through the seams of the tilt door. I remembered that it was my turn to fill up the little stove before we fell asleep. Just as I was putting in the wood, Clarence turned over again and said, "How did you make out in the war years? Could you hear about how the war was going?" Well, I told him we did hear some news because I had an old radio that I had bought from Rev. Lester Burry up in North West River. I had it at Square Islands. After I got it all hooked up I was afraid to move it, as I thought I wouldn't get it all together again. It was a big, high, floor-standing model with a lot of batteries. There were "A" batteries, "C" batteries and "B" batteries which were the largest ones. So I would come out of the country and Uncle Alex would say, "I wonder how the war is going. We haven't heard anything since last fall when we moved in by boat and now it's February." So I would get ready. It was only thirty-six miles round trip to Square Islands, and to hear the war news would be worth it, as I used to walk twenty-four miles just to get one Christmas card.

So off I'd go. The radio was in the house we had built from the timber we had sawn with the old pit saw the first winter I was on the coast. The radio was up in the loft where we used to sleep. I'd get a long stick and put up the antenna by the side of the hill. Then after getting enough food for the night I would hear all the news and go back and tell the folks at the head of the bay all they wanted to know. They really only wanted to know if our side was winning.

One night I remember being out there and turning on the radio full blast. It was a very cold night, and I had to get my wood first. All I could tune in was BBC in London. I curled right around the stove, trying to get some heat; I still had all my clothes left on; it was so cold. All of a sudden, Winston Churchill, who was prime minister at that time, came on and he told the Germans to come on; they were ready for them. And he would dry the English Channel with their dead bodies and walk over them to France. I got right up and started to jump. I felt like going right back to the head of the bay that night and telling the folks what I had heard on the radio. Mr. Churchill went on with his speech, but I could never remember one other word, just that one challenge to the Germans. I didn't go back that cold night, but I was off early the next morning. When I rounded the last point up the bay, I could see that some of the people were waiting for me to hear the news. All I had to say was that our side was winning. After I got in the house I told Uncle Alex what Mr. Churchill had said in his speech. I think it was better news to Uncle Alex than if he had had a silver fox in his trap!

I believe Clarence was sound asleep before I had finished the story, and then I had a nap. That night in our tilt far from home we had laid the foundation of a little settlement now known as Charlottetown; that was twenty-five years ago. It couldn't be found on the map the first year we started. None of the bush

pilots for Eastern Provincial Airways could find us until they
sent their chief pilot in, Marsh Jones. He came himself and
found us and put us on the map. Today, April 10, 1977, as I
write this story, I look through my office window and see four
aircraft sitting on the ice at the same time. The first is a Cessna
owned by Labrador Airways, based at Charlottetown for charter work anywhere along the coast and piloted by one of my
sons, Sandy Powell; the second is also a Cessna owned by the
Wentzell brothers – this is the only village on the coast to own
its own aircraft; the third is an Otter, the passenger plane that
operates out of Goose Bay and is overnighting at
Charlottetown; the fourth is also an Otter that brought us mail
from St. Anthony, Newfoundland, and piloted by another of my
sons, Lester Powell.

 Charlottetown has become one of the youngest and fastest-
growing settlements in coastal Labrador. It now has schools just
as modern as any on the island of Newfoundland, and seven
teachers. But all this didn't happen overnight. It took twenty-
five years of sweat, toil and sometimes tears. In the chapters
that follow, I will give the story as it happened, from time to
time.

18
Hanging Up the Traps

On April 15 I went back over the trapline, and from my third tilt in I picked up all of my traps and hung them up at Jeffries' Pond. I took the beaver traps that had the long chains on them and put all the other traps on those long chains and carried them down on the long point. I put a big ring over a stump and thought that perhaps someday I might return and once again tail those traps. I picked up all the traps I had on Hawke River and the southern waters of Hawke River, except the small ones which I left in their places. All the others I carried back to the open tickle and tied them together with wire under a big leaning juniper. The next day I headed back home, leaving all the other traps in their places. I still had a trapline with three tilts on it, and I thought that even though I was at the lumber business I could still find time to make some trips that far back on the trapline. It would be hard to give up the trapline altogether.

The lumber business remained to be seen! We weren't even sure we could make a success of it in Labrador. If we could, it would mean that many traplines would soon be idle, as people would have to move together and leave their little places that were scattered around the bay.

It was early the following summer when we had our first visit from our provincial Member of the House of Assembly, following confederation with Canada. We were fishing at Square Islands when a little motor yacht came in and anchored close to my stage. I went aboard and a man shook hands with me and told me he was our Member of the House of Assembly,

Harold Horwood. So I shook hands with him again, heartily; at once I thought this was the chance to get some help for our sawmill. I soon told him my plans for the coming winter and that we needed some help to get going. If he could help with the motor we needed I thought we could manage the rest ourselves. But the answer was very disappointing when he told me that if he got an engine for me, everyone in Labrador would want a sawmill engine. Then he opened a little cupboard door and hauled out a bottle of rum. He offered me a drink, but I told him I didn't drink. I wished him good-day and stepped back into my little boat. There was no time to fool around if he wasn't going to be of any help.

In August I went to Dead Islands where Clarence Perry was fishing, only about five miles north of Square Islands. We once again talked over our plans to go ahead with the sawmill business, and I told him I was going to Newfoundland to see my brother, Roland. For sure I would get some help from him. But I told Clarence I could be gone a good while before I could get the needed outfit all straightened out. The main thing I wanted to know was that he wouldn't back out on me while I was gone. He told me I could depend on him not to back out. And I knew I could. I hadn't known him very long, but I soon found that Clarence was a man of his word at any cost.

The first week in September a vessel came in to take our fish that we were selling to Fishery Products Ltd. She was called the *Eric Bartlett*, skippered by Captain Gus Davis from Wesleyville. After we got our fish aboard I asked the skipper if he would give me passage to Newfoundland. He was a very kind man and told me he would. After I told him why I was going to Newfoundland he was better than ever to me. We left Square Islands and went back to Snug Harbour where the fish weights and barrows were landed. I also got paid for my share of the voyage. At five o'clock that evening we left, heavily-loaded with a cargo of salt bulk and codfish.

The next morning we passed through Quirpon where the vessel hove to for a few minutes. Soon a man came aboard; he was the skipper's father who ran a fish plant in Quirpon. The skipper told his father he had a fellow on board from Labrador who was going to "get the rights" (that's the words he used) to start a sawmill up in Labrador. His father said, "Very well," and pushed off again in his little boat. We headed south.

That night it was very rough crossing Notre Dame Bay. There was so much water going down in the forecastle that we all had to leave and go back into the pilothouse where we stopped all that night. The next day we arrived at Badger Bay where there was a fish plant with a lot of large flakes around it for drying fish. That was where the fish were to be unloaded and dried under the sun. That night the skipper took me ashore to his home and his wife got us supper. She had red hair and told me her home was in Quirpon before she got married. The captain's house was large, and he told me it was once owned by a famous sea captain, J.P. Windsor. The next morning Captain Davis brought me back to the wharf where a passenger boat came and picked me up. It was owned and operated by John Sturge of that place. He was running a passenger service from different points around the bay to Gambo.

We had a storm of wind going right up the bay. The boat was powered by a Calvin motor, maybe a forty-four-horsepower; it was a long ride up the bay, but the fare was only $2.00. From there I took the train that arrived in Port Blandford at midnight. My brother was at the station to meet me. Somehow Effie, my wife, had sent a telegram to him, advising him I was on my way to Port Blandford. I didn't know Roland at first. He was dressed up in a dark suit with a light hat. When we were last on the trapline together we wore our light dickies and muskrat caps and skin boots. Roland had had that big whisker, too. Now I was meeting a man who had just walked out of an office. However, he knew me at once and soon I was over at his house. After lunch he told me to go to bed and we would talk tomorrow.

The next day, before he would do any talking with me about the sawmill business, I had to go all over his farm with him. At that time there was still no hydroelectric power at Port Blandford, and the road only went from one end of the town to the other, so that was as far as you could drive. Roland had a gas pump installed and he told me that someday the road would go through and he could make use of it. While I was looking at the pump with the figures that showed the price, a man came along with a can to get one gallon of gas. Before he could get in, Roland had to walk up to a little house that he had built for a lighting plant and start the motor with a crank. It was an Armstrong motor. Then he walked back and put the hose into the can. After the gallon can was full he had to walk back again and shut off the motor. I thought to myself that this was slower than back home!

We went back into the house and I told Roland what Clarence and I had in mind. He thought it was a good plan and was ready to help in any way possible. So the next day he went to St. John's with me on the train and we ordered one ten-horsepower Acadia stationary motor, ten drums of gasoline, lubricating oil, a saw mandrel and saw, belt, rollers, and a lot of other things. Then we had to have enough food for about ten families. We needed a horse and spare shoes for him, beside hay and oats. However, Roland went fifty-fifty on the total cost. Everything was on order to get back to Labrador on the next trip of the S.S. *Kyle*. A few days later, when the *Kyle* sailed from St. John's harbour and I was on board, I learned that the boat could only handle our food supplies on that trip. The next trip she would have our horse and engine, etc. A few days later I was back in Square Islands with all the food supplies landed.

19
A New Way of Life

On September 25, 1950 Clarence and I once more went to have a look at the timber in what was called Old Cove at that time. The timber that was suitable to cut for good sawing logs was about three miles from the saltwater. We landed, moored the boat, and decided to boil the kettle before we walked back to the timber. The spot where we stopped was right where Powell's Supermarket stands today. There was a big rabbit path that ran close to the shore. Soon we had the fire going and were roasting caplin over it. This looked like it would be a fine harbour for shipping. Right in the bottom was a little cove that would give shelter to the little boats with a big brook running into the saltwater. We thought this would be all that was necessary to make a future settlement. But we still felt that day was too far away to even mention.

It was a nice evening. The leaves were falling from the birches and blowing on our fire. The trees just hung over the water. Although we had reached the point where we had to go on with our plans, there was still that feeling for the trapline. I felt that maybe I was stepping out on a limb that might break off and leave me with nothing!

Soon Clarence and I were heading around the third pond and close to the foot of the mountain brow. This was the spot! Lots of timber and as big as you wanted them. I was sure some of them must have been growing 'way back when the Spanish-American War was on. Here was a virgin forest waiting to be harvested by man, a forest that would change our way of life.

We were to start this operation only twelve miles from the seacoast through an uncharted channel. We hoped that someday
we would watch the bright lights of ships entering our new harbour, but this was only a dream.

On the next trip of the S.S. *Kyle* we got our motor and the
horse. After checking it all over, we found that we had no
rollers for our mill and no harness for the horse. These were
two things we just had to have, but this was the last trip of the
coastal boat for the season. We got several men and started to
cut our road from the saltwater to the first pond. I couldn't tell
them we had no harness for the horse and no rollers for the
mill, as this would discourage them. There had to be some way
to find the answer. So when the *Kyle* went south again I put a
letter on her to my father to check out and see what happened
to those missing items and if they were found to try and get
them across the Strait of Belle Isle somehow on a boat, just as
long as they got across to the Labrador side; we could get them
from there.

Sometime in late November somebody picked up the message that had been sent over Gerald S. Doyle's News Bulletin
in St. John's that our horse's harness and the rollers would be
on the M.V. *National II* going to Fishing Ship's Harbour. It was
a late time of the year to go to Fishing Ship's Harbour in a
small boat. First, we had to get the men started in the woods.
There was no way that we would be able to build houses at the
saltwater the first year. Our plans were to put the mill in the
woods where the timber was, have the horse haul the logs to the
mill, then use the dog teams to haul the lumber to the saltwater
where it would be shipped later on in the summer. This meant
that with the sawmill in the woods we would have to get some
houses built there and a horse barn, so there would be no hopes
of having time to build a school the first winter. Maybe the second.

So that fall we built four log houses and the horse barn. The
horse was still up in the bottom of the bay, so our family would
have to stay up in the bay this winter to look after the horse

until the bay froze up enough to walk the horse on the ice. Then the food had to be looked after because some of it was freezable. So all hands were hard at work back in the timber area. The only building that was put up in Old Cove, which is Charlottetown today, was the crate that the horse came in. We put a roof on it and used it for a little storage place to put the hay for the horse and some oil and gas.

By the last of November all four houses were in good enough shape to move into; we built the horse barn last. By now the head of the bay was well frozen, so if I was to make Fishing Ship's Harbour to get that horse harness, I had to go soon before that froze over, too. I took one big boy with me by the name of Jim Dyson, and with our fourteen-foot boat and a seven-horsepower outboard motor we started off for Fishing Ship's Harbour. It was pretty rough all the way along, but finally we made it. It was a real ghost town. Nobody was there. There was snow on the wharf and no sign of tracks anywhere.

One mile away was George's Cove where one family was living by the name of Ward. Billy Ward was supposed to look after the fish that were going to be loaded on the *National II*, Lewis Dawe's vessel. So we decided to go on across the run to hear the news from them. It was dark when we arrived there and very cold. We moored our little boat and went to the Ward house for lunch. Mr. Ward told me he had heard on his marine band radio that the *National II* had broken down in Seldom on her way up to Labrador. So it was hard for us to know just what to do. Our bay was freezing up and if we didn't soon leave we wouldn't be able to get back. But this was a chance we had to take.

The weather was very cold and windy each night, and we knew that as long as the wind kept up the bay would remain open. After five nights the boat arrived and blew her horn off George's Cove. Then it went on to Fishing Ship's Harbour. We soon chased her over and when she got tied up the skipper brought along a box with the horse harness in it and another very heavy one with the birch rollers. Our little boat was loaded when we got all this aboard. The wind was blowing a fair breeze from the northwest and Jim Dyson never slackened the bailer from the time we left until we got to Square Islands. There we got more gas and headed on up the bay. We were iced up very badly by the time we turned Burnt Point and headed into Old Cove. It was after dark when we landed the rollers. We put the harness in our little shack. We saw nobody, as the men were three miles back in the woods in their little log houses. Nothing mattered now. We had everything we needed for the winter.

We then got in our little boat again and headed across the bay where we hauled the boat up on land. We still had three miles to walk in order to get to our house at the head of the bay. A few days later the ice was strong enough to bring the horse down to where the men were working. They could now start hauling the logs to the mill with the horse.

I was free to take a few days on the trapline. After a week I came back with some very nice lynx; it would be difficult to keep clear of that trapline! By now the price of furs had dropped very low and many furs weren't even saleable. So as much as we liked the trapline, we couldn't make a living at furs any longer. It would have to be the lumber woods in any case, and we were off to a good start.

It was the first of the year before they got the engine working. The ten-horsepower wasn't much power for those big sticks; many we were squaring down into 12" x 12" and it was slow work. The best the men could do with the saw were two thousand square feet per day, and this was from seven in the morning until nine o'clock at night. By the last of April we had seventy-five thousand square feet of lumber sawn. This amount was mostly all hauled by dog team three miles from our mill to the saltwater, ready to be shipped to Newfoundland. Then we had to saw several thousand for ourselves which we had to get out of the woods before breakup in the spring. We had to build a bigger store at the landwash for our supplies if we were to continue on. With just about all the lumber on the bank in safety everything looked good for another season. It seemed that our first winter had been a success, so I thought I should put some name on our settlement that we hoped someday would grow from what it was at that time – one little 5' x 8' and one big pile of lumber from the first winter's work! The problem was to pick a name. We had little settlements all over the bay – Campbell's Cove had three families, New York had one family, Newtown had about five families, and Wild Bight had two families. So I thought that maybe someday this place would be the capital of the bay, the same as Charlottetown is the capital of Prince Edward Island. But I really didn't know how to spell that long word. I tried it anyway. I got a can of paint and a brush and on a board I spelled out what I thought was Charlottetown. Then I marked in small letters beneath it, "In God We Trust." As soon as the paint was dry I nailed the name to a tree over the big pile of lumber. The first person to see the name was Mrs. Roy Penney who was driving her own team of dogs. She was going from her little log house close by the mill to the head of the bay where we had the supplies to look after

One of the first houses in Charlottetown. It mightn't have been pretty, but it was warm!

those families. She saw the name painted on the sign-board, but couldn't read it. The next fellow was John Penney. He saw the name on the board, and couldn't read it either! So, Mrs. Roy Penney, on her way back to her house with the groceries, thought she would just have to find out what this said, so she went to the house of Margaret Perry and told her what she saw and couldn't read it. Both of them went back to see the words. Margaret Perry soon read the name and said it was Charlottetown. So the cove that was once known as Old Cove among the trappers now had its new name, Charlottetown.

It wasn't too long before I had a store built on the landwash that spring, a building 20' x 30'. Then the ice started to give out on the ponds, so all hands had to move out of the woods and take the horse back up the bay to our other homes while the ice would still hold us. There was very little food left for the horse. So we all moved back up the bay. One week later we all moved out to the seacoast to our little fishing communities, leaving the horse in the bay by himself. We left the barn door open and put all the hay that was left inside. Two weeks later I went back to see how the horse was getting on. I came part of the way in boat and walked the last six miles over the ice. When I arrived at the barn there was no sign of the horse, and we never saw any sign of the animal after that. Her name was Nellie, and she weighed one thousand pounds.

When the navigation season opened we shipped all our lumber for the town of Spaniard's Bay in Conception Bay, Newfoundland, and we got almost $90.00 per thousand for some of it. This was a big price in those days, and then with a very good fishery that summer things were looking good for the coming winter. When we got the money for our lumber, all hands paid off their winter food bill and had a few hundred dollars in their pockets. My brother, Roland, also got all his money back the first year, but no interest.

It was now the summer of 1951 when Clarence Perry and myself got together and made plans for our second winter. People from every little settlement were wanting work. We hoped there would be some way to give everyone a job, but this wasn't possible yet. There were still plenty of problems that had to be solved. We had to move slowly as our resources were still limited. So we set our figure for the winter – to cut enough logs to manufacture one quarter of a million feet of lumber. This would require a new diesel motor and at least three horses that could stand up to the strain in the lumber woods. I would have to move my house out of Campbell's Cove at the head of the bay to the new place called Charlottetown and also build a horse barn there to house three horses. Plans were for all the other families to stay on in the woods close to the mill. Two horses would haul the logs to the mill and one horse would haul the lumber to the saltwater, helped by the dog teams. All plans were made.

In September 1951 I once again boarded the coastal boat, the *Kyle*, and headed for St. John's, Newfoundland, where I bought a twenty-six-horsepower diesel motor from the Great Eastern Oil Co., plus fifty barrels of diesel oil and one barrel of diesel lube. This was all that was needed for the motor. After looking the second time at the motor and considering the weight of it, I knew this big unit would be a problem to drag three miles into the woods, even with a horse. So I asked them to take off the two big flywheels before shipping. This would make the package in three pieces. It would still be plenty heavy, as the wheels were six hundred pounds alone. After some time I managed to secure three horses – one was nine hundred pounds, another twelve hundred, and one big black one fourteen hundred pounds.

We got all our supplies from Ayre and Sons Ltd., in St. John's. Flour was the most important thing, so I ordered two hundred and forty-five bags, one hundred pounds per bag; six tons of hay for the horse and fifty bags of oats. We had a busy fall getting all of this stowed away, but with a big shed now at Charlottetown we were doing well. At least we thought we were doing well, until the vessel was delayed a long time in bad weather on its way to Labrador. We weren't aware of this.

We were now busy getting our little house off its shores up in Campbell's Cove in order to tow it to Charlottetown. The house was only 12' x 22' and one and a half stories high. This was a fair-sized job for us with very little to do the work with. We finally got it to the landwash at low tide, then tied a lot of oil barrels on it to keep it from going too deep in the water. When the water rose it floated off and with the wind in our favour we made good time, pulling it with boats all the way. That night we had it on the beach in Charlottetown, ready to haul ashore with the horses.

But that night we got word that the vessel had arrived at Square Islands with our hay and was waiting for me to go out and pilot her into the channel to Charlottetown. At that time nobody else would take it upon themselves to pilot a vessel through the uncharted channel, so I always had to go. This spoiled the day, getting the house out of the water that day. It was almost dark by the time we got the last of the hay landed, and only then did we discover that it was all spoiled, or at least most of it. When it was put into the hold of the ship in the warm, it heated and went mouldy and fousty.[1] There was no way any animal would eat it. It was still plimming[2] and bursting the wire that tied it. I told the skipper, Harold Kelliway. He said there was nothing to worry about as all the cargo was insured. I told him that navigation for our part of the coast was closed for the season, and a cheque for the insurance couldn't feed three horses for the winter! And a lot of men and their families were depending on this woods operation. I then wrote off a message to Ayre and Sons Ltd. and stated that our cargo of hay was spoiled and for them to contact the Canadian Railway to send a special boat to Labrador, adding to the order twenty bags of flour. I also told them to send us a blind message over Gerald S. Doyle's Bulletin. My idea in ordering the extra flour was that more effort would be made by them to get flour onto the coast than hay at that time of year! We had plenty of flour for our

---

[1] A bad odor.
[2] Swelling.

winter, but I knew this would be our only hope in order to get the hay.

It was long after dark when I got back from piloting the vessel out through the channel again. Tired and sleepy, Jack Shea and myself hauled up our little boat and went into the house that was now floating close to shore. We went upstairs, and without getting anything to eat we were soon fast asleep. We woke up in the night with a storm of wind blowing right in the cove. The house was pounding on the rocks; it was pitch black. We lit some matches and looked downstairs. The water was right over the stove and all the oil drums were gone. The house was sitting on the bottom. There was no danger of getting drowned; it was all sandy beach. At highwater the end of the house that was on the beach kept striking the rocks. We decided to stay there until daylight, no matter what happened. The old house wasn't much before, and now with this shaking up it would be worse than ever to live in this winter!

20
An Unforgettable Trip for Hay

When daylight broke, the kitchen door was washed off its hinges and there were sculpin and flatfish all over the kitchen floor. They had been driven in by the storm. One sculpin was right on top of the stove. The tide was starting to fall and the wind was dropping back, so we got out through the loft window and made it to safety. Before long some of the men got around and after we had a lunch and the water got low, we started to haul the old house ashore onto land with the horse. We were having one awful time of it with no jack to raise the house in order to get the poles under. We were all about ready to give up when Clarence Perry said there was only one way to do it. He went and cut several big sticks about thirty feet long and got the old house rolled up on those. Then the old horse, Queen, soon had the house on dry land where we could shore it up. This was the first house in Charlottetown. It was now 1951, and this would be the only house there that winter.

I was supposed to look after the horses at Charlottetown until the ponds froze up. Then they could be moved into the mill. But if we couldn't get the hay onto the coast we would have to shoot those three fine horses to save them from starving to death. They were now picking among the mouldy hay; this might keep them alive while they weren't working.

The second week of December the channel to Square Islands was still open. This was very unusual for this time of year. I didn't have any traps tailed up, but there was still hope to tail up a few if I could get that hay for the horses. Our house was very uncomfortable for a woman and children. We couldn't get enough heat in it to dry off the boards. One part of the house was where we kept the supplies for the families that worked in the woods. Many people from the little settlements around the bay would also come and do some trading. As soon as it froze up we would have quite a few people coming to trade from many miles away. There was Norman's Bay, Hawke Harbour, and other places.

This was our second winter at the sawmill business and there would be no teacher or school again this winter. But our plans were to have the teacher the third winter. But I wondered if we'd even have the school or teacher by that time if we didn't get the hay for those horses. Our winter's operation hung on a single thread. There was nothing to do but to live with that hope. Many homes around the bay now had their little radios and could hear the Gerald S. Doyle Bulletin that came on twice a day from St. John's. Day after day people listened, waiting to hear the message. But it wasn't until the second week in December that we got the message saying that the S.S. *Burgeo* was leaving St. John's with flour and hay on board for Ben Powell and that he was to meet her at Square Islands. Now there was hope! Normally our bay would be frozen up at this time of year, right out to Square Islands. Fortunately, this year the channel was clear all the way into the wharf at Charlottetown. We still kept our trap boat out in the water, hoping to get the message sooner than we did.

The next morning was very calm and not very cold. I got lots of food and asked Frank Roberts, who was working with us at the time, to come out to Square Islands with me, as I had to pilot a boat in with our hay. I wanted Frank to come with me because he was the sort of fellow who could always say something funny that would make you laugh, even when things went wrong. Soon Frank was at the motor and I was at the tiller and we were heading to Square Islands. The water was as calm as oil. In a little while we were going through the Narrows of the bay and then along by Narrows Island where the small birch hung over the water at high tide. I looked ashore and there were white partridges sitting in the limbs of the small birches. I headed for shore and told Frank to shut off the motor. The water was so high that the nose of the boat went right up under the trees and the partridges never moved. I picked up the gun and fired. The first one fell right down into the boat. I was going to load the gun again when I noticed the tide was starting to run out. I looked behind us and saw that we had gone in over a bar of rocks. I told Frank I wasn't going to kill any more partridges until we got back over the bar. We did have quite a time before we got out in deep water again. I said to Frank that the best thing for us to do was to head for Square Islands. I believed there was a storm coming on; it was a calm day and the tide was very high, which made me believe there was something behind it. When this happened in December, it was unusual. Frank said something funny, so we went straight for Square Islands and left all the partridges behind. We had one, and that was enough for supper.

We just got to the wharf when the storm struck from the northwest, snow and wind at gale force. We didn't want to take any chances throwing out the anchor to the boat as we would be blown over the wharf. As the wind was blowing off the wharf the boat wouldn't get hurt. We went to the house and got the fire going and the kerosene lamp lit. We had lots of birch wood in the house, so we had no wood to get in the storm. We fried up the partridge and then made up a bed on the floor close to the stove. We put one mattress under us and one over us and all the bedclothes we could find in the house. Most were old coats with split tails! We must have had the pile three feet high, and we got in with all of our clothes on.

The wind howled all night. When it got light enough to see we noticed that snow had drifted all over us, about six inches of it. We got out and started the fire. I thought to myself that I would sooner be in on my trapline where I could fill up my stove in my little tilt and then lie back on the four sticks for a bunk with a chunk of wood under my head for a pillow! That

would be real living. I didn't like the seacoast in the wintertime.
But now we had to try to do the job we had come to do. Frankie
wasn't saying anything funny now. He was getting the snow out
of our bed. It was blowing through the seams in the door and all
around the window. We couldn't get any heat from the stove
and yet we had a big fire in. So we decided to go down to the
stage and beat up the blubber puncheons.[1] We had lots of them.
They were made from oak, and with all the blubber left on the
wood we figured they would just about melt the stove if we
used them for burning! From Monday night until Saturday
night the storm never slackened, wind and snow. We caulked
up all the seams we could in the old house and kept feeding the
puncheon staves into the old stove. We warped that stove right
to pieces.

On Saturday night I got a bad cold, what with all that draft
and snow blowing over me. I was miserable, so on Sunday
morning I told Frank we just couldn't stay on that island any
longer; I really didn't feel that well. There was only a little
wind, but there was no way to get back in the bay, as we were
sure the Narrows of the bay would now be barred for the rest of
the winter, with all the snow and frost we had had. Our only
chance would be to try and get to Pinsent's Arm across the
other side of the bay where several families lived.

After we got all the snow out of the boat, we got a kettle of
boiling water and threw it over the pumping gear of the motor
and the inlet. After some time we got the motor going. We
looked across the harbour and the side that the wind was on
was just dry with eider ducks. Many were king birds, the most I
had ever seen on the water at once in such a small area. They
weren't moving. They all had their heads tucked under their
wings.

Our boat was moving very slowly. I looked over the side but
couldn't see anything wrong. The motor seemed to be running
normally, but we weren't making any more than one mile per
hour. Then we struck this main patch of ducks; there wasn't one

---

[1] Chop up the tubs to use for fire-wood.

of them that flew away, as far as I could see. We just made one path through them and the gap closed behind us again. Neither one of us made any attempt to haul one in the boat. When we rounded the first point we ran out of the ducks for about fifteen yards, then struck another patch. We kept moving in that patch until we got to Little Island Tickle; we were just going through the tickle when the motor started to steam. It was frozen again. We couldn't cross the bay until we got the engine pumping. We managed to make it back to our stage. The ducks were the same – we just made one trench through them that closed behind us.

I was feeling very sick by now and had a really bad throat. We got the fire going again and boiled two big kettles of water which we threw on the engine again. The main trouble was the inlet, which was freezing on the bottom of the boat. We got a long nail and cleared it out and started off again. We were hardly moving and the duck situation was the same. Until this day, I had never before made a trench through ducks that never tried to get away. After a whole week of storms the ducks were probably taking a good rest in the cold with their heads under their wings.

We made it across the bay by dark, then went along by the land until we reached Pinsent's Arm where we were welcomed by Daniel Campbell and his wife. Once I got in the good warm house and had some homemade medicine, I began to feel much better. The next day the Arm began to freeze up so there was no other choice but to get the boat out of the water. If we were to get back to Charlottetown it had to be on snowshoes.

Daniel Campbell got all the people together who lived there and with the block and tackle we got our thirty-foot trap boat out of the water. Only then did we discover why our boat was so slow moving in the cold weather. The frost had driven right down through the bottom of the boat and it was iced right over, about one foot thick in places, so it was like trying to steam through with an iceberg! If the wind had blown off shore when we were crossing the three-mile bay, we would never have seen land again. Although things seemed bad we were having some luck and at least we were still alive.

Day after day passed and it wasn't until four days before Christmas that we heard the whistle of a steamer blowing at Square Islands one fine morning. This was for us, and here we were at Pinsent's Arm. There were now strings of slob ice reaching across the bay and pans of ice everywhere; there was no way for us to get back to Square Islands. Only the steamer would be able to get through this slob. It so happened that the steamer had one passenger aboard for Square Islands, Tom Campbell, who was coming home from the hospital in St. John's. He knew the channel over to Pinsent's Arm and got the captain to take him over where he could go ashore and stay with his brother until he was able to get back in the bay. Meanwhile, we got a little boat on a komatik and were hauling this across a point of land with the dogs. We could see one lake of water that ran from Soddy Island out in the bay. Then we saw the steamer following this lake of water and coming toward Soddy Island. Daniel's dogs did well, and we finally got the little boat out to Soddy Island. By that time we could see the lifeboat coming ashore toward Soddy Island. This was a little flat island that stood to the north of Pinsent's Arm out in the bay. Soon the lifeboat was at the island and Tom Campbell jumped ashore. As he jumped ashore I jumped back in his place. The men in the lifeboat asked me where I was going. There was no way that they were going to land freight here under those conditions. I told them to take me aboard the steamer so I could talk with the captain.

The ladder was hanging down over the side of the ship when we got there and I could see the captain on the bridge, saying nothing. I went right to the bridge and said good-day to him. Then I told him he had supplies on board for me. He said he had supplies on board for Square Island and he had been there and no one was around. So he decided to carry the freight all the way back again. If we had no boat to land it, there was no way to get it ashore. I told him this was a matter of life and death. He had flour and hay aboard for me and should death result this winter, he would be held responsible. He had a boat in the water with a motor on it which could carry the supplies to the island where we could then look after them. The captain turned to the mate; the sailors were all on the bridge by now. He told them to get the hatches off and make it smart!

The first thing that came out of the hold was the flour, then ten bundles of hay. This was the first load. I jumped on top of the hay in their boat and went with them. We only got a little way when we struck a pan of ice and knocked the bottom part of the outboard motor off; the blades were clean gone. We pushed ourselves back to the ship again and the mate passed us another brand new eighteen-horsepower Evinrude motor. Nobody said a word. We all got farther in the stern of the boat to keep the blades underwater more. We held to the channel of water until we made it to the island and soon we had that load landed. The boat went back for another trip, but after four trips the slob closed in the channel of water and the little boat couldn't make it back again. So the steamer went back with the balance of our hay. I would say we had a little more than half of the amount that had been on board. Under those conditions we were happy to even get this much landed on the island.

We were about twelve miles from Charlottetown, and we would be able to haul these supplies by dog teams as soon as the ice got strong enough. We stowed the hay in the middle of the island and the people from the Arm bought the flour to help us out. We went back to Pinsent's Arm for the night where Daniel's wife, Dorothy, had a big dinner of ducks cooked up for us.

The only way we could get back to Charlottetown was to walk through the woods. That night Daniel got two pairs of snowshoes ready for us and a game bag with a lunch. The next morning we were off early, and Daniel said he would come along with us about five miles to put us on the right trail. We had to take a trail that would lead us over to the foot of Gilbert's Lake before we would change trails to go back to Charlottetown, a distance of about eighteen or twenty miles.

The travelling was good in the open where the wind had blown the snow clear, but it was bad in the woods where the snow was deep. Daniel got us on the trail and then he went back to Pinsent's Arm.

I took the lead, but I hadn't gone far before I told Frank we would have to stop and boil the kettle. I still wasn't feeling very well from the cold. We lunched up, and when we were ready to go I said to Frank, "Daniel Campbell is one of the Campbells whose name will live on long after he is gone. What more could a man do than to give us his snowshoes, game bag, and food, and then come five miles with us?" Frank agreed.

We moved on. At dark we reached the foot of Gilbert's Lake; there were still seven or eight miles to go. I was dragging by then and getting more tired. Frank was carrying everything and I was walking ahead, finding the trail. By midnight we made it home, tired and hungry, but the job we had gone to do was now done; that was the main thing. Clarence Perry came out of the woods when he heard we were back and told me that everything was going on schedule. The men had more than four thousand logs cut and ready to be carried to the mill. He thought there was enough good hay among the had to last the horses until the new year. We would manage through the winter, but there wouldn't be any extra hay to waste. Every bit would be needed to get that two hundred and fifty thousand feet of lumber on the bank at the saltwater.

Time passed quickly. Soon it was New Year's Day and the bay was frozen up. It was time to get the big motor into the woods and start sawing. We were seeing dog teams arrive now from all the remote places and we marked on our calendar each day that a team arrived at our house to do business. We counted one hundred and twenty from January 1 until the last of April. March was the highest month – thirty-seven teams, and everyone had lunch at our house! Many also stayed overnight.

21
The Iron Jigsaw Puzzle

It was February when we got the message that we were to have a mail courier to bring the mail from Port Hope Simpson to Charlottetown, twice a month. William Russell would be the courier. We thought this would be a great thing. The mail would be flown to Port Hope Simpson, then carried by dog team to Charlottetown. We would receive first, second and third class mail; soon we were receiving papers and even C.O.D. parcels.

Our logging was going well. The next job was to get the big motor into the mill and set it up. First, we hauled in the wheels, then the motor was placed on the big double sleds with two tiers of planks. Without too much trouble we got it into the woods and onto its large birch bedding that we had sawed. After getting it bolted down, we started to put the wheels back on. We noted that when they had taken them off in St. John's, they shoved the pulley that ran the belt back on the main shaft. They probably thought it might get lost on its way north, so this would be a sure place to put it. Now we had to take this pulley off in order to get the wheel on. Then the pulley would go on again, outside the wheel. In St. John's they had no problem with this, but we had nothing to get the pulley off with. We tried every way to move it, but it was just stuck on the shaft. After spending three days and still not moving it once inch, we decided to use some big wedges between the pulley and the side of the engine. The logs were piling up around the mill, about five thousand of them, and most of what we cut was already there.

We pounded those wedges with the axe, and finally the pulley began to move slowly. But it had to come more than that, about one foot before it came off. We spent another two days at this and used more pressure and bigger wedges. Finally, there was a crack and the whole side of the motor went into pieces! Part of it was cast iron and couldn't take the strain of the wedges. Everyone had long faces once more. The man who found it worst was a Mr. Colbourne from Newfoundland who had come to Labrador to team the big black horse. He was supposed to be a real teamster, as he had spent many years at it. He planned to make a big winter's wage that year and now the side was gone out of the motor. He had no chance to make any money, and this went to his head. He couldn't sleep at night and started going out in the woods to walk around. Some of the women were afraid he might get worse, so we had to drive him to the nursing station at Mary's Harbour, about fifty miles away. The trip was made in a short time on dog team, and Mr. Colbourne stayed there for awhile. He never got back to the woods again.

Meanwhile, Clarence Perry got a bucket and picked up every piece of the broken motor, some of them not as large as your fingernail and others as big as a chocolate bar. Very few were any larger. After looking it all over we found this was only a plate that kept lubrication on all the working parts, such as the cam and timing wheels. The main bearings on the crank were inside this, so there was very little strain on this. But it had to be tight or the lubricating oil would leak away and the engine would lose its oil pressure. The plate was several feet on the round, but the whole rim was still on the motor like a picture frame. The rim was only cracked off in one place, so Clarence said he felt he could fix it. He took the rim off and carried it all into the little workshop we had for doing horseshoeing and sled-making. Nobody was allowed in after he emptied his bucket of small parts onto a piece of plywood. Then he cut out a piece of sheet metal the same size as the plate and got a piece of fireproof paper that came in the cases of Eddy matches. This went next to the sheet metal. The jigsaw puzzle was being put together.

Just how many days and nights Clarence worked at that I don't know. Each piece had to be drilled with a hand drill; if it was really small he put one small stove screw in it. If it was bigger, several screws had to go in it. By the time Clarence got all this done, the boys had the pulley off the motor. When the frame went tight on the motor, there was hardly a seam to be seen. It worked perfectly and has worked ever since. In 1977 the old motor was still working by means of the jigsaw puzzle that one man had put together. It hasn't been apart since.

We were ready to put oil in the tank of the motor. It was a cold day, and when we opened the barrel of diesel it was too cold for it to run; it reminded me of a barrel of butter. We had to get a fire under the barrel, then heat all the oil lines with a blow-torch to get the oil to the motor. We still couldn't get it working. We were afraid there was something we hadn't done right, so we went to Port Hope Simpson and got Gus Penney, a tractor driver. He said there was nothing wrong, only the cold weather. We couldn't turn her fast enough with our hands to start it. So we got it really hot with fire and a blow-torch and finally she went. While the weather was cold we never shut her off; she ran day and night.

The lumber began to pile up at the saltwater. We were averaging three thousand feet every day with our push table. This was good work. By the last of March, we had over two hundred thousand sawn and put on the landwash. This was good work with all the setbacks we had had. We now felt there would be no problem to reach the quarter million mark in another three weeks. A bad storm in April slowed things down somewhat and buried both the logs and the lumber.

22
Two Dead in a Storm

Stanley Campbell arrived at our house that April and said that Edward Cadwell and his son, Manuel, were lost in that snowstorm. Edward had left Port Hope Simpson with food for his family and the last time he and his son were seen was just before they crossed our bay in Charlottetown. I hurried to the sawmill where the men were sawing and told them to shut off the motor. There were two people missing in the storm. We had to go at once and help in the search.

We left on three dog teams and took the trail where he was supposed to have crossed the bay. I often thought that though we were all scattered in little places all over the bay, when there was a need for help, all hands soon joined together as one big family. Soon we were heading down the side of St. Michaels Bay, one dog team close behind the other. I was hoping we would find them alive that day, as I wanted to get back to our shack again that night if I could. My wife had another small baby now and not much wood left at home; I had come away in too much of a hurry to get more. We had three small children now, and Effie was having a hard time in the house which had been shaken up hauling it ashore. After being full of water, it never dried out the whole winter, and in the cold weather there was no heat to be found at all downstairs. Upstairs in the loft you could find some. We had made a shelf right along over the stove where we used to put the bottles of cake flavouring and other freezable things. If the fire got low at all, you could hear the bottles cracking with the frost. We used to take turns keeping the fire going. I would stay up until two o'clock in the morning, then go to bed. Effie would then get up and stay until daylight.

When there were problems at the mill, I would have to go in and try to help, thinking I would be back again the same evening. Sometimes I wouldn't get back until three days later, and this would make my wife very uneasy about me. She would be out in the old house for days by herself, and there was no one else living in Charlottetown that winter. Before the men started to haul the lumber to the landwash in the early part of the year, she wouldn't see anyone in the daytime.

I recall one very cold spell of windy weather. Our house seemed to be colder than outdoors. In my clothes box over in the corner of the kitchen I had an old weather-glass, so I decided to take it out and hang it on the wall to see how cold it was. When I took it out of the box, it showed ¯2°. This was too cold for comfort for women and children. Somehow by spending most of my life on the trapline, I had gotten away from a way of life which should have given more attention to my wife. But I just never gave this a thought. I did put a lot of confidence in Effie, not because she was my wife, but because she was a Campbell, and the Campbells were just wonderful and capable people.

Until today I often think about dear old Aunt Maggie Campbell going on her trapline at the age of seventy-five, with her snowshoes. If she didn't bring back furs or rabbits, she would have her hands full of herbs to make homemade medicine. I often heard her tell the stories about when she lived up around Mulligan by Grand River. One day her grandmother was catching trout through the ice. She had a pile of them beside her when she heard a noise. Turning around, she saw a big white bear close to her! She grabbed her ice chisel and stuck her skin mitt on the point of it. When the bear opened his mouth to bite her, she drove the mitt on the chisel right down his throat and then ran for home. The men were all out on the trapline at the time, and she never saw the bear again.

There was another story she told me about her own Aunt Maggie, the woman whom she was called after. This Maggie went to her traps one day and found a big wolf caught in a trap, leaping the full length of the trap chain. She loaded her muzzle-loader and fired. She had one of those big lead balls; she missed his head and the lead ball when through the guts of that wolf. A string of his guts came out, and with another leap that wolf broke the chain and went for Aunt Maggie. He almost had her, but his insides got hooked on a stump. He continued to leap at her, but his guts had him moored. The old woman had to walk back to her boat and load the muzzle-loader again; then she returned and killed that wolf dead! It was this calmness that I always remembered about Uncle Alex Campbell when I was with him and we were in trouble.

Aunt Maggie Campbell in her seventies returning from her trapline. She had no furs, only an armful of herbs to make medicine.

Our dogs soon had us down by the side of the Long Labrador Trail. It was this trail that Edward and his son were supposed to follow north across the bay. But no track could be found. When we got to the point on the back of Square Islands, we looked out in the middle of the run. Right where the trail was supposed to cross, there was a komatik with food on it, but no dogs. We went on the land where we found the team of dogs in their harness and the bridle had been put over a rock. We followed south along the shore where we saw the track of the man and his son. Someone was ahead of us for sure, and we hoped to find them alive. A little farther on, we picked up two mittens. About fifty yards offshore was a hole in the snow where we found the man dead. We could see small tracks going back and forth from the island to where the man had perished in the snow. Then the small track left the ice to go up over a high snowbank on the island. The boy had then fallen and rolled back onto the bay ice. He never moved after that. Both father and son were dead. The father had died first, then the twelve-year old son, who had kept going back and forth to his father until he dropped. There was a slight shell on the snow before the storm had come, so the new snow had all blown off, making it easy to follow the tracks on the shell.

Then we followed the tracks of the komatik and hauled the two dead bodies to their home. It was a sad time when we arrived. Mrs. Cadwell had just lost a baby that fall suddenly and now her husband and oldest son. Sometimes death strikes hard in those little places. Just in a short time this settlement lost five people – John Campbell III went through the ice on his dog team and was drowned; then Aunt Louie took a stroke and died, so in all they had two double funerals and a single one.

Yet there are times when nothing happens for a long while. When the first John Campbell came and settled in the bottom of the bay, he was one of the first settlers. So as soon as he got his log house built, he wanted to mark a suitable spot for a graveyard. He knew death could come at any time to anyone, and if it happened in the winter with eight feet of snow, it would be a problem to find a suitable place. He marked the best spot I ever saw. It is a big long sandy place, and once the sod comes off, you just need your shovel to dig away. It wasn't until forty years later, on January 3, 1934, that John Campbell died. He was the first to be buried in his marked burial place. Today in that graveyard rests some from four generations of Campbells.

All three dog teams returned home to Charlottetown, bringing the sad news to the people working in the woods. Many were closely related.

From Newtown to Campbell's burial grounds. Two bodies would be laid to rest.

23
First School and Teacher

By the last of April, the horses were running out of hay, although they still had oats. All the logs were sawn and the lumber was piled on the bank. After we had taken enough lumber for our own use, to build a new house in Charlottetown, we did up the old house for the teacher's house. Then there were three families moving from Hawke Harbour – Robert Williams, Joseph Williams, Jr., and Uncle Joe Williams. All of them had to have lumber to build new houses in Charlottetown. As soon as a school could be built, people would move in from little settlements around the bay. On the bank we had two hundred and forty thousand feet of lumber for sale.

The next job was to get the three horses out to the seacoast where they could get something to eat. Charlottetown was still only a wooded area with no grass. Even after the snow had gone there would be nothing for a horse to eat. So we took the three horses to Dead Islands. On this barren place most of the snow had blown away and old dry straw was all over the island. A horse couldn't live on this, as there was no sap in it, but they could get the roots that were starting to grow. We thought this might keep them alive until we had hay come on the first coastal boat when the navigation season opened. Clarence moved out on the island to look after the horses. Two survived somehow on the roots. The third one, Queen, the big mare, was the oldest and her teeth weren't so good for pulling the roots from the ground. She finally died. Clarence tried to keep her alive every way he could, but a big animal requires a lot of food to keep on its legs. The last night the animal lived, Clarence lay close to it all night in his sleeping bag. The other two horses were younger and managed to keep alive somehow until food arrived.

We shipped all of our lumber as soon as navigation opened, but were disappointed to learn the price of lumber had dropped during the winter. We had to sell one-third of our lumber for less than it cost us. After all our winter's work, we only broke even after all expenses were paid. But we planned to carry on the following winter, hoping things would look brighter the next year.

In the summer of 1953, we did very little fishing at Square Islands. We went back into Charlottetown in August, and by early October we had our new house ready to shift into. It was 16' x 28' with an upstairs high enough to walk around in. This house was all built from two-foot plank, studded right around, then sheeted up on the inside and clapboarded on the outside. This would be a fairly warm home. One part of the house downstairs would be the shop where we would look after the supplies for the loggers. One part upstairs would have to be used for the teacher to keep school in until we could get the school built. This would be at least after Christmas.

In September I went to Hawke Harbour and got Hayward Green and his family. He was to be our teacher for the winter. Clarence Perry floated in a house he had bought in Dead Islands, twelve miles away. Several houses were going up now around the cove – Walter Canning's, Roland Bursey's, Harry Marshall's. Nobody would be living in the woods this winter. The sawmill had to be moved to Charlottetown, but before we could do this, we had to saw the material for the school.

All the fathers who had children going to school got together and decided to give free labour to cut the material, saw the logs, and build the school which would be 16' x 24'. We had a road cut three miles around the ponds and through the woods right to the mill. We all got together, several men cutting, and I teamed the horse, the big black one. Three men were sawing, and in one day we had all the material we wanted for the school, except the finishing material which would have to come from Newfoundland. The biggest battle we had was dragging the timber three miles over the bare ground. We had to cross a lot of brooks and now the frost was coming. The water flying over the lumber made it all icy. Several men started building while I did most of the teaming. Later John Shea, a single man, offered to give free labour to help team the other horse. In about a week, we got the lumber out. Then the biggest job was to take each board and scrape the ice off. It was now early October and I would have to get the material in for the finishing work.

The Rev. Lester Burry was the man who had to do with the school board for the area and he was now at North West River, more than three hundred miles away. I decided to go to Fishing Ship's Harbour and send him a telegram to get us the material before the navigation season closed. This was the message I wrote:

> To Lester L. Burry, North West River:
> We have all rough material cut and on site for school, and foundation is laid. Please help us with finishing material. It will be now or never.
>
> Regards,
> Ben Powell

This is the telegram I received back a few days later:

> To Ben Powell, Square Islands via V.O.P. Fishing Ship's Harbour:
> Re tel. This is your authority to purchase material for your school to the amount of $500.00 STOP Teacher's salary will be paid by school board.
>
> Regards,
> Lester L. Burry.

My second telegram then had to go to Saunders and Howell at Carbonear to order the material. The weather was getting bad, and I had to spend a couple of days in Fishing Ship's Harbour after sending the telegram before I could get back.

Everything was going well until a big herd of caribou travelled the area between Charlottetown and Gilbert's River. One by one the men started to go caribou hunting, until there was only one man left working on the school, besides myself. We were determined to get the roof covered before we left. But it was a real battle to stay on the job with the caribou so handy, and then with the trapping fever in one's blood, it keeps any trapper restless.

The school was all covered before winter set in. The teacher was now teaching his fifteen students upstairs in our home. He had a rough bunch, and it was a bit uncomfortable for my wife, but we just had to live with it. The worst part was when they would leave school for the day; they would all ride down over the rail on the stairs and make a terrible racket. This would disturb the small children who would be sleeping in the house.

Early in the new year, the school was finished enough to shift into and nobody was sorry. Then we had to go and get our sawmill out of the woods and put up a mill in Charlottetown. In two weeks this was done. With lumber still dropping in price, we decided there would be no point in cutting more than one hundred and fifty thousand feet of lumber. We only had two horses for the winter, so we picked out a spot of logs about halfway into where the mill had been before. This was smaller timber, but easier to handle.

Everything was going normal, and under these conditions nobody was complaining. There was plenty to eat and drink and people were happy. Then we got word from the post office department that we were to have air mail service to Charlottetown once a month. This looked better than ever. Mail would be brought right to our doorstep by plane. The news got around and all hands were excited. The teamsters told me to let them know if the plane came when they were in the woods, and

Charlottetown's first school, 1951.

Mr. Green in the school wanted to know when the plane came in case he was in school. So I promised that if the plane came and they didn't know about it, I would let them know.

One day we heard the sound of a plane overhead. Everyone

The author's sawmill at Charlottetown.

was out running and waving. Mr. Green came out of the school with a flag and all the school children after him. The two horses came out of the woods with their teamsters. Everything was alive in our little town. Soon they had a flag flying on Goose Island and another on Burnt Point. The big plane circled several times, then went out of sight. She had no wheels down and no skis, so I couldn't see how that could be the plane with our mail. It must have been a search and rescue plane doing some work. When they saw so many people running around with flags, they made several circles to see just what was going on! Uncle Alex said to Uncle George Kippenhuck, "I thought that plane was going to land, as she came so low and calmed her wings." Many of the older people thought airplanes flew like birds, with their wings going up and down. They weren't aware that their wings were fixed in one place!

Days passed and there was no mail plane. One day Charlie Larkham and his wife, Dorcas, left Rexon's Cove on their dog team to come to Charlottetown to do some trading at our store. About ten miles out the bay, they saw something on the ice that looked like a company of caribou lying down. So he called his dogs ashore and got out his rifle. After awhile nothing moved, so he decided to walk toward it. What did he find but a pile of mail bags, blue and white ones! The mail plane had left Gander, Newfoundland with our mail but couldn't find Charlottetown. We believe he saw some men in the woods cutting firewood for the summer. Rather than bringing the mail back to Gander, he put it on the ice, thinking those woodcutters would see it and take it to Charlottetown. But the woodcutters knew nothing about it. The trouble was that we still weren't officially on the map and the label on the mail bags said Square Islands, the summer post office that had now moved to Charlottetown for the winter after the fishing season ended. This was where the plane had been searching for some sign of life.

We reported it to the general post office in St. John's and they reported this to Eastern Provincial Airways. This company sent their chief bush pilot up to Labrador to find Charlottetown and put it on their map once and for all. But this wasn't so easy, even for chief pilot Marsh Jones. He also searched the area around Square Islands. Finally, he saw two houses at Wild Bight where he pitched and asked directions to Charlottetown. A few minutes later, we had our first mail plane. Once marked on the map, there was no problem finding Charlottetown again. Now we are enjoying three mail flights a week in 1977, when the weather is suitable.

An Otter aircraft landing with mail, 1977.

24
Charlottetown's Biggest Accident

Things were going well – one mail plane a month, all school-age children were at their studies, and everyone had fresh meat at least every Sunday for dinner, either caribou, rabbit or porcupine. In another few weeks, all the logs would be sawed for the third winter of the sawmill business. We were off to a good start; our only problem was that the price of lumber was dropping.

On April 20, 1954, the sun rose in a clear sky and shone on a field of thin bay ice that was no longer safe to travel on. Lakes of water were starting to open from every little brook that ran into the bay. In Charlottetown, the stillness of the morning was soon broken by the noise of the diesel motor and the sound of the thirty-six-inch blade that sliced off the lumber from the hard, icy logs. Every man was working hard to finish up the job before the last of the bay ice was gone. No definite working hours per day and no holidays were ever considered by those hardworking men who were willing to settle for little that this world had to offer.

It was fifteen minutes to six and soon time for supper. Some boys came along by the mill; the biggest fellow was Gerald Green, the teacher's son. Clarence told them to move on or they might get hurt. Even a slab from a boxy stick could hurt anyone who came too close. But when the men turned their heads to put another log on the table, Gerald Green put his hand on the long crank that was sticking out. His mitten hooked in the key that kept those big flywheels on. Soon he was wound up, going around at the same speed as those big flywheels, which was six hundred and fifty r.p.m.'s. His boots went flying over, then his clothes started to tear from his body, and before the men could get the motor stopped, the boy's arm was torn from his body, tight to the shoulder. His arm pitched a long distance from the motor, across the cove. As his body started going through a hole in the flooring, Clarence caught him in his arms and carried him into our house. He sat on the floor with him in his arms. Soon they got some clean rags and bandaged him up the best they could. I went out to the cove to get the arm and held it under my coat. As I passed the name Charlottetown high over my head, I noticed again the words I had painted underneath – "In God We Trust."

This accident would be a bad one even in a city, but at least you could get a patient to a hospital. Only a couple of springs before this, a Mr. Green had broken his leg while launching his boat. There was no way of getting him to a hospital, and he died.

Our nearest hospital was one hundred miles away at St. Anthony, Newfoundland. Our only hope would be to get him to Mary's Harbour, over thirty miles away, but how could we get there over the bay ice? No one had used the ice for several days now. The few families that had shifted out to their summer fishing places had already gone. I was still going around with the boy's arm under my coat, wondering where I would put it so I wouldn't frighten the women. I walked into the pantry and put the arm in the flour barrel. This seemed like a strange place for me to put it, but I believe now that I had a reason for doing that.

Uncle Alex Campbell used to tell me the story about Mr. Jeffries when he came home from his trapline once. He found that his little girl's legs were frozen to her knees, so he took out his hunting knife and cut her legs off at the knees, then stuck her up by the stumps in the flour barrel to stop them from bleeding. I believe that at that very moment my mind must have gone back to the problem that that man of old had to try and solve in his own way. With the problem we were facing at the moment, I went to the flour barrel without really knowing what I was doing.

There was no time to waste. We had to try and save this boy's life. The only ray of hope would be to put a boat on a komatik, with a bed in the bottom of the boat. The father would stay in the boat with the boy to try to keep him from rolling out. Two men would be on each side of the boat to help haul it out of the water when it broke through the ice.

All the men had a quick lunch, and shortly after six o'clock they started off with their dogs pulling the boat and the father and his son in it. The crew was John Shea, Clarence Perry, Harry Marshall, Roland Bursey, the father, Hayward Green, and the boy, Gerald, going on twelve years old. They had gone only a little way when we saw the dogs fall through the ice. They went down in one hole and came up again, only to go down in another. This was bad, because the dogs would have to be hauled back by the trace through the hole they went into to keep the trace clear. Then the boat would go down and rock around. The men would pull it up again. Soon they rounded the point. We would know nothing else until they returned. We just had to live in the hope that they would get to that nursing station where something could be done to stop blood poisoning from setting in.

The next morning, April 21, I was up early. There seemed to be a cloud over our little town that day. If only we knew where those men were and if the boy was still living! But we could never know until they returned.

I was the only man on our side of the harbour; on the other side was Walter Canning. Until that time there was still no bridge to cross the brook from one side of the town to the other. As we were the only two men left in the town, we figured there was no point in just sitting around waiting. Time would seem too long. So I decided to go back to the mill and take hold where those men had left off. It would be slow, but I could saw twelve hundred feet of lumber per day. As I walked to the mill, it was a bad sight – boots and clothes were all over and the green motor was spattered with human blood. As I picked up the clothes, wiped off the blood and cleaned the end of the crankshaft, I thought to myself that we were really at war – not a war of one nation against another where man kills man. But we were in a battle against poverty and isolation; we were fighting for a better way of life, not for ourselves but for our children and their children. Could we ever win? I felt sure we were beyond the point of no return. Now with all of our forces gone to the front, I would stick to the gun until the men returned and I believed they would. But it wouldn't be until their job was done.

Many days and many nights passed. As we looked out the bay we could notice the ice melting very fast. Soon the men would be able to come back by boat. They finally did return and we listened to their story. The first night after they had left Charlottetown they got nine miles out the bay. Their dogs were beaten out and so were they. The ice was too bad to go any far-ther. They turned to the north, taking them three more miles away from Mary's Harbour, and spent the night at Newtown. That night they discussed the plans for the next day, and they decided their only chance was to go to the seacoast. There was no way they could do it on the bay ice, where there were three bays to be crossed. If once they could make Square Islands and if the Arctic ice was off the land, they could go along in boat.

The next morning they left for Square Islands. After some time, through the worst of conditions, they found that the coast was blocked with drift ice. There wasn't one hole of water big enough to put a boat in. They spent the remainder of that day there and the following night. The next morning they could see that red streaks were beginning to go down the side of the boy's shoulder. They knew he wouldn't last many more days in that condition, especially if there was no change in the ice.

Clarence moved out of the house, unnoticed by the other men, and started to climb the very high hill that stood right over the harbour where he could see many miles around. The whole Atlantic was one field of Arctic ice, as far as the eye could see. It was disappointing. Just below the high hill was the old grave-yard. Most of the railing had fallen down, and through the faded grass could be seen the wooden headboards, some fallen down, others leaning, and a few still standing upright. Holes had been dug down through some of the shallow graves by animals that had brought up some bones. It must have run through Clarence's mind that perhaps there would be another body laid to rest there soon. But this was not possible. The little graveyard had been filled many years ago. Many who had been buried there had lived on this island over the years; when sickness had struck at certain times of the year, no help could come from doctors and hospitals, so these folks just died and were buried. The day came when no more could be buried in that burial place, so the dead now had to be buried in John Campbell's spot eighteen miles up in the bottom of the bay.

Clarence looked again at the field of ice and knew there was nothing anyone could do to move it. It was just an act of God. Clarence wasn't a praying man, but that morning, April 21, Clarence Perry prayed to his Maker to move that barrier of ice that separated them from the nursing station thirty miles away. That man prayed right from his very soul that morning, and before he got off that high hill he could see the ice starting to scatter. Lakes of water were fast-making. He hurried and told the other men to come and launch the motorboat; the ice was moving. After getting the boat launched they had to break into our store and get our five-horsepower Acadia motor that had been stowed away for the winter. They put it in the boat, and with everyone working they were ready by dinnertime. They started off with a canvas house over the boat, and to their surprise had no trouble at all. Before long there wasn't a pan of ice to be found in the ocean and a light westerly wind came on.

They made Mary's Harbour sometime after midnight, only to find a big pan of ice in the tickle, barring the whole entrance to the harbour. They went ashore on the point, lit a big fire and shouted. Soon people came across in a boat and took their patient to the nursing station. The next morning the men made it back to Square Islands and their patient was air-lifted to the hospital at St. Anthony. They had saved his life. Today he is married and is living in St. Anthony, but he has only one arm.

25
A Pulpwood Operation for Charlottetown

The following summer we got word from our lumber agents that the price of lumber was very low and they could only take from us long lengths and wide lumber and wouldn't buy more than fifty thousand feet. This seemed bad. We couldn't survive another winter with all of this lumber on our hands. So once again Clarence Perry and myself got together and talked over the possibility of cutting plywood. We wondered whether we could find a market for it in Newfoundland; it certainly looked like the lumber business would be out for the time being.

By now we had a new M.H.A., Dr. Frederick W. Rowe, so I wrote him and drew several maps of where our timber stands were, including estimates of the number of cords that were in each stand of timber. I asked him if he could get a market for our pulpwood. I got a letter back shortly afterward saying he was working on it, and as soon as he had something definite he would let me know. I was a bit surprised that Dr. Rowe would even be able to read my letters, as I was a very poor writer and speller. But it seemed like the message got right into his hands. I got another letter saying I was to go to Grand Falls and meet B.W. Potts, a woods manager for the Anglo-Newfoundland Development Company.

I stepped out of the fishing boat on September 1 and stepped onto the coastal boat heading for Grand Falls, Newfoundland. I got off at Twillingate and joined a passenger boat that was operated by a fellow named White. This boat went as far as Lewisporte, where I joined a train and went right to Grand

Falls. A taxi driver asked me where I wanted to go, and I said to a boarding house. He took me to a place that was operated by a lady named Mrs. Benson. I left my suitcase in the hallway and she asked me to come into the dining room for some dinner. I was sure hungry for some kind of food. Soon I was settled down among a crowd of well-dressed businessmen. Nobody spoke when I sat down on a chair to wait for dinner. Soon the old lady told all those fellows in their shiny suits of clothes to sit into the big table. I sat into a little table farther over in the corner and a big plate of corn meat hash was set before me. I thought this was great. As I looked over on the other table, I could see that it was decorated with all kinds of fancy food that I didn't even know the names of. I believe they called them salads in those days. I had never seen any of that kind of stuff before in Labrador and I didn't want to. How could I have made that sort of mixture on a trapline! My mother never even had it at home when I was a boy in Carbonear.

I had almost eaten my whole plate of hash when the phone rang over my head. The old lady soon answered it. It was a ring from B.W. Potts, the woods manager. He wanted to know if she had a Mr. Powell there, and she said no. Then she told him to wait a minute. Mr. Potts said again that this gentleman was from Labrador and was going to send them pulpwood. She stooped down and asked me if I was Mr. Powell. I told her I was, so she told Mr. Potts that I was there. He said for me to come to his office at three o'clock that afternoon. The old lady came back and asked if I wanted any more dinner. She had thought I was a fellow who had just come out of the woods on his way home. She told me she had a lot of those fellows who got their dinner from her, then left their old caps on the chair and never returned to pay for their meals. I told her not to worry, that I was doing all right. I had a good dinner. I thought to myself that I often had to settle for a lot less, with a day's walk before me.

Then those men at the other table started to ask me questions about Labrador. It seemed as though they knew as much about

Labrador as I knew about Grand Falls! But I had no trouble answering their questions about Labrador; that was my home, and I never wished to change Labrador for a town like Grand Falls. I had spent too much of my life away from civilization to ever want to get mixed up with it again. I was meeting many people, but I couldn't find anyone so happy as the ones back in my little hometown. Even when I lived in Campbell's Cove with only three families, everyone was happy. They had time to stop and speak to one another. But now everyone was rushing back and forth in the cities and very few would even speak to each other.

It was time for me to go to the office of the Anglo-Newfoundland Development Company. As I climbed the steps of the office, B.W. Potts was there waiting for me. We shook hands and went into an office and sat down at a big hardwood table with a lot of papers on it. He told me he had no problem getting all the wood they required to run their mill, but Dr. Rowe had contacted him and wanted to know if he could use some wood from Labrador. He said he was very interested to know just what kind of paper the Labrador wood could make, so someday they might have to go to Labrador for wood. He said further that the only terms he would give us was that we would have to get the wood right to the mill in Grand Falls. This seemed to me like a big job; that meant it would have to be brought by ship to Botwood and then thrown out into a boom and trucked to Grand Falls. I asked him what his price was, delivered to the mill. He said $22.00 per cord. I didn't know if this was reasonable or not, as I really didn't know just what would be involved and there was bound to be a lot of shrinkage. So I asked him if he could do a little better. Well, he told me he could pay $23.00 a cord, but that was the price. I said I would sign the contract for $24.00 a cord, landed at the mill. He got really upset and pounded his fist on the table and said he didn't need my wood, that he could bring it in from Nova Scotia cheaper than that. He said he was only trying to help me out. So I told him to hold on for a moment, that he knew I had no experience in the pulpwood business, and by the time I could even get all my costs that would be involved from the time I took the wood from the stump to the time I delivered it to his mill, it would be too late to start the operation this year. So I was willing to sign the contract at a gamble for one thousand cords at $24.00 per cord. And furthermore, I asked him if he was in my place and I was in his, would he settle for the first offer? As he shoved the papers along for me to sign, I thought to myself that I had gambled with him and won, but the biggest gamble would be to get that wood to Grand Falls!

Until that date, nobody had gotten any able-bodied welfare in Charlottetown. I hoped it would stay that way for some time to come. Then Mr. Potts asked me how I would get back to Labrador. I told him that when the boat returned that week, I would return on her. So that evening he sent a man with me to have a look at the mill. We started right where the wood went in and was crushed and we followed right along to where it came out as paper. It was very impressive. Later Mr. Potts sent for me again and told me that if I wanted to get to Labrador in a hurry to get the operation going, he would send a plane to take me to Square Islands. This really was wonderful of him. What more could he do? He told me the plane would be leaving Russy Pond, Gander, the next morning, so he would have a car pick me up at the boarding house.

The next morning I was up early, but the old lady was up long ahead of me and had a good breakfast for me, all alone in the dining room. There was no sign of any of the other men who had been there the evening before. The car came for me and I shook hands with the old lady and thanked her for putting me up. Soon we arrived at the little plane dock near the pond, and in a short time we took off on the trip to Labrador.

The day was fine until we were out over Notre Dame Bay, where we struck a thunderstorm. After trying every way to get around it, we had to turn to Baie Verte where we spent the night. It was there that the pilot shook hands with me and told me he was from Quebec. His name was Benny Levar. We had a lunch at the priest's where the pilot stopped for the night. I went to another house where the woman took boarders. She had a name that I could never remember. The next day I arrived home. Soon we were making plans for the winter.

26
First Communications System

People were moving in from other places all the way from Seal Islands to Fox Harbour. We were telling anyone who wanted work that they could have it. The thing that bothered me most was the lack of communications with many families that moved in and the type of work we were involved in. There were sure to be accidents with all the sawing and cutting with axes. But now there was an air ambulance stationed at the St. Anthony hospital. All we needed was a two-way radio to contact them, and if the weather was suitable, they would be able to arrive at our settlement in one hour. I got to work, trying to line up a good second-hand radio. It would be hard to afford a new one that year with so many things to buy and only half our lumber sold from the winter before.

After contacting several companies, I finally purchased a second-hand two-way radio from John Lickie in Halifax for $550.00. It was a seventy-five watt output. Spiliday and Dindal Ltd. was the name on the old rig that had been salvaged from some old fishing vessel in Nova Scotia. But it was working fine. This was the very first communications system we had in our area. It was installed that fall, and for the next twelve years that old radio handled a lot of messages, until the Bell Telephone Company came in. We could talk directly to the hospital at St. Anthony, and I believe our radio saved a lot of lives over the years. When the weather was fine, they could send the air ambulance right to Charlottetown to pick up our patients. We also had schedules with White Point, Battle Harbour, where they would relay our messages to any part of Newfoundland. The old set was licensed under the number, C.J.N. 397. We had many breakdowns over the years, but I had some spare parts and I learned a lot about the old set. I had a bulb on a wire that I hooked onto the antenna. Then I would get a screwdriver and shift the taps on the antenna coils until this bulb would get bright. The brighter the light, the better the signal. On Christmas we had a big time in the house singing songs and playing the violin, and we broadcast it over the radio. For a long time after, I received post cards and letters from people all over Newfoundland who had picked up our programme and enjoyed it and wanted to let us know about it.

The fall that the whaling factory burnt down in Hawke Harbour, the whaling ship was still out at sea catching whales and wasn't aware that the factory had burnt the night before. So I got the message through on the two-way radio and soon the ship was at the ruins of the old factory.

Another fall the weather was stormy for a long time and Canadian National couldn't get any report from one of its ships that was storm-bound up at Hebron, more than five hundred and fifty miles north of us. One night I was able to contact the vessel and pass the message on to Canadian National in St. John's the next day. They were very pleased to receive it.

Lots of nights I have talked to boats in Halifax, and I have also talked with Department of Transport men in Cabot Tower in St. John's.

Only this year, on March 12, 1977, did I receive a letter from the Federal Building in Corner Brook, Newfoundland, advising me that my old double-band radio could no longer be used. All radios had to be replaced by single-sized radios. I quote part of the letter from R.J. McNeil, Acting Manager of the Department of Communications in Corner Brook:

> Dear Mr. Powell:
> Your radio-telephone was one of the very first on the coast of Labrador and has served the peo-

ple of that area in time of need. I'm sure your contribution has not gone unnoticed or unappreciated by your many friends and neighbours. Unfortunately, with the great increase in radio usage and changing technology, we now find ourselves faced with having to do away with the old double sideband emissions to make way for more radio users also. Your particular set has outlived the need it once satisfied.

Wishing you every success in all your endeavours.

Yours truly,
Department of Communications
R.J. McNeil, Corner Brook

The third year that I had my radio, we experienced another accident at our sawmill when Frank Clark lost his finger with the saw blade. Once again it happened to be the last ice in the spring. We contacted Dr. Gordon Thomas, superintendent at the Grenfell Mission hospital. He told us to check the ice carefully and see if there was enough for a plane to land. If so, he would have to arrange for one to come in from Goose Bay. The ice was full of holes, but after some time we found one strip of ice that had the thickness that was required for Beaver aircraft. I called Dr. Thomas again and told him we now had the ice marked with bough tops and wondering if there would be any chance of getting our patient out that afternoon. His exact words were, "We will evacuate your patient this afternoon to Goose Bay hospital, as the weather in St. Anthony is down." Those were words of comfort that we weren't able to hear in times past. But somehow we managed to hang on to see the times change slowly.

27
A Stick in My Son's Throat

That following spring, our son, Tony, was two years old. We had shifted to Square Islands for the fishing season. One day, Tony was coming over a flat rock that ran from our stage all the way to our house with a long, thin stick in his mouth. He fell down and drove the stick down his throat; there it broke off, leaving him in a choking condition. We tried every way to get it out, but it was too far down. Whenever we tried to work at it, the little fellow would almost choke.

That spring the radio was out of order. The motor that sent out the carrier wave was gone. I had spent awhile working at it, but there was nothing I could do; the motor had to be replaced. Once again our island was surrounded by drift ice. Some lakes of water could be seen out in the bay. There was no point in trying to take the little fellow by boat to Mary's Harbour, as we might only get out in the bay and get stuck in the ice for weeks.

Harry Morris had a boat at our wharf with a house on it, and it was powered with a Calvin motor. I thought this boat would push its way through the harbour ice, and then if we got out in the bay, we could make Fishing Ship's Harbour where there was a radio set that used to contact White Point twice a day in the summertime. The problem was that if we got there after his scheduled hour in the evening, we wouldn't be able to get the message to the hospital until the next morning. By the time the plane got to Square Islands and back to the hospital, it could be too late. As it was, the little fellow was going black in the face on times. I went to work on my radio. The one at Fishing Ship's

Harbour only had one set of crystals, 16-15. This meant the operator could only contact White Point, Battle Harbour. If my set was working, I had several frequencies and I could contact boats on 22-50 KC sometimes. I thought I would take the crystals out of my radio and put them in my pocket. Then if we made Fishing Ship's Harbour and were too late for the last schedule of his radio, maybe my radio crystals would fit and we could contact some boat in St. Anthony harbour that could get the message to the hospital.

I took the crystals out, wrapped them in paper and put them in my pocket. I arranged with Harry Morris to try and take me to Fishing Ship's Harbour. We took plenty of food and were soon underway, shoving and shaking the boat through the ice in the harbour. After several hours, we made it out through lakes of water that reached part way across the bay. Then we made slow progress through loose ice until we got almost to Ship Harbour Head. This was it. The big tide had the ice bound on the land as far as we could see. We could see no water. We worked around the pans for about an hour, but there was no way out. I told Harry that if he didn't mind I would walk ashore over the ice, then over the cliff at Ship Harbour Head and on to Ship Harbour. Harry thought it was a good idea. He said he would stay there in the boat, and sometime the ice would slacken and he would make it to Ship Harbour.

It wasn't long before I was ashore at Ship Harbour Head where I climbed over a high cliff. I made it safely, then walked to Ship Harbour where I had a lunch with the Penney people who fished there. When I told the story of where I was going, George Parr told me he knew the best trail that would take me to Fishing Ship's Harbour and it would be the shortest cut. He had walked the trail before and it was a bit rough, but he figured we could make it before dark. We were soon off at a fast walk up and down the deep valleys. All the valleys run inland from the seacoast. We came to one pond in the valley with a beaver house in it, and there were beavers striking their tails on the water all around us. We then came to a cliff that was very high. I told George there was no way to get down this one. It looked as though we'd have to go around, which would take us a long time, as this deep gulch ran almost to the saltwater. But George said there was a place just ahead where we could get down. We came to a tall tree that ran right to the top of the cliff where we stood and were close to the side. George said this was the place, so he caught hold of the tree and went to the bottom of the cliff. I thought we must be like Jack and the Beanstalk!

The next valley was the back of Snook Cove where some families lived. We passed on the back of this cove and came out behind Fishing Ship's Harbour. Now we could see the high radio poles and we went up to the old house where Bay Roberts Fisheries Ltd. operated a summer fishing business. The manager was Lewis Roach and I soon told him the story. He said, "Well, well, well. And our radio is off the air for the night and I have no way to contact anyone until morning." Then I told him about the crystals I had in my pocket and that I thought they would fit his radio. He said he had never seen the inside of a radio and he knew nothing about it. But he told me I could have a look at it. I took the case off the radio and took out his two crystals. I put mine in, which were marine crystals – one to transmit and one to receive. Then I told Mr. Roach to turn on the power and see how things worked. The red light started to blink, then he started to transmit, "This is station V.O.P. Fishing Ship's Harbour radio. I have an important message for St. Anthony hospital. Any vessel in that area reading this transmission, come in, please. Stop." Then there was a silence for about a minute. But it was broken by a rough voice that said, "This is the vessel, *Norma & Gladys* at St. Anthony tied up to the Grenfell Mission wharf. Go ahead with your message. Over." Once again Mr. Roach squeezed his mike and said, "V.O.P. back to the *Norma & Gladys*. Please contact Dr. Thomas and advise him that we need air ambulance sent to Square Islands to pick up a small boy with a stick broken off in his throat. In choking condition when we left." Again the *Norma & Gladys* came back, "Have copied your message and will deliver it to

Dr. Thomas at once at hospital. Over." Mr. Roach said, "Roger, roger. Thank you very much. V.O.P. off and clear with the *Norma & Gladys*."

The *Norma & Gladys* was owned by Skipper Charlie Kean. I knew the old man well. He had hauled our lumber from Charlottetown to Newfoundland and was a real old friend. Now he was going to do all he could to get that message into the right hands as fast as possible. Mr. Roach then gave us a lunch and we started back as fast as we could for Ship Harbour. We had gotten the message through and that was all we could do. We hoped everything would turn out all right.

Sometime that night we made Ship Harbour. I thanked Mr. Parr very much for his help as a good pilot over that rough trail. I was very tired and lay back for a rest on the bench at Roy Penney's house, but it still wasn't easy to get to sleep when I didn't know whether Tony would live until help arrived. And then I thought of Harry Morris back in his boat in a jam of ice off Ship Harbour Head. I wondered how he made out. There was very little wind, so I didn't think there was too much to hurt him, and Harry could take care of himself in any case.

The next morning I headed out along the shore and didn't get too far before I could see Harry's boat moored close to the land inside Ship Harbour Head. Soon I was on board and we didn't have too much trouble with ice on the way back. When we reached Square Islands, we learned that the air ambulance had flown over that morning, but couldn't pitch because the island was surrounded with drift ice. However, we were glad to learn that about three hours after we had left Square Islands, Tony started vomiting up blood. Effie could see the end of the stick and she made one last try with her fingers and got it out. The little fellow got on fine.

28
Last Winter at Pulpwood

Everything worked out well that winter as far as filling our contract with the pulpwood industry. We got our one thousand cords out of the woods and had some on the land and some in Salt Water Pond in a boom. We only went salmon fishing that summer; there was no time for codfishing as we had to go back in the bay and ship our wood. While the men were getting it boomed and doing all the necessary things for loading, I had the first vessel on her way to haul the wood. She was only a small boat owned by the Earl Freighting Service in Carbonear, Then I got another one from Yarmouth called the *Vagabond Prince*, owned by Lawrence Sweaney. That boat hauled five loads for us that finished off our winter's cut. The wood was very heavy and the boats could only take about two-thirds the amount they thought they could take. Then when they threw this heavy wood overboard in Botwood, quite a bit of it stuck on the bottom in the mud. This made a big shrinkage in the amount that had been scaled aboard the ship and the amount that was scaled out of the trucks at Grand Falls.

It had been a lot of hard work and there were plenty of headaches and very little pay. We were at it day and night while the wood was being shipped. There was no way those vessels could lay at anchor idle, so when the last chunk went on board, I would have to pilot them out through the bay. There were no markers anywhere. In those days the steamers had no radar either, so it was quite a responsibility to get those boats out through the Narrows of the bay on dark nights. In some places, we had to be careful not to go too far out of the channel or the boat would land on a shoal. But I made all of the trips with no problem. I often think of the difference nowadays – if a vessel hasn't got its two radars working, she ties up until they are both operating!

After we got settled up on our winter woods operations, I could see it was a big gamble. For us to carry on without insurance on the wood could lead us to disaster. There was too much danger involved. It was a different situation for a company to be in the pulpwood business, but it was risky for one individual to try and carry on an operation to give work to everyone in the area. Every woods operation that had ever started in Labrador only lasted a few years, then it went out, even when they were getting help from the government. So it would be difficult for us to carry on when we weren't getting any money from anyone. It was all from our own resources.

I told the woods manager of the Anglo-Newfoundland Development Company that I wasn't anxious to follow on the next winter. However, he wanted us to go on with the operation the second winter. He said the Labrador wood was much better than the Newfoundland wood for making paper, owing to its hardness. A trial run of the Labrador wood had shown that it was making much better paper than the standard wood in Newfoundland. So he told me he could give us two more dollars per cord than what we had received the year before and he would step up our contract another five hundred cords. He would also insure our wood, so this seemed to give us more security for another winter. I once again signed the contract to deliver one thousand five hundred cords of wood to the mill in Grand Falls.

We were busy planning our winter woods operation again. We now had another horse on order, which would give us three that winter. More people kept moving in to earn their living by cutting pulpwood. By November 15 we had all of our supplies in for the winter, but no hay and no horse. I sent a message to Dr. Frederick W. Rowe on our radio-telephone and he advised me he had arranged with Canadian National to send back the *Kyle* on a special trip with our hay and the horse. After waiting some time at Square Islands, the old steamer, the *Kyle,* arrived. In charge was Captain O'Keefe, and he said he had no orders to go to Charlottetown. After a long talk with him on the bridge, l told him he would have to carry the cargo back to Newfoundland and we would have to shoot our horses if he wouldn't come into Charlottetown. He then said that if I could pilot the vessel into the bay, he would go. On this last day of November, she dropped her anchor in Charlottetown. Then the captain turned to me and said he was going to wire a message to the office in St. John's, telling them he was anchored at Charlottetown. He didn't know whether they'd even know where that was! Then he had a big laugh and went off for coffee!

The bottom of the harbour was now frozen over. We were going to have to land our hay on the ice after we took it off the steamer by boat. We would also have to take the horse off in a boat and find some suitable place to land him. Just as we had the horse in the boat and had tied his halter strap around the thwart, the steamer blew and the horse made one jump. He pulled the thwart right out of the boat and drove all of his hooves through the side of the boat, then jumped right over into the icy water. He started for the land, trimming along by the edge of the ice. There was an island rock halfway to land that he got up on for a spell, then he saw the rest of the way to land. It was two or three hours before we could catch the animal after coming out of the icy water, and it was a very cold day. We finally got him into the barn and put a warm blanket on him. He got on all right.

That winter, everything went well. We cut our contract of fifteen hundred cords and the Anglo-Newfoundland Development Company of Grand Falls sent in their two scalers to check against our scale, just to make sure we had the amount the contract stated. They were supposed to be able to scale all this in about three days. After their work was done and they were ready to go, the weather turned bad and the plane couldn't get in to pick them up. They were delayed sixteen days in that bad weather! They were two unhappy men. The plane arrived on the sixteenth day and they both grabbed their bags and ran for it. They jumped into the seats and never so much as said "Thank you" or "Good-bye." Those people were used to travelling in Newfoundland where they could do most of their work on schedule. In Labrador things were different, and you just had to learn to wait, regardless of how bad you wanted to get out.

We got our wood on the bank and put one big boom in Little Brook Pond. We cleared the brook and built a dam to raise the water so we could drive the wood right to the saltwater. All went fine until loading time. I had a steel boat come up from Montreal that was supposed to take all of the wood in three trips. We got the first two trips loaded on schedule. While she was gone on the second trip, we had a big storm of wind from the southeast and our big boom of wood broke. The wind was up to one hundred miles per hour. Nothing could stand against those lops and that wind. Our wood was scattered all over the bay. When the wind changed, I wired the Anglo-Newfoundland Development Company and told them not to send the boat back as the charter was about $500.00 per day. There was no way this could pay off picking up the wood and carrying it to the ship in a boom. The woods manager thought I should have the boat back, but I refused to do so on the same conditions of the contract and this company was supposed to have the wood insured. It turned out that the insurance was only against forest fire. With that in mind, I knew there was no way a woods operation could profit, unless there was more security for the contactor.

I took a firm stand against cutting pulpwood for Newfoundland. The Company sent a private aircraft to see me with some of their forestry engineers on board; they thought I should carry on for another winter. But I just refused to do it under those conditions.

29
A Good Season

We decided to stick to the lumber business and try to sell our lumber in Labrador, as the prices were still low in Newfoundland. Present markets were uncertain and transportation costs had gone up from $15.00 per thousand to $18.00 per thousand to have it sent there. So we sold one horse and kept two for the lumber business.

In the fall, a fellow by the name of Sam Silver, a Canadian Jew, came on the coast. He was going to put up a big mill at Port Hope Simpson and another at Paradise River so he could go into the lumber business on a large scale. He visited me to ask if I would saw for him that winter; he would pay $85.00 per thousand at the mill. This was the best deal we had ever been offered. It was certainly better than selling in Newfoundland for over $100.00 per thousand.

We sawed one hundred and twenty thousand feet of lumber for him. Some of this was to go to Port Hope SImpson to build a sawmill, the remainder to Paradise River to build a sawmill and warehouse. However, by the time he got the last of the lumber from the mill, he went bankrupt and we only got paid for the first thirty thousand that he took. We didn't get a cent on all that went to Paradise River. We tried every way to get some money off him, but he claimed he had none. He was dead broke. This was nothing new for coastal Labrador, as every operation that ever started went out after a few years. But Silver never even got started!

This left us in a bad position for the next winter's work. We couldn't call ourselves broke because we were broke before we started. We were at the bottom of the ladder already, and if we went anywhere it had to be up a step or two. So we decided we would have to sell the second horse and only keep the smallest one. It was a staggering time, but we had to keep going. It had been toil and sweat the past winter, and now it had all gone down the drain.

We had several young married couples just starting out who were willing to work as long as they could earn their bread and butter. Many of our old teamsters were gone now and several of our sawmill workers had learned how to operate a sawmill and had gone out on their own. For awhile there were seven sawmills in operation in Charlottetown. Some men were only sawing for their private use, building new homes and boats. We had two sawmills going that winter, one on the north side of the harbour and one on the south.

The following summer we were encouraged when codfish went up to $5.00 a quintal. The fishery was very good that year. Family Allowance was coming to every family. Old age pensions increased so that the few old people we had working for us could now manage on their pensions; before this they had worked fixing up the horse roads so they could make enough money to live on. There were salt rebates coming to the fishermen and they were receiving little cheques on their fish that they had sold the summer before. Times were changing. For the first time, we began to see some one-dollar bills that began to stay in our village long enough to get wrinkly and worn. Before this, bank notes would pass through and wouldn't be in the village long enough to get worn.

Many of the old people who never had the chance to go to school and had never travelled far from the area thought the money was coming straight from Premier Joseph R. Smallwood's pocket! And nothing could change those old people's minds. There was one old lady by the name of Aunt Mary Ann Williams who was old enough to know about a lot of the hard times on the coast. Her husband had died many years before. Whenever someone died, she would come to me and say, "Another lucky one is gone, and I am still living. But I don't care as long as I die before Joey Smallwood, because when he dies we are all going to starve to death." We have very few of those old-timers left now. Soon they will all be gone.

Our only hope now was the sawmill in the wintertime and the fishing in the summertime. The fur on the trapline was just about done. The market was down and most furs weren't even saleable anymore. I kept one trapline going just around the head of the bay and the nearby lakes. These furs I stowed away, thinking that someday they would come back again in price.

The following winter we sold our lumber to Fishery Products Ltd., which operated several fishing rooms along the coast and needed lumber to keep their fishing rooms in good shape. They have always been reliable people, as far as paying. So we had no problem getting our money for the lumber that year. We had gone up the ladder one step! Then we had a good cod fishery that summer and the price of codfish was still going up. In 1960 we decided to build a longliner so we could go north and bring back a load of codfish. My sons were getting old enough to

Labrador's first longliner, *Miss Charlottetown*, 1960.

manage such a boat, so after getting a permit from the Department of Fisheries, we built a forty-five foot longliner at Charlottetown that we named the *Miss Charlottetown*. This was Labrador's first longliner.

We worked hard that winter, sawing lumber to sell and at the same time building this boat. Some of the young fellows were now teaming the horse, and they had to learn a lot before they could do the job like the old teamsters. I recall one morning when the teamster came and called me out of bed at five o'clock, saying he couldn't get the horse to stay in the staves. He kept leaving the sleds behind him. So he asked if I would come out to the cove where he was trying to get the horse into the woods. As soon as I got out where the horse was, I could see he had the collar put on upside down and the traces kept falling off the hooks on the hames. After awhile he was off again to the woods with the collar on the right way. He never had to be shown the second time! I must say we had hard-work-

The author aboard the *Miss Charlottetown*, 1976.

ing men in Charlottetown. There was no welfare among them. They worked for their living and worked hard. The lumber business was going well. In the winter of 1961 we had a shop built on one side of our house, the full length, and on the back of the house we had a new post office built. We were certainly getting established so we could serve our little village better.

30
We Lose Everything

February 23, 1961 was a cold day. All of the men were in the woods, including our oldest sons. I was in the post office getting the mail ready for the mail plane that was expected the next day. Then I heard Effie shout, "The house is on fire!" Both of us rushed upstairs, thinking the fire had started around the stovepipes. We just reached the top of the stairs when a fire extinguisher exploded, knocking us both back over the stairs. It was awhile before I came to. As soon as I did, I knew there was nothing I could do upstairs. The fire was too far advanced.

I thought of the money in the post office where I had been doing up the remittance for the C.O.D. parcels. This money belonged to the post office people, so I had to try and save it. I scravelled back and packed all the post office equipment in a box and got it outside the door. Then I went back to the house and tore the two-way radio off the wall and threw it out in the snowbank. By that time, the flames were bursting through the door and several men were out of the woods and getting up on the roof to tear off the boards around the stovepipe. Our son, Lewis, then came with the horse and went for the roof, too. Now that I had all of the post office money safe, I went for the shop. This was where all of the food was that we had to depend on for the winter. But as I got to the shop door and opened it, the flames came bursting through the side of the house. I grabbed something in my arms and went for the door. I had just gone through the door when the ammunition started to go off. We had a lot of it in the shop as this was one of the main things people have to have as part of their living off the land. When kegs of powder started to go off, all hands had to get clear. In a matter of minutes, everything fell in. We never really knew where the fire started.

I stood in my shirtsleeves and this was all that I had. I didn't save another garment. Once again we were back where we had started. The worst thing was that all of the food was gone. Mr. Wentzell had a shop across the harbour, but he never had enough food in it for all hands. My brother-in-law, Sandy Campbell, took us in and gave us food and shelter from the cold weather.

We got right to work and took our old equipment out of the little garage. The first thing that went up was the two-way radio. I got a message to the welfare officer in Mary's Harbour and he arranged with the Red Cross to send us bedclothes. That evening, Pastor William Gillett of the Pentecostal Church in Charlottetown came down with a coat under his arm and gave it to me. It was badly needed, and I wore that coat for a long time. Then Frank Clark gave free labour to put shelves in the little garage that would have to serve as the shop for the remainder of that winter. The nearest place to get enough supplies was Battle Harbour. The government paid to have them airlifted to Charlottetown. The third day, we were back in business on a small scale. No one went hungry, and we managed to keep things going.

We stayed at Sandy Campbell's until the weather got warmer, then we took the horse out of the barn and fixed that up enough to stay in until we got a new house built the next fall. The children would be able to sleep in the hay with their blankets. We had plenty of spiders and every kind of insect crawling over us in that old barn, but we had to live with it because we had no other choice. The main thing in life is to hold one's health and strength; everything else can be replaced when you have your health and strength, even though it might take a long time. When I was on my trapline, crawling on my hands and knees, I wouldn't think about home. No, that was too far away. I just hoped my strength would last to reach my little tilt. Now with everything burned to the ground, we just had to think about getting back to where we were before we got burned out. We had a little insurance on our home, but none on the shop or the winter stock which had to be paid for.

That winter some of our neighbours helped us cut logs for a new house. Because we had the sawmill, we had no problem getting all the rough material we needed. We had everything ready to start building as soon as fishing was over. That summer we landed over two thousand quintals of codfish and the price was very good. We got enough of the house built to live in that winter; one part was used for a shop and another part for a post office. We had it all in a nutshell. But it would take several years to get back to normal again.

31
Bigger Ventures

We had one more good cod fishery and that was all. The fish started to get scarce. Our longliner, the *Miss Charlottetown*, wasn't big enough to go far enough north and take all of the

The *Blanche Marie I*, 1966.

fishing gear that was now needed to make a profitable voyage. And my other sons were getting big enough to go into the boat, too, so we needed a larger one. We asked the government for a permit to build a fifty-six foot boat, but the government didn't think we could build a boat that big, so we had a difficult time getting started.

But in 1966 we launched our new boat, the *Blanche Marie,* called after our two daughters. As far as we knew, this was the largest one to be built in Labrador. She was sixty-two feet long and sixty-five gross tons. This was the real answer for the north. She could carry twelve hundred bags of salt and a deck load of gas and oil, besides the cod traps, salmon nets, and all of the outfit.

The first two summers we did very well, then the fish got scarcer. We could see that in another year or so the fish would disappear altogether. And failure did come, all along the coast. About two-thirds of the fishermen had to go on able-bodied welfare. My son, Lester, who had been skipper on our boat for several years, was now married. With the fishery having gone from bad to worse, he said he could no longer stick with it. His younger brother, Sandy, who was not married, would have to take over the vessel and hope the fish might come back again.

Lester went to flying school and later became a bush pilot. If the cod fishery continued to be a failure on our coast, we would have a problem surviving on the sawmill business, as it was only seasonal. But there could be a way out yet. One day I was going through my old file on the pulpwood business and I came across a piece of paper with my name on it. It was an article from *The Evening Telegram,* the St. John's newspaper, and it said, "This paper is made from Labrador wood, the first to come to Newfoundland." It went on to give more details about the operation. I knew a fellow in New York City, New York, who puts articles in *The New York Times*; this was his business. So I wrote to him and asked him to put an ad in that paper for me, saying, "Anyone interested in coming to Labrador for sports fishing, contact Ben Powell," and I gave my address.

The scrap of paper made from Labrador wood would be payment for the ad.

It worked fine. Soon I started getting many letters from people all across the States, so we had to get right to work and build a fishing lodge in White Bear Arm of St. Michaels Bay. We operated there for two summers, then shifted our fishing camp to the mouth of Gilbert's River so we could fish the big Gilbert's Lake with boats. At the time of this writing, we have been operating there for five years.

The author's fishing lodge, at the mouth of Gilbert's River used mainly by American sports fishermen.

32
Snowmobiles Take Over

It was the following year after we built our big boat, the *Blanche Marie*, that the first snowmobile came to Charlottetown. Things began to level off a bit. We now had two schools. The way of life was changing. Slowly the younger generation began to do things their way and the old way of life in the North was gradually dying. But the craving I had for the trapline would never die in me. I thought it would be wonderful to drive over the trapline on those snowmobiles and just see what was left of my little tilts. I thought it would be nice to bring back a souvenir from each of my tilts to put in my office. I knew it wouldn't be possible to get the traps I had put together at the far end of the trapline because they were now far under the snow and ice. But there were so many memories that could be brought back from such a trip.

My first plan was to get some gas brought in part of the way so I would have plenty to make the trip. So I did this. I carried all of the gas I could manage on the snowmobile and left it in two different places. The next morning I was up before daylight. My next plan was to go right to the Hawke Bay Mountains. Many people wouldn't trust those units to go very far and they were still keeping their dog teams. Even the manufacturers recommend in the owner's manual that it would be safer to travel in the company of more than one snowmobile on the trail. But somehow I felt they were safe to travel on and I was willing to take the chance.

I didn't tell anyone where I was going. My wife, Effie, was

over in the St. Anthony hospital; her mother had died that month and Effie lost a lot of rest being up with her in the night-time. It was a little more than she could take, so she ended up in the hospital. If Effie had been home, she would have tried hard to stop me from going on this trip. But now that I was getting ready for the trip, it would have taken a lot to stop me. Nobody else in the village knew the trail I would take to the mountains. Other trappers had been there but went on other trails or followed the river to the mountains. My way was my own trail. I knew it well, but no one else did. So if I broke down halfway, nobody would ever find me. I decided to draw out a map and mark the trail I would take right to the mountains. On the bottom I wrote, "Leaving for the mountains. Hope to be back tonight," and I left the map on the table. The first one to see this would be the servant girl who would be up at 6:30 a.m. By that time I hoped to have a good start.

Soon I was ready with six gallons of gas tied onto the seat and a lot of quart containers tied on all around the snowmobile, wherever I could tie one on. I took nothing to eat, only three chocolate bars and one tin of pop. Soon I was looking back at a few dim lights from some of the houses where people kept their lamps burning all night. The first sign of daylight started to show in the east. I was heading up White Bear Arm, the travelling was good, and I left a clear track from the snowmobile behind. I thought that if I had seen this kind of track in the snow twenty-five years ago, I probably would have gone and smelled it to try and find out what kind of animal had gone along, not even showing the print of its paws, but just sliding right along like a grandfather otter would do!

Soon Aunt Maggie's Trap Point was in sight. This point was the far end of Aunt Maggie's trapline. She must have been eighty years old when she last travelled this line. The last time I looked at the tree where she had her trap made fast to, there was just the chain coming out of that big tree. Over the years the tree had grown and had covered the staple and ring of the chain altogether. She had only been a girl when she first set up

John Campbell and his granddaughter, Rachel. His wife, Martha, is cleaning a black bear skin, 1930.

this trapline.

As I travelled on, I looked once more where I had once lived in my little log house one winter with my brother, Roland, and then the second year in our studded house. Those were fond memories. I was now passing over the very spot where once I was hanging on for life on the bottom of my fourteen-foot boat. Looking to the north, I saw Campbell's Cove where I lived after I got married. John Campbell's house still stands today, but everything else is gone; almost a century ago this house was built, and many hundreds of offspring have spread to different parts of the world. I still wonder what made people so happy in those days with so little to speak of. Some of the old pictures are still on the wall, and often there were labels taken off fruit cans. A can of fruit was so rare that the pretty picture was always taken off the can and put on the wall. The empty can was put away as it could serve many uses. Now what a change! We are paying garbage collectors to throw away all those cans with all the nice pictures.

Then I headed up over Salt Water Pond and struck the

Middle Trail. There at the end of the trail, high in the tall, slen-
der trees, I could still see the marks of rope where I used to
make those trees work for me to haul up my boat. They were
taller now. I was to take the Middle Trail, not the wester'd one,
as it was very rough. I would skip my first tilt on Gull Lake. It
was real fun to just sit down on that snowmobile and watch the
many ponds and lakes go by. Almost every mile would bring
back old memories. Soon I would be on Clifty Lake, the place
where something almost always happened. There was the little
point where once on Christmas Eve I had eaten the very last
crumb of food and was still a long way from home. I tried not
to think of this. There seemed to be a lump come in my throat
just thinking about those days. Those days I hoped were gone
for good. Things had changed now. At that time there wasn't
even a Charlottetown. Now we had a fine little village, and the
traplines were almost all forgotten. Most of the old trappers
were gone and very few of the younger generation would ever
go back over the old trails.

Just then, as everything seemed to be working fine, bang
went the drive belt on my snowmobile. I was really disappointed as I had planned to have a big day. I had a spare one with
me, but when I put that one on, there would be no other spare
and I was only starting the day. I had never put a drive belt on
one of these units before, but I managed to get it on after a little
while. I decided to go only as far as my Three Mile Pond tilt. I
wanted to get one of the top logs for a souvenir, as the first
teacher we had had cut his name in one log. Soon I was driving
on again. Well, I thought, this is the lake where something is
sure to happen.

I thought about one spring when Roland Bursey and myself
went to the White Hill Mountains for a caribou hunt. We left
our dog team on Clifty Lake, and after going over the White
Hills, we could only see the very old tracks of caribou. It
looked as though we would be going home without any caribou. Just before I got to Clifty Lake, I slipped by the side of the
mountain, fell down and broke the stock of the gun, knocking

the site to one side. I tied it up as best I could. We were just about back to the dogs on the lake when I looked out and saw four caribou about two hundred yards away. The big stag was taking the lead and he seemed really lazy; he would take a few steps and then stop. I knelt down on one knee and took aim at him. There was no way I could strike him; my sight was out of place and by the time Roland got his gun ready, they had jumped into the woods and gotten away from us. The strangest thing I could never understand was that those dogs were all sitting up watching the caribou and they never made a move or a bark. I don't know just how long those caribou had been there before we got there. Poor old Roland thought it was very hard as we would have to go back to our families without any caribou when they had been so handy to us. He just couldn't get over it. I told him they just weren't for us, so that was it.

I then drove east around the mountains and soon I was on Three Mile Pond where my tilt was. This was my best tilt. I had a little spring of water just below it and it was still running. The can was tied on the tree with a brass fox snare; this was where I used to put the minks to keep the mice from eating them while I was gone to the other end of the trapline. The stovepipes I had put over the stump were still there and not rusted at all after those many years. But there was no sign of the tilt; everything was gone. I started to dig down to the ground with my snowshoe and all I could find was some birch bark that I used to have on the roof. There was nothing to take back for a souvenir. Never again would I enjoy the good nights in that old tilt that was so warm. I only had a wooden bed with a chunk of wood for a pillow and my cap under my head, but it was real comfort. There was a feeling that one would have only after hauling his toboggan all day when he was wet with sweat, then he'd get in the tilt for the night. There was a little pile of wood on one side of the stove and on the other side would be the splits all cleaved up small; the wood was so straight-grained that you could cleave it as small as you pleased. With the cracking of the wood in the stove, I would straighten out for a rest with my back to the heat. That heat would strike my wet body and there would be a feeling beyond words. Only one who had this experience would ever know what it was like. As you slumbered off care-free, you certainly weren't worrying about the stock markets in the States or whether you had a rich uncle who might leave you some money when he died. The thing that is most on a trapper's mind is wondering what will be in the traps tomorrow just around the bend of the river. This is what makes the game so interesting. It's not what you've got, but what you expect the next day or week. I was just standing there where once stood my greatest home in the country.

I could recall the one trip when I came and got all of my wood, stowed it up on both sides of the stove, got my lunch, and after the moon rose decided to go to the head of the pond and see my mink traps. After making this trip, I was almost back to the tilt when a big horned owl attacked me. I didn't have a chance to hold my gun; all I could do was to bat him off with it. He'd sail back at me again and again and kept it up for at least a half hour. I kept edging toward the woods and at last he went off into the trees and started making all kinds of noises.

There were some other times at the tilt when things weren't so good. A few times I came to my tilt and dug down to the ground with my snowshoes to get an old fox or lynx carcass for something to eat. From being under the snow since the fall of the year, the carcass would be turned right green, but I would find some little part on the legs that I could cook and it would keep a fellow alive until he could find better.

I decided I would have to move on down the feeder where I had the gas hung in a tree. Soon I was gassed up and was think-ing as I left that old tilt of the five different people who had overnighted there. Only two of us were left now, and that was my brother, Roland, and myself. Uncle Alex had been out on the trail when he almost went stone blind from a tumor that was growing on his brain. He made home but only lived a short while after that. Then there was our first teacher who wanted to spend one weekend in the little tilt. He later got the measles and died. Eric Pardy from Cartwright was in on the trapline with me one fall and later died not far from his home on the trail. So there were only two of us left, Roland now in Newfoundland and I back on the trapline on a snowmobile.

I drove down to the big feeder pond and through the Narrows. Just between the two ponds I looked ashore and thought to myself, "Well, this is the place where my hair almost stood on end one time in the fall of the year before the snow was down." The narrow path went from one pond to the other. The animals had it beaten hard on the ground. Up above, the willows had it all closed in and it was just hard to get through. I was going along this morning, trying to get down to the big pond where my last trap was and get back again before dark, when all of sudden I heard this terrible noise coming toward me. Everything was cracking before it. The trees were so thick that there was no way I could get to one side of the path to let it pass. I thought I would be tramped to the ground like a rabbit. I started to pull the gun coat off my rifle, but the trees were so thick that there was no way to even get the rifle stuck out ahead of me. All of a sudden, the animal jumped to one side of the path and went straight out of sight. All I could see was the big willows shaking and what looked like the horns of a caribou. I followed along until I got to a muddy place in the path and I could see it had been a big caribou with a wolf tightly behind him. Well, he sure gave me a scaring as I couldn't see what was going on. Sometimes the wolves do this when they get hungry; they single out a caribou and drive it in a narrow path, then they bite the main arteries and the caribou will bleed to death.

It was on this very same marsh one time in the spring that I was dragging a heavy load. It got really warm out so I cut some boughs to take a rest on for awhile and fell asleep. While I was sleeping, a caribou walked right up to me, smelled me and then went right back into the woods. When I awoke, I saw the track and didn't know what was going on. As the wind was blowing away from me, the caribou didn't smell me, so this big hunk of venison got away while I was sleeping. Well, I thought, this is a great country!

Right in this very spot was my choice place and the Indians' choice place until I took it over. They were remarkable people who never destroyed anything more than was needed. Where I was passing, I could see one dry juniper where for many years the Indians had been taking part of this tree to make their snow-shoes. They never cut the big tree down but left it standing. They'd only take from the tree the amount of wood they needed and when they needed it. The thing I was most impressed over with the Indians was how they wanted to save the forest. When they found a beaver in a brook, they would stake off the brook by driving sticks in the brook. This would keep the beaver close to the house so they could trap them, and each of those pickets they drove into the mud had to be chopped in two so it would make two pieces; in this way, the wood went twice as far. To cleave a stick in two that is six or seven feet is quite difficult, but the Indians were willing to do this in order to save the for-est. I believe very few white men would be willing to do this.

I was now ready to leave the last of the big water to go around the north side of the mountain. In each hour on my snowmobile, I could cover the same distance as a whole day's walk towing my komatik. This deep cove that was now close by could never be forgotten, because it was where I saw the Indian wigwam. In all my days on the trapline, it was probably close to a hundred years before that date when the Indians lived in that wigwam. The sticks were mostly all rotted away. This was a good, sheltered spot and I used to pitch my camp there often before freeze-up time.

One fall, I was camping there and while I was out to the lynx traps one day, it came right mild with southwest winds. The young ice[1] started to get watery so I made a shortcut for the camp, about ten miles away. But the shortcut turned out to be different from what I thought it was, as I had to follow a small deep brook that hardly had enough ice to walk on. Finally, it got dark, really dark as it does in the early fall. About every ten

[1]The first ice that forms in the fall.

minutes I'd fall into the brook that night, sometimes right up to my neck, but I could always reach the willows by the side and pull myself out again. Often in the night I made it to my little canvas camp, wet, hungry and tired, with no wood cut. This was the first job, which wasn't easy without light. I had to feel through the trees for a dry stick. Then I'd take a chip off the tree and smell the tree to see if it was dry or not. Finally, I'd get a good stick, and with a candle in the camp door, I'd cut up plenty of wood for the night. Then I'd have a good lunch and with the stove red hot I would take off my clothes and spread them around the stove to dry. As soon as I got my underwear dry I put this on, then filled up the stove with wood again to dry the rest of my clothes. Then I would fall back and go right dead to sleep as I was so tired. It was after midnight then. With such a big fire, the boughs got dry and caught fire, but I was so dead asleep that I never awoke until the hot ashes started to fall in my face. When I looked up, I was looking at the stars on a starlight night. My camp had burned to the ground. I jumped up and started to grab for my clothes. Very little was left. I was standing in my underwear, staring at the stars. I had left my skin boots and my game bag outside the tent door, so this was one thing in my favor. I got together the rags of my clothes and part of the camp that wasn't burnt and wrapped them around me; my game bag could cover my back.

It was three o'clock in the morning when I set out for the Three Mile Pond tilt. It was a bit chilly at that hour in my underwear! The frost was starting to strike good when I got close to the tilt. After a day there, I fixed up the rags enough to keep out the frost until I made home. I never camped in that place after that.

I was now moving around the side of the mountains fast. Soon I would be to my third tilt; this was the one where I almost got smothered with that big feed of beaver meat so I had to cut a hole out through the logs to get air to breathe. Now I had reached the very spot where the tilt was supposed to be, but there was not one sign of anything left. Over the years, everything had decayed. Many big windfalls had dropped right across the very spot where the tilt was once built. This had always been a leaky and a cold tilt, but it gave me a lot of shelter over the years. I had spent too many nights in this tilt to ever be able to count them. I certainly wouldn't get any souvenir from this tilt. There just wasn't anything to see. If only the snow was gone, I would be able to get all the traps that I had left on the big otters' rub just to one side of the tilt.

I had to move on; the day was going. Still the Hawke Mountains were a long way off. When I broke my drive belt, I hadn't planned to go this far, but now I was to the last pond on the Southwest Feeder. Soon I would be on the lead of marshes that should take me to the southern back waters of Hawke River, six marshes, one after the other, and from this end I would take the smallest one first and each one would get bigger. Now, on my snowmobile, they only seemed like the steps of a stairway. It wasn't long before I was at the big marsh. I had to laugh to myself as I was now in the spot where once I saw the dung of a black bear. The dung was white in colour, and I knew this shouldn't be. I figured he had stolen the flour that I had hauled up to my tilt at the open tickle. I had put it into an oil barrel with a little door in one end. Somehow, I knew the bear had gotten the door open and had eaten the flour that I was trusting to for the fall. But it wasn't the first time that that had happened to me. The bears had eaten my flour many times, but this was the first time I had gotten the message about ten miles from my tilt!

I stopped and checked the gas tank. It was getting pretty dry, so I filled up again with the gas I had in the quart containers and soon was heading for the tilt at the open tickle. This was a great day. Everything was going just wonderful, but I couldn't take the chance of going much further. It wasn't long before I was driving along by the open tickle and then through the path that comes from the east. I could still see the form of the logs of the little tilt. I had built it from dry juniper, a very hard wood that took a long time to rot. As I began to take the snow off, I could see that the top part was gone, but all the side logs were still there. It was only four logs high. The old bed was still there and the chunk I had used for a pillow was all covered with fool's gold that had fallen out of the seams. There was nothing I could see that would be any good for a souvenir. Then I looked overhead and saw my old scaffold, still tied there with fox snares. So I reached up and took one down. The thought struck me that this was the spot where Clarence Perry and myself had made plans to start the sawmill business that led to the little settlement of Charlottetown. This place now has two schools, seven teachers, two churches, and six shops. All of this took twenty-five years, but it was worth it. Clarence Perry had gone back to Newfoundland, as his mother made him promise before she died. Our little settlement is still growing while the old traplines have died away. The tilts are gone, never to be rebuilt.

I thought I would go just as far as the river and then I should return, but the travelling was too good to stop now. But with everything working so free, it was the next bend of the river and the next; this went on until I reached Mountain Brook, which used to take me all day dragging my toboggan. This time it had only taken one hour. Here I was at the mouth of the brook where I had learned from the Indians how to put up my camp stove on three sticks, rather than four. The heavy timber along this brook was wonderful to look at; it reached up so far in the air and leaned from both sides of the banks toward the middle. It was like driving through an arch. All at once, my motor began to sputter and make funny noises. I stopped and hoped it was nothing serious. I looked in the gas tank; it was dry. I had gone farther than I thought I would. I was on Mountain Brook and just ahead was my old camping place. The little island in the brook was still there and the beaver dam that barred off half the brook. All of this brought back many memories. This was far better to me than a trip to the Holy Land. It was like someone being away from home for a long time and then returning.

Soon I was gassed up again and left the red gas containers hanging on the limbs of the small trees that hung over the river. I thought that if I never returned, somebody would see those and know I had gotten this far. I only had about five gallons of gas left, but the tank was now full. To be on the safe side, I would only go around the next bend and then head for home. But it was the next and the next again, and then the big barren mountains loomed up, straight ahead. I couldn't turn back when they seemed so handy. I just had to go on. In awhile I was climbing those mountains on my snowmobile, the highest ones in this part of Labrador. I came to a stop on the second highest peak, then took my camera in my hand and looked back. It was like I could look all over the world. Only then did I realize that this wasn't a wise thing to do. Should bad weather come, I would never make it home. I was no longer as young as I used to be; I was getting up in years and was partly crippled in one leg. At one time, I hadn't cared where night overtook me. I could manage to put up a fair bout as long as I had food to eat, but now all I had were three chocolate bars and one tin of pop.

Well, here I was at the spot that one time took me eight days

The White Hill Mountains.

to walk, pulling my load, and that was going a straight distance. This didn't seem far on a snowmobile if all worked well, but if one little thing broke, I was stranded. I would never be able to make it back on my own on that little lunch. As I looked back over the long stretch of wooded country, I could see the White Hill Mountains about thirty miles to the southeast. All of the hard trips I had made seemed to come up before me. There had been many times when I had just made it, when I was down to my last crumb. But I was always taking those chances; this was my life, and it was hard to get away from it.

Over the years, we had to bring our horses back and forth from Square Islands to Charlottetown in the spring and in the fall as there was no grass for them in Charlottetown. It was all green trees. So those horses had to be moved to the seacoast where there was lots of grass. This was a big chance to take, putting them in fishing boats and bringing them back and forth. One fall I had the horse in the boat with my wife and children, and there was no lifeboat at that time. We were halfway in the bay when it got dark. A fair breeze of wind was blowing and the horse must have gotten thirsty. He was trying to get his

Fishing boats at the author's wharf at Square Islands.

head overboard to get a drink and began to move around in the boat. I was expecting him to drive his hooves through the side of the boat any minute. I had to get forward in the boat and hold his head while Effie steered the boat until we made the beach in Charlottetown. Then the animal jumped to safety onto the beach. I recall how Uncle George Kippenhuck came along just as the horse jumped ashore and he said to Effie, "Well, that man hasn't got a grain of sense to take his family in the bay after dark with that big animal." I had no quarrel with Uncle George; he was right, but somehow those chances had to be taken. There was no other way out because we didn't have any bigger boats. Uncle George is now the oldest man in Charlottetown and he very often tells me how the old Campbell people, Uncle John and Aunt Martha, were always giving him good advice when he was a young man and he always tried to

The Powell home (centre) and Powell's Fisheries Ltd., Square Islands, 1980.

take it. They would tell him never to fire at anything unless he was sure of what he was pointing his gun at; never to go on bad ice, even if you think you could get over it, as someone else could follow your track and get drowned.

When the first church minister came to Charlottetown, Uncle George told him the story about the time Aunt Maggie put the skin mitten down the white bear's throat. The old minister said he didn't believe it, so Uncle George told him that Aunt Martha Campbell had related that story to him and she didn't tell any lies. Then Uncle George asked him about Daniel in the lion's den. The minister said that God was with Daniel. Then said Uncle George, "The same God who was with Daniel was with Aunt Maggie." Up until today, Uncle George doesn't forget that minister not believing the story.

I filled up my tank with more gas, then took a picture of the snowmobile on the mountain. I pulled a bit of bark from a tree and put it in my pocket as a remembrance of the old mountain. Many times I had been there before, but never so unprepared as now. I bowed my head and with a little prayer I asked my Maker to bring me back home safely. I started the snowmobile and rode down the mountain.

For three and a half hours I kept the throttle at one speed. I was afraid to drive too fast in case my drive belt broke, and I had no replacement. My fingers were almost dead when that time was up. I was in the middle of the big marsh on the southern waters of Hawke River. I stopped and let the motor cool off, then ate one bar and drank the tin of pop. I checked over the motor and everything seemed to be in shape. After tightening up a few nuts, I started off again. In another hour I was driving down the Southwest Feeder of Hawke River, and here I noticed the tracks of a lynx crossing the point. I wished I had a trap to set there. This whole area was where my traps were, but they were all under the snow. Others were on the otter rubs and could be gone after these many years. Often the beavers will cut off the sticks that the traps are tied onto and throw them out into the water. Then I thought about my souvenir, the snare I had taken from the tilt place at the open tickle. So I pulled it out of my pocket. It looked as good as new. It was made from five parts of brass wire. I fixed up a good place and barred it off on both sides and tailed the snare. The following Saturday I returned and found a big lynx. I took him out and tailed the snare again. The next Friday I had caught another. By now the snow was almost gone on that point of land, so I had to put the snare closer to the bottom of the stick. There was hardly enough wire left to fasten it on good, as the stick was much larger than the butt. The following week when I returned, I found that the lynx had gotten into the snare but had gone with my souvenir around his neck. So that was the end of it. However, I did all right that winter with lynx; I sold them some years later for $500.00. When the price came back again, I had quite a lot of furs to sell, and did well.

The author on the trapline, taking a large lynx from his trap and lashing it to the toboggan.

I headed back to where I had left my gas on the trip in. From this point, there would be no problem to make home on another three gallons of gas.

By now it was getting dull out. The day was well spent and I had had a lot of fun. As I rounded the last end of the White Hill Mountains, I realized that in another hour I would be at

The author with a big lynx on his back.

Mountaineer Pond, which was only one mile from Salt Water Pond. Uncle John Campbell had called this Mountaineer Pond because this was as far as the Indians would bring their wives to the settlement called Campbell's Cove. They'd come out to trade their furs for food with Uncle John Campbell and put up their camps at this pond. The wives would stop in the camps while the men went on to trade furs. About halfway from the pond to John Campbell's house, they would leave their guns. They would never bring them to the white man's house. Only the chief could speak English, so he would have to do all the talking. My wife, Effie, who lived with her Grandfather Campbell, said she could remember seeing as many as sixteen Indians sleeping on the floor of her grandfather's house overnight. Then in the morning before they would leave, the chief would take each of the Indians' bags and empty them out on the floor one by one, to show that they weren't stealing anything from the white man's house. They only had what they

The lynx has been lashed to the author's toboggan.

traded their furs for. Many times they would bring furs that
didn't have much value, as the animals were caught too early
and Grandfather Campbell would tell the chief that he couldn't
value the furs very much. The old chief would say, "You pay
me well for my furs and I will pay you well for your goods." So
in this way they always kept on good terms. Until the year John
Campbell died – 1934 – he and the Mountaineer Indians were
always good friends. After he died, the Indians never returned
to the head of St. Michaels Bay to trade, since the one they had
called John the Baptist, their friend, had died.

Soon I would be home. I was now on the saltwater ice, driving along one quarter of a mile from John Campbell's old
house, the only one left in the head of the bay. It was dark now,
but through the green trees I could see a white tombstone sticking up through the snow in an unfenced graveyard. This was
John Campbell's. Six more miles and I would see the lights of
Charlottetown shining across the bay of ice. It had been a great

day, and I was home again safe and sound.

The next thing I thought I should do was to contact the manufacturers of the snowmobiles and give them my opinion of what I thought of their machine. It had only recently arrived on the coast, and this might be of some help to them. So I wrote to Bombardier Ltd., Valcourt, Quebec, and told them what I thought. In my opinion, that machine would take the place of the dog teams in the North. I knew from my first trip on the trail that this would be a dependable machine in a few year's time. The company replied to my letter at once and was very happy with my comments. At the same time, they had contacted their distributor in Corner Brook, J.W. Randell Ltd., who sent me a telegram at once and offered me the dealership for this area of Labrador. Today we have more snowmobiles in Charlottetown than we had teachers in all of coastal Labrador twenty-five years ago!

The graves of John Campbell and his wife, Martha.

33
Mr. Jeffries

In the previous chapters I have written, I have mentioned the names of many ponds, lakes and mountains. Some of these I have named myself; others my brother, Roland, has named. The names of rivers were determined by earlier settlers on this part of the coast. The most remarkable river is Gilbert's River. It has two names; the outer part is called Gilbert's, and the inner part is Jeffries'. Mr. Jeffries was one of the early trappers and a very notable man. So the people from that part of the coast called the inner part after Mr. Jeffries. This was long before my day. However, I did see what was left of his old log house at Gilbert's Bay.

As far as I can learn from the oldest people in this area, Mr. Jeffries was an Englishman who came to the coast in the latter part of the eighteenth century, either on a man-of-war boat or on a pirate ship. Along this time of the century, Britain and France were having wars, and many young men were being pressed for war. Mr. Jeffries got close enough to the Labrador coast to make land, maybe by swimming ashore at night, and settled up in the bottom of Gilbert's Bay where he married an Eskimo woman and later had one daughter.

The mother and the little girl would stay home while Jeffries would tend his long trapline that ran sixty miles inland. He trapped mostly martens in those days. I have seen very few in my time. They are smaller than a house cat but much alike. A marten trail would be blazed a long distance, mostly straight. The trapper would cross a river and pond and follow on by putting his traps in rotten stumps. The marten cat would follow along this trail and often get caught in the traps. So this was the life of Mr. Jeffries in the wintertime.

On one of his trips at the trail, he crossed Hawke River. While on the far side, a great mild came on and it rained for many days. The river overflowed its banks and he couldn't get back across. His food was scarce. He waited sixteen days for the rainstorm to cease. His biggest worry was for his wife and little girl back in the bottom of Gilbert's Bay. He had only left enough wood at home for a regular trip; now he had been away over twenty days, and even if he got back across the river, he was a long way form his home. However, the weather can change quickly in Labrador; after the sixteenth day the weather turned cold, and he once more crossed the river on ice. After several very cold days, he finally reached the little bank just above his home. All he owned was in that little log cabin.

The night before, it had snowed a little, and he noticed that there were no tracks in the snow around the door. He hurried down over the high bank and opened the door, only to find his wife sick in bed and his little girl trying to tend on her. His wife had gotten a cold out in the woods in the wet weather trying to get wood while he was stranded out on his trapline. As the little girl ran toward her father, he could hear by the sound of her feet striking the floor that her legs were frozen, right to the knees.

Mr. Jeffries had to solve his own problems, as many people had to do in Labrador. He hauled out his hunting knife right there and cut the little girl's legs off to the joints of her knees, then stuck her down in the flour barrel to stop the bleeding so he could tend to his wife. After getting the fire lit, he went into the woods and brought back herbs to make homemade medicine to cure his wife. Soon she was well, and very slowly, the girl's stumps healed up and she was able to walk around on them.

The following summer, when the Grenfell Mission boat made its usual trip along the Labrador coast, the medical people learned of Mr. Jeffries' daughter. They went to the bottom of Gilbert's Bay and found her, happy on her stumps. The Grenfell doctors, with the consent of her parents, took her away to St. Anthony, Newfoundland, and from there to the States, where they gave her two plastic legs and put her in school where she was well-educated and later was able to speak several different languages. But the girl wan't happy in that strange land. She wanted to return to her little log cabin in the bottom of Gilbert's Bay. She didn't like her plastic legs and just wanted to walk on the two stumps. She did return and married a man from the mouth of Groswater Bay. They lived close to the side of the Long Labrador Trail and were great friends to many who travelled that way. They served hundreds of meals over the years. I was told by a river warden from that area that the girl died as an old lady a couple of years ago.

Gerald Green in 1985 returning to look at the motor where he lost his left arm.

34
The First Nursing Clinic[1]

More improvements were slowly coming to Charlottetown. In 1965 the Newfoundland Bell Telephone came in, and in 1971 we got our first hydro power. Our greatest problem still remained unsolved – how to get a nursing clinic.

For many years we had seen the nurses and doctors come to town by dog team and then snowmobile. Our medical help was

The Grenfell Mission hospital at Mary's Harbour, 1951.

[1]Information provided by Shirley M. Flewitt.

limited by weather conditions, as they often had to travel fifty miles from the nearest nursing station at Mary's Harbour. One or two families in Charlottetown always opened their homes for the nurses and doctors to work in. They were only too happy to do this, even if it meant personal inconvenience to their families. In the back of everyone's mind, we hoped the day would come when a resident nurse would be stationed in Charlottetown.

And so we began to plan that way. We were modest and practical in our desires and our hopes were not too demanding. But as often happens when projects are undertaken without personal gain in view, the abundant is supplied. On a night in March 1974 the principal of the William Gillett Pentecostal Academy called a meeting. A fair representation of the community was present to discuss the possibility of building our own clinic. At that time, we could not imagine the proportions to which it would grow. We would have been happy just to have a small place where the travelling medical people would work with some degree of convenience. Our starting point was an anonymous gift of $2,000.00 which was presented to the school principal to be used specifically for the construction of a clinic. Thirty men of Charlottetown pledged themselves to cut and saw twenty logs apiece to provide the rough lumber for framing. A committee was formed to plan and supervise the operation: Ben Powell, Sr., merchant; Frank Clark, Sr., fisherman; John Kippenhuck, power plant operator; Alexander Campbell II, chief operator, power plant; Henry Hilliard, fisherman; and Shirley Flewitt, principal and teacher, Pentecostal school.

It was truly a community effort. There was no promise at that time of any outside help, but with faith in the value of the project and a confidence in many hearts that what we were doing would merit God's approval and help, we forged ahead. We did what we could. By June the logs had been cut, sawed, and piled on the site. The schoolchildren, down to the smallest kindergartner, helped. How often did we see two tykes carrying one piece of 2" x 4" between them to the construction site! They were eager to do their part. Bake sales and jumble sales were organized; donations started coming in until by the end of June there was a reserve of $4,000.00 to use the next fall for the actual building.

The two teachers, Joan M. Cartledge and Shirley M. Flewitt, went home to Ontario for the summer and secured newspaper space in the *Hamilton Spectator* to tell of the need. People responded with monetary donations. Two hospitals in the Hamilton area offered used equipment and hundreds of dollars' worth of blankets. Service clubs, churches, and individuals responded from many places both in Canada and the States. Some gifts came from the affluent, but many came from elderly folks with no source of income but their old age pensions. Out of love and concern for the Labrador people, they gave what they could.

In September, Henry "Hank" Roberts, affectionately known as "Skipper" by the Charlottetown people, arrived with his wife, Doris. They spent ten weeks with us so Hank could supervise the construction of the clinic. He brought with him many years of experience as maintenance supervisor at National Steel Car in Hamilton. We will never be able to reckon in dollars and cents the help he gave in planning, purchasing, supervising and in just plain hard labouring. A group of local men worked with Hank, not knowing whether they would ever make a dollar. Over twelve hundred hours of free labour were given. A registered architect drew and donated a plan. Hank took off the required material list and sent some of the men to Newfoundland with $5,000.00 to purchase what they could. It was a work of faith all the way. It would be untruthful to say there were no discouraging times, but there was never any real doubt in the hearts of the committee and the labour force that our task would be completed and our mission to provide a medical facility would be accomplished.

We applied to Canada Manpower for a grant via the Local Initiatives Program. Out of a total of 111 applications approved that year in the province of Newfoundland-Labrador, ours was the first to be accepted. We are grateful to the men who saw our need and approved our grant. The deciding factor was the fact that our people had shown initiative enough to go ahead themselves, with no promise of help from anyone. Now we had added impetus. The grant provided the funds to finish the building and a double blessing was that the men who had given so selflessly of their time in the past would now get paid to complete the work in the major part of the winter.

Donations kept coming. Furniture was purchased. The International Grenfell Association finished the water and sewage systems. By the spring of 1975 our clinic was basically completed. Only $5,000.00 remained outstanding on the entire project. The Pentecostal Assemblies of Newfoundland, under the leadership of Pastor A. Stanley Bursey, assumed the existing debt and the responsibility of the ownership and maintenance of the building. The International Grenfell Association, under the directorship of Dr. Gordon Thomas, agreed to take over the operation of the clinic and provide a resident nurse. For over eighty years that Association had been responsible for the medical services on the Labrador coast. A visiting engineer put a replacement value of $90,000.00 on the building! We had come so far, all with the help of God, from the few thousand dollars and the few hundred logs a year before.

During the summer of 1975 a dental unit was donated, a much-needed and much-appreciated contribution. It is the best on the coast. It was given by three dentists and a school superintendent in Ontario. One of the dentists came to Charlottetown and personally installed the unit. Since that he has donated a dental X-ray unit.

December 1976 marked the first birthday of the Charlottetown clinic. The first permanent nurse, Isobel Muir, invited all the adults to the clinic for a time of fun, food and fellowship to celebrate one year of successful operation. It was also a time of remembering what we had gone through to have our clinic. It was beyond anything we had dreamed of that winter night in March 1974. Today it stands as a monument to the dedication of people who gave time and money to a cause they believed was worthwhile.

In the midst of all this, we don't ever want to forget the noble efforts of the past. Nurses and doctors came on harsh wintry days over hazardous trails; they travelled on stormy waters in the summertime to attend their patients; men and women of Charlottetown worked long hours comforting the sick and travelling rough trails to take others to the nursing station miles away. Among those we especially think of Mrs. Alex Campbell – Aunt Lennie, whom I have mentioned before – who served as a midwife for many years. More recently we recall her daughter, Mrs. Ben Powell – Aunt Effie – carrying on the good work of her mother. She was also the custodian of all medicines for many years. Almost everyone in Charlottetown and the surrounding small communities benefitted from her care and concern.

Many fine, dedicated nurses, doctors, dentists, eye doctors and public health specialists have used the Charlottetown clinic. Even the dog population has benefitted. A team of veterinarians used the clinic at one time to treat the dogs for rabies!

You just never know what will result from a challenge on the Labrador! This all started with a few people, a few dollars, many prayers, and a big dream!

The Charlottetown Nursing Clinic.

35
A Young Man's Dream Comes True

The first printing of this book was in 1979. Now, more than a decade later, I'm still receiving letters from far away, letters from people who want to know how our little settlement of Charlottetown, that was started in 1950, is progressing. So I decided to write another chapter for this fourth printing of *Labrador by Choice*. I can sent a copy to all my friends to answer the questions they ask.

It has been officially announced that our Charlottetown is

Nathasha Cadwell (the youngest kindergarten student) cutting the ribbon at the official opening of a new gymnasium and a newly renovated school.

now the fastest-growing settlement in Labrador.

February 13, 1993 was the day when a young man's dream became an old man's reality. That was the day when scores of people from all along our coast as far north as Nain, as well as many from Newfoundland, came to take part in the official opening of a new gymnasium and a newly renovated William Gillett Pentecostal Academy. The story is told in the February 22, 1993 issue of *The Labradorian*:

> The people of Charlottetown were recently delighted to celebrate the official opening of a new gymnasium and a newly renovated Pentecostal school. The school now possesses the facilities to offer a wide array of educational programs at all levels of schooling, comparable to any school in the province of similar size.

> The school's new gymnasium provides an ideal location for a broad physical education, extracurricular, and community sports program. Coupled with this is a combined computer room and library, with some $65,000 worth of computer equipment. This state-of-the-art technology allows students and teachers to access a variety of resources to support and enhance the regular curriculum. In addition, the new industrial arts room, a number of renovated classrooms, and the science room offer other specialized areas for the 83 students at the school.

> Visiting guests for the official opening on Feb. 13 included Domino Wilkins, superintendent of the Pentecostal Assemblies Board of Education, and Pastor A.E. Batstone, executive director of the Pentecostal Education Council. Other members of the school board in attendance were Pastor B.Q. Grimes, vice-chairman, Pastor H.E. Perry, secretary, and Pastor G.N. Norman, Labrador representatives. The master of ceremonies was the assistant superintendent responsible for the area, David Rideout.

Letters of congratulations were read from Labrador MP Bill Rompkey, Eagle River MHA Danny Dumaresque, and David Swan of the local Gospel Hall assembly. The mayor of Charlottetown, Sandy Powell, expressed his council's appreciation for having such a fine school in the town. He also encouraged students to take advantage of every opportunity to gain a good education.

The principal of the school, George Jefferies, commented on the students' excellent results on various test measures, such as Canadian Test of Basis Skills (CTBS) and public examination results. For the past two years the school has enjoyed a 100 per cent pass rate among its Grade 12 students. Mr. Jefferies described the broad range of courses now being offered to the students, including French, physics and advanced mathematics by distance education. In his concluding comments, he thanked the parents for their continued support and the school board for its commitment to providing educational facilities of this calibre.

The superintendent of education, Mr. Wilkins, expressed the school board's appreciation for the cooperative planning at all stages of this project, which saw substantial improvement in the building with a minimum increase in the total school size. The end result indicated that a lot of work had been accomplished for the $400,000 cost of the renovations and the extension. Special recognition was given to the contribution of the local school committee, under its chairman, Pastor B. Pelley, for its involvement in the discussions and planning which led to the completion of this building project.

A highlight of the opening exercises was the outstanding performance of the school choir, with students from Kindergarten to Grade 7. Parents and guests were delighted from the very beginning, when the choir sang both the English and French versions of "O Canada". Other selections chosen for the occasion were "He's Still Working on Me," "It's A Small World After All," and the "Ode to Labrador."

At the conclusion, Natasha Cadwell, a Kindergarten student, cut the ribbon to declare the school officially opened. This was then followed by tours of the school to view the new facilities and observe the various displays set up by the students. The response from everyone indicated a great sense of satisfaction and pride in the new facilities.

Mr. Wilkins, speaking to the large audience, said that the Charlottetown school is as modern as any in St. John's or, in fact, anywhere in our country, with nineteen computers and all the other modern things in our school. All the parents were happy to know that their children have the opportunity to have a good education. The school children stood and sang the "Ode to Labrador," first in English, then in French, which surprised many of the people.

Today we have ten people working in the Charlottetown Community Hall. Roxanne Notley, Co-ordinator for the Labrador White Bear Development Association, is involved mainly with rural development in assisting five surrounding communities to develop the area's vast potential, which includes creating and promoting economic growth.

Lisa Dempster is Outreach Worker for Canada Employment and Immigration Centre, which provides employment-related services to five surrounding communities. Her duties involve employment counselling, assisting with proposals and other funding applications, Unemployment Insurance problems, job placements, and career counselling.

Todd Russell, Northern Cod Adjustment and Recovery Counsellor, is employed by Canada Employment Centre, in conjunction with the Department of Fisheries and Oceans. His position was a result of the moratorium placed on the northern cod fishery on July 2, 1992. As a counsellor, he assists fisher persons in making the career choice that they feel is best for themselves.

Selma Noel, Secretary, is employed by Canada Employment and Immigration Centre. Her position involves carrying out secretarial duties for the NCARP Counsellor.

Asaph Wentzell, Fisheries Officer, is employed by the provincial department of fisheries. He monitors and enforces rules and regulations of provincial fisheries, and provides licenses for different fish species to surrounding communities.

Ronald Rumbolt, Fisheries Guardian, is employed by the provincial department of fisheries. He assists the Fisheries Officer to carry out his duties.

Raymond Turnbull, Fisheries Education Co-ordinator, is employed by the Labrador College and Marine Institute. He is involved with the local fishermen committee in Labrador by offering fishery-related training as per their request.

Jessie Nippard, Town Clerk, is employed by the Charlottetown Community Council. She is involved with all and any duties or concerns relating to the community (i.e., land applications, poll tax, water and sewer, etc.).

David Campbell, Maintenance man, is employed by the Charlottetown Community Council. He is mainly involved with the water and sewage system, ensuring its smooth operation. He also maintains the building.

Susie Roberts, Janitor, is employed by the Charlottetown Community Council.

We have an airstrip, which is a busy place, on the south side of our settlement. Labrador Airways brings mail and passengers most days when the weather is suitable. Labrador Travel Air is based at our airstrip and operates four aircraft – both wheels and floats – and takes freight and passengers anywhere in Labrador or in Newfoundland. There are also several private planes based at our airstrip, but owned by residents of Charlottetown.

In 1992, the sum of around $2,000,000.00 was spent to put

Labrador Travel Air is owned and operated by the author's son, Tony.

water and sewage services in our community. We have a large new hydro plant that supplies us with electrical power. This plant also supplies Pinsent's Arm, twelve miles to the south of

The contractor putting water and sewage services in Charlottetown.

us, with power. For the past twelve years, we have had a huge snow groomer that grooms a two-lane trail to settlements north and south of us.

So we have a lot to thank our Government for. We have come a long way since Friday, October 20, 1950, the day when the first freight was landed in the little woody cove, called Old Cove.

At the age of seventy-three, I call myself semi-retired. But I still work long hours in my office and I do the accounting for two divisions of my company. I still take time to do the things I liked best in life, like going into the wilderness, doing some hunting, trapping fur-bearing animals, stopping at my tiny cabins, and enjoying a lunch in a quiet and peaceful land.

Our lifestyle has changed. We no longer travel on foot, but on snowmobile. A distance that at one time took us all day to travel can now be done in one hour.

Driving up these beautiful lakes and rivers, with the air so clean and fresh, I often try to forget the hard times I experienced as a young man. But those living memories don't go away. Every wind in the river brings back more memories of the past. I often squeeze the throttle and go faster, trying to put those sad memories behind me. However, as I bring the next woody point into sight, I am reminded by the tall trees that this is another place – a place where I once survived a terrible storm. With no food, there seemed to be no hope that I would ever see home again. But I survived those storms. Only once did it take me forty hours to get back to my log cabin that was hidden in a forest in no man's land, but even then I was still many days' walk from home.

On September 20 – a beautiful autumn day – I decided to take my fishing rod, get into my small boat and go across the bay to Peter's Brook. I would still have a couple of hours before dark, plenty of time to catch a meal of trout to take home for supper.

Soon I headed across the bay. The light, warm wind made ripples on the water. Minutes later, I moored my boat close to the mouth of the brook. Walking along the shore, I was surprised to see so many small fish jumping into the air at the mouth of the brook. I soon realized that they were salmon smolts and parrs.[1] In the previous fifteen years, I had seen very few of these fish in our brooks and rivers. Now they were back as in the earlier days when the brooks were teeming with them. Of course, in those days there were lots of large salmon, as well.

Sitting down on a large round rock at the water's edge, I watched the fish as they jumped, the setting sun sparkling on them. I made no attempt to cast my lure into the water because it was against the law to catch small fish.

I noticed that the sun was no longer shining on the fish. I decided to walk in the narrow footpath that went up along the side of the brook to a place we called "the Steady," which was like a little round pond. This was where you often caught big sea-trout and salmon. Those days were long gone, and I wasn't expecting to get any salmon. Over the years our streams had been over-fished, and only a few salmon are left.

I went up the footpath, with tall trees standing on both sides. With the sun gone down, it was starting to get shady. Reaching the Steady, I went to where the large brook was running into it. Again I was surprised to see so many small salmon jumping. Still I made no attempt to cast my line into the water.

Looking closer, I noticed that the salmon were jumping after the black flies that were flying around just above the water. Turning and looking up the brook, I received a greater surprise. There was a large speckled lake trout in a little pond. Somehow it had gotten stranded there. Its fins were sticking out of the water. I could see that the fish had been there a long time, because its lower fins were almost worn off as it tried to get out. I was also surprised to see fish, hawks, owls, minks and otters around the Steady.

I reached down and picked up the trout. It had large red spots that shone on both sides. The fish made no attempt to get clear.

[1] Young salmon.

I thought to myself, "What a great supper this trout would make for us! I know how great it would look in the frying pan on the stove!"

The fish moved its mouth several times. Only then did I notice that it was a female trout, full of spawn. While trying to reach the spawning grounds at the lake, she had been stranded for several days in the pool. The sun had gone down and the air was getting cold. The trout was being held in the hands of an elderly man whose mind was going back to the days when he was a young trapper. Late in September and early in October, the brooks would be filled with trout and salmon. But now there are very few left. Seeing the parrs jumping into the air, I thought, "There's still hope if we stop over-fishing."

I walked to the edge of the Steady and gently put the shining fish back into the water. She slowly swam out to the deep water. I knew she had spawn enough to put a hundred fish back into our lakes and streams.

Leaving my fishing rod by the brook-side, I hurried over the footpath to the pond where I had a small boat. I turned it over for a long winter ahead, which would keep the ice and snow out of the craft.

I returned over the footpath. It was dark when I reached the brook. Picking up my fishing rod, I headed out to my boat that had been left in the mouth of the brook. It felt great going beneath the trees, the silence being broken only by my clothing rubbing against the underbrush hanging over the path.

Reaching my boat, it was too dark to see the parrs and smolts I had seen jumping earlier. I got the motor running and headed for home, driving only at half-speed and keeping my head below the windshield because the air seemed cold.

Lifting my head, I saw in the distance the sparkling lights of our town. There was one bright red light on top of the hill over-looking our settlement. At the airstrip building, another bright light was sending its beam in all directions. For a moment I had to ask myself, "Am I dreaming?" I started to count all the streetlights and the large lights on the hydro power building,

One of Charlottetown's houses today.

but there were too many. Slowing down the motor, I re-counted them.

Suddenly, my mind went back to November 16, 1950. On that dark night, a twelve-year-old Eskimo boy and I headed into this cove. In the darkness, we tried to keep clear of the sheets of ice that were floating around. I now thought to myself, "If only we could've seen just one light in this woody cove! It would've meant so much to us that night when our clothing was iced over and our stomachs were aching from hunger."

Fifty-three years after being a young trapper, our lifestyle has changed so much. Thinking about how we survived that terrible trip brought tears to my eyes. We had built five log cabins back in the woods. The men were hard at work cutting more logs. I learned that our horse horns and birch rollers for our sawmill hadn't arrived, but I couldn't tell our men that without those things our operation was unable to carry on.

One day someone heard a message on radio that our packages had been shipped on a boat that was going for codfish to Fishing Ship's Harbour. There were three miles of our bay already frozen over. I got a young Eskimo boy – Jimmy – to go with me. We pulled our fourteen-foot boat over the three miles of ice. Using our seven-horsepower outboard motor, we headed to Fishing Ship's Harbour.

Arriving there later that night, we were cold and hungry. There was snow on the wharf, but there was no sign of life. So we went to George's Cove Island, where we found shelter. At daylight four days later, the boat blew her whistle and headed into Fishing Ship's Harbour.

We pounded the ice off our boat and motor and headed to the boat. Shortly later, we motored out into the ocean. The large package of birch rollers had the little boat well loaded. As we reached the ocean, it was rough with white lops breaking in all directions.

I told Jimmie that if he could keep the water bailed out of the boat, I would try to steer clear of the whitecapped waves. Turning back-on to the waves, he bailed for all he was worth. We moved slowly, the wind blowing in a northwest direction.

It was late that evening when we rounded Cape St. Michaels. The wide bay opened up, the whitecapped waves coming toward us. I could see no ray of hope for us in our overloaded boat. Looking down at Jimmie, I saw that his sealskin mitten was frozen to the bailer and his clothing was iced over. But still he showed no sign of giving up. I looked toward the shore, thinking we might find shelter from the waves, but the shore-line was a cliff of ice that rose a hundred feet from the sea.

We slowly moved on, our boat now iced over. By dark we were getting into smoother water. It was no one other than God who finally brought us to a sheltered cove on that cold, dark night.

In my boat, I again lifted my head. I saw smoke rising from several fires along the shore where people were cutting and burning brush. This was one of the "make-work" programs that was taking place in our settlement. At one time, we knew nothing about such programs; life was a reality back then. Now it's like a dream-world.

Back at the wharf, I moored my boat. Walking toward the

house with my fishing rod, I wasn't disappointed that I had no trout. We had plenty of food to eat. I was happy, knowing that within a few more days I'd be able to go around the bay and set up my traps and hunt wild birds. Those were always the greatest days of my life.

At seventy-three, I have to slow down a great deal. When the travelling gets good for snowmobile, I still plan to go over the mountain trail north of the White Hill Mountains, where I once had a little cabin. That is where the small birds are happy to see me arriving, because I always have food for them. They like to pitch on my hands. It's great having so many wonderful friends out in the wilderness.

The author and his brothers, Roland and Herb.

The author pictured with his family at his youngest daughter's wedding, 1985. Six of his seven sons are aviation pilots.

Summary of My Years

I've touched both joy and sorrow,
   As the old days passed to new,
      And little lessons I did learn
         And with each one I grew.

– Benjamin W. Powell, Sr.

An old house at Campbell's Cove.

* * *

The Old House Will Soon Be Gone –
But the Name Will Still Live On

It was back in the days of fur trading,
    John Campbell his life just begun,
Made friends with the Mountaineer Indians,
    And started to build his new home.

Now the old house stands a memory,
    Of those days of long ago,
Where Mother and Dad gave all they had
    To keep hunger away from their home.

If you turned back the pages of history,
    Their names you'll find written in gold,
A century has passed and the house it still lasts,
    While its builder has gone from our shores.

You may reach it by land or by water,
    You may see it from high in the air,
But the greatest of all is the story once told
    How the old house stood there so long.

It was never recorded in history,
    How that white man survived in the North
While he filled every need of the family,
    And with others he shared their good luck.

Now the paint on the old house is faded,
    The glass in the windows is gone,
The floor that never wore carpet,
    Tells the story of life long ago.

The old iron pot and the kettle,
    The gun rack now lay on the floor,
The stove with the big barrel oven,

No longer will heat the old home.

Every chair, the table and dresser,
  Nowhere could the trademark be found,
Hard work of that old fur trader,
  From the forest the trees he cut down.

If you lived in the days of John Campbell,
  The years that his life was in bloom,
And you followed the trails in the country,
  They'd lead to that old trapper's home.

If you followed that lonely footpath,
  As the sun sinks low in the west,
It would shine on a marble tombstone,
  Marking the spot where they laid him to rest.

— Benjamin W. Powell, Sr.

* * *

The M.V. *Blanche Marie II* after arriving at Ironbound Island.

The Loss of the *Blanche Marie II*

Come all ye gallant fishermen and listen to my tale,
About the crew of the "Blanche Marie" that weathered out the
   gale
It's a life that's tough and sometimes rough for those men who
   go down to the sea,
To earn their bread from the ocean bed by hauling the cod gill
   nets.

The "Blanche Marie," a masterpiece, designed by the skill of
   man,
To build a boat, to fish our coast, there was nothing else in
   mind
It was late up in September when the "Blanche Marie" got away,
She took on board provisions to last her for her stay.

She carried a crew of four young men just in the prime of life,
Who knew the game called fishing, and handled the splitting
   knife.
Their destination Ironbound, the home of the great big fish,
For there are those commitments all fishermen have to meet.

Twenty-seventh day of September when everything looked gay,
With cod gill nets and red bobbers they started to shoot away,
The next day it was Sunday, their nets they didn't haul,
But went onto shore to take a stroll, a paint can in their hand.

And on a rock bottom those letters, they put the date of their
   arrival
And the bottom line it seemed to shine, those words, "In God
   We Trust."

The weather it was average, the fish were coming fast,
Every man was happy, and hoped the fish would last.
Her stern was getting heavy, the salt was getting shy,
The skipper said, "Another week, we will fill her to the hatch."

At twelve o'clock on Wednesday night the forecast it was good,
They started to get ready, their gill nets they would pull,
But before they could get ready, the wind came on to blow,
And with it came a heavy sea and also heavy snow,
Which caused them to get ready, their vessel to secure,
But before a man could get on deck, all shorelines had let go.

Skipper Sandy told his crew, "There is only one thing left to do,
And with the use of radar we will ride it out at sea."
Ironbound, a windswept rock, many miles at sea,
Could give but little shelter to their ship, the "Blanche Marie."

Fourteen hours they battled the storm, the seas ran mountain
*   high,*
The winds and snow that struck the ship, nobody will ever know.
When daylight broke upon them, the land they chanced to spy,
"We will head her once more windward, and give her another
*   try."*

The radar now had vanished from the water that went below,
And the next to go was the radio, no signal could be sent.
The sound of the Stempro motor was like music in their ears,
As she had never failed them, in all their fishing years.

They still had little shelter as they got closer to the shore,
When above the sound of the ocean came a terrible roar.
Then Skipper Sandy said, "My boys, I am sure you know the
*   score,*
First we lost our nylon ropes, then our anchors and chains,
Then we lost our lifeboats, and now we have lost our blades."

The skipper then gave the orders that they must all leave the
*   ship,*
"But nobody give up courage, until we reach the beach.
Our ship has done her duty, as any ship could do."
But they could not see the driftwood that had hooked her down
*   below.*

Tony was the first man to go over the bow,
He said, "My boys, this is the third shipwreck, but I hope I make
   it now."
Eugene was the next man to walk up to the bow,
He wondered how his folks at home could do without him now.

He thought about the fish he would have to leave behind,
While every cent was needed in his little home.
Two men now in the water, two men left on board,
The skipper said to Gillingham, "It's your turn now to go."

Gillingham, an able man, a man from Gander Bay,
Who had fished in the "Blanche Marie" since her maiden day.
"I cannot leave you, Sandy, I want you by my side."
And with one shove it was enough to put both of them over the
   side.

Four men now in the water, their ship they saw no more,
But an angel from the heavens, guided them to shore,
To that very spot on the windswept rock, those letters seemed to
   say,
"Still four of us, and in God we trust, to take us home from
   here."

Four days on that lonely island, no rescue came in sight,
They found a hook and two little fish that served their appetite.

No word came from the "Blanche Marie" for eight long days or
   more,
When Bert Winters from Makkovik said, "It's time to search our
   shore."
He searched the cape and every place until he reached
   Ironbound,
And here he found the shipwrecked crew and got them safe and
   sound.

With thoughts of home, the author composed a poem to his wife, Effie, in his tilt by candlelight, using a piece of charcoal on birch bark.

Now my tale is ended, just another shipwreck of the sea,
We will try and replace our ship, to serve our oldest industry.
— Benjamin W. Powell, Sr.

* * *

The author about halfway around the White Hill Mountains. His life depended on his gun.

Mine Alone

Darling, there are many things
I keep within my heart,
The hardships on the trapline,
Can never be forgot.

Outside it's very stormy,
Yet my candle is burning bright,
I have no pen or paper
As I write this poem tonight.

Memories of good times we had,
The thoughtfulness you've showed,
And all the special pride I feel
Because you are mine alone.
                                              – Benjamin W. Powell, Sr.

                              * * *

The Old Trapper's Song

Forty years I have been a trapper,
And lived up in the north.
My axe, my gun and my snowshoes,
Are all a trapper has.

No money I had in my pocket,
No shops I could find on a trail,
A trapper must live by his courage,
Is the game that all trappers must play.

When I left my home on the Island,
I was only just a kid.
The government had told us all industry was dead,
And eighty thousand Newfies could no longer earn bread.

I stood one day at the seashore,
  Feeling so very sad.
No way to earn my living
  On the Island of Newfoundland.

So I traded my home on the Island,
  For a log cabin up north,
And there by the light of the candle,
  I'd put on my caribou scoff.

One day in that northland I married
  I just wanted to make it my home.
My wife did the work in the cabin,
  While I hunted the trapline alone.

Forty years now I've spent in this northland.
  With its freedom a challenge to all.
I never think of retiring,
  Or returning to my homeland again.

Should ever you ask me the question,
  "Oh, why did you settle up north?"
I could easily give you the answer,
  By telling a hard time I had.

For sixteen days it was storming,
  The snow it was falling so fast.
My food it had to be rationed,
  And I knew that it would never last.

At last I had reached the lakeshore,
  Still I was searching for food.
My stomach was aching with hunger,
  My clothes they were torn in all rags.

I counted the miles to the river,
I counted the miles to the bay,
I knew at the little log cabin,
The light was burning for me.

My snowshoes seemed so heavy,
My gun seemed to have fired its last shot.
The axe that I used to get firewood,
Only added more weight on my back.

Still many miles from my cabin,
The big White Hills just ahead.
Twelve times I lunched with only hot water,
Each time my belt I tightened in.

Only one mile from my cabin,
Still I kept dragging along,
Thank God! I see the light shining,
Once more the lone trapper made home.

Life in this northland is rugged.
You just live with the ice and the snow.
My wife lived a life of long-waiting,
As her dad too was a trapper, you know.

Should ever you feel you're unhappy,
And you live in a big city or town.
Remember the life in the northland,
And the trappers who call it their home.
                                    — Benjamin W. Powell, Sr.

One of the author's new trapper's cabins.

Dear Friend, Trapper Ben:

My visits with you and over your trapline in 1974, 1976 and 1977 have been and are among my most pleasant memories and nicest trips, even though I have been very fortunate to have seen most of North and South America, Africa, Iceland and Europe, including the Norwegian countries.

Being with you on your trapline proved to me the value of your art and experience in trapping. All of my trips with you were great; it is difficult for me to choose the greatest. However, I will always remember seeing the remains of one of your little old line camps and the whale riband disc snowshoe form to make snowshoes. Also the form for making moccasins and the hand-hammered Vale trap which you so kindly gave me. You might recall that you thought the latter was well over one hundred and fifty years old. These two items, along with the other things you gave me, are hanging in my home where I see them and dream.

Ben, the trip of more than one hundred miles in 1976 over part of your trapline and to the beacon station at the top of the tallest mountain was surely a memorable day. Remember the ptarmigan we saw at the very top?

For days I could reminisce. May the Lord spare you and give you the good health to enjoy many more good, fruitful years on your traplines. My thanks and very best wishes to you and yours.

Cordially,
Henry Veghte, Jr.
Stage Pico Pines
Mendon, Vermont 05701

Charlottetown, 1977.

By Benjamin's Wife, Effie

In April 1978, I asked Ben if he would consider a trip to Florida as since our marriage over thirty years ago, we have never had a holiday together outside coastal Labrador. After a little consideration, he said he would go for one week. Shortly after, we arrived in Florida and then to the beautiful Castaway Hotel. As I looked through the big windows seven stories up, I thought it was the greatest sight of my life – the long, sandy beach, the warm air blowing from the ocean, and the blue, sunny sky.

I then opened my handbag and took out my little diary and asked Ben to write me a verse in the book before we would go down to the seashore. He stopped for one minute and then took the pen and wrote this verse:

As I sit near the window
  and watch the waves roll on the shore
Among the thousands of people
  I saw five from Labrador.
With the sailboats on the water
  and the suntanners on the beach
I wouldn't trade my trapline for the place
  called Daytona Beach.

As I read Ben's verse, I knew from the start that sunny Florida could never change Ben's love for Labrador. So many years devoted to the freedom of the north could never change.

As he says in his own words, "Labrador, our last frontier

with its virgin forests, its lakes and streams, many still untouched by the white man, its vast natural resources which are slowly opening up, still holds a great future for our younger generation."

The author and his late wife, Effie, in Florida.

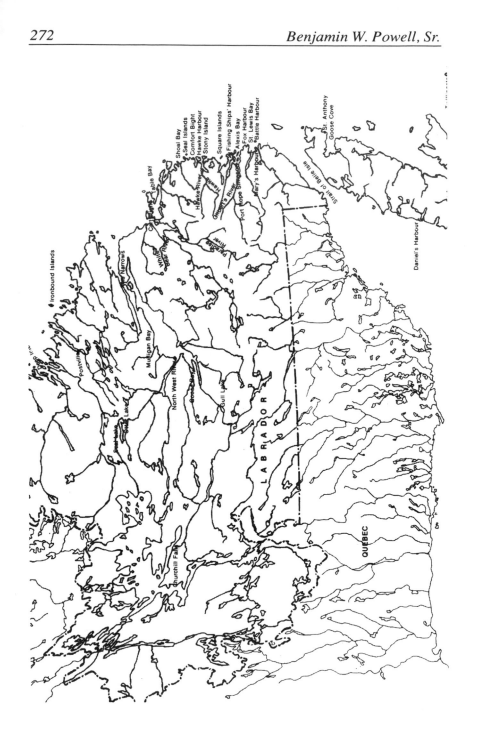

P. O. BOX 346

PHONE 673-3272

SPRINGDALE AVIATION LTD.

SPRINGDALE, NEWFOUNDLAND
A0J 1T0

Ben W. Powell Sr.

Charlottetown, Labrador

Dear Uncle Ben;

    I thought I'd drop you a note to compliment you on
on your book "Labrador by Choice". I read it and thoroughly
enjoyed it. As a matter of fact I passed it on to a friend
of mine who was in hospital. At that time he was having
a lot of problems with his contracting business and was
at his wits end.

    T ran in to him again recently and he was back on his
feet both physically and financially. He brought up reading
your book while he was so ill and ready to pack it all in.
Once he started reading "Labrador by Choice" he realized
that you had it just as rough or more so trying to make a
go of it. He said his sense of selfpity left him and He
was determined not to give up either. He told me that it
took alot of determination and will power but his business
did get back on track and is thriving today.

    In closing I would again like to commend you on a fine
effort and I look forward to your next book.

Sincerely,